MARTHA NEEDLE

For Mary, a great cousin and friend who'll
never be forgotten.

And also, for the late Bob Watt - a really
good man, who gave me my first break.

MARTHA NEEDLE

The spellbinding story of Australia's
most infamous femme fatale

BRIAN WILLIAMS

NH
NEW
HOLLAND

'Well-behaved women seldom make history.'

- Laurel Thatcher Ulrich

A Remarkable Story.
— *Brisbane Courier,* **1894**

One of the most remarkable cases that has ever come before an
Australian Criminal Court ... The case of the heartless murderess
Martha Needle stands out as one of the most awful, if not the very
worst, in the records of crime.
— *Herald,* **1894, Melbourne**

There are murders that seem to stand alone in their unspeakable
horror and atrocity. They completely absorb the public mind ... And
it somehow happens that murders committed or inspired by women
have the maximum power of arresting public attention.
— *Advertiser,* **1894, South Australia**

One of the most sensational stories of the day. Step by step they were
confronted with extraordinary facts.
— *Argus,* **1894**

The condemned woman presented to the very last the inscrutable calmness and cold indifference which characterised her from the time of her arrest.
– *Sydney Morning Herald,* **1894**

Poisoned her family as a matter of business – Australia's arch fiend … One could search the corridor of the ages and unearth all the storied butchers of antiquity without ever finding a match for unsurpassably appalling Martha Needle.
– *World's News,* **1935, Sydney**

The epithet bestowed on Martha Needle could not have been more appropriate – The Black Widow of Richmond. The beautiful and ruthless poisoner is up there in the rollcall of Victoria's serial killers.
– *Herald Sun,* **2012**

Gravestone inscription composed by Martha Needle
for her three deceased children:

Little lips that murmured mumma
Still and silent now they are;
Tiny feet no longer patter,
Hushed forever 'neath the clay.
One by one they wandered from me,
And I linger here alone;
But their sweet and loving mem'ries
Blossom through the loving years.
By their loving mother –
M. Needle

Newspaper obituary written by Martha Needle
following the untimely death of her third child:

I had three little treasures once,
They were my joy and pride,
But one by one they all have gone.
They all have early drooped and died.
All is dark within my dwelling,
Lonely is my heart today,
Now unheard, unpitied, unrelieved,
I must bear alone my load of care.

Contents

CHAPTER 1

The Life and Crimes of Martha Needle

The extraordinary Martha Needle was not only the most treacherous poisoner in Australian history but she also clearly stands out as one of the nation's worst murderesses of all time. And from an international perspective, she still ranks among the world's most prolific female killers.

In her day, Martha was as big as Ned Kelly – and she even shared the same pugnacious lawyer. The legendary saga of this attractive yet cunning mother and housewife not only fully transfixed the community in late 19th-century Australia but it was also dramatically reported around the globe as 'the story of the century'. To this day, Martha's story has continued to be widely chronicled as one of the most mind-boggling poisoning cases and copybook murder investigations in world history.

Pivotal to the entire backdrop of these shocking crimes was the intriguing character of Martha Needle – a seductive and manipulating young woman who could exude the poise and sexual charm of an alluring temptress, yet be equally dastardly. The world press had not luridly dubbed her the 'Black Widow' for nothing. In her wretched rampage, she deviously used arsenic to exterminate all those around her who stood in the way of her personal ambitions or unfettered greed – even her own children.

Martha's story had it all: family conflict, betrayal, gruesomeness, a media frenzy, shattered societal expectations, dodgy lawyers, guileless doctors, questionable police, an attractive accused, romance and even a hint of sexual scandal. It is little wonder that before the case even went to court, it aroused an immense and unprecedented interest in puritanical, Victorian-aged Australia.

Martha lived in brutal times. Although she was officially only convicted of one murder, she paid the ultimate price for her deeds. After a landmark investigation and trial, she was marched to the gallows and judiciously hanged by the neck until dead – even though many members of society were outraged by the state-endorsed execution of a woman.

But amid such an emotional outcry, a multitude of scandalous secrets also fell through the well-oiled trapdoor with the tight-lipped poisoner on that grim morning. By the sheer magnitude of her deeds, Martha may have entrenched herself into the pop culture of Australian folklore but there were a colossal number of twists and turns in her story – many of these previously unknown or unexplained until now.

After spending four years studying the case across a number of Australian states, highly regarded author, lawyer, historian and educator Dr Brian Williams has uncovered many rare documents and archives, some concealed from public view at the time of Martha's court case and execution. These include medical records, unpublished reports and even a stash of private correspondence written by the Black Widow herself, in which she reveals her innermost thoughts and seeks the impassioned sympathy of those around her. And all the time she was plotting her next move and maintaining a façade of warm innocence.

While awaiting her murder trial in this grisly case, Martha sat passively as four bodies – all ultimately found to contain arsenic – were exhumed from their respective graves. Unfazed by this unfortunate development, she had mocked detectives with the retort:

> So they found arsenic did they? A few more of my friends have died lately, I can give you their names. Would you like information about their burial? It would be useful if you wanted to dig them up. [1]

Regretfully, the already overwhelmed detectives never took up Martha's stunning offer. One even helpfully replied, 'No, I have quite enough at present'.[2]

Compelling new evidence is now fully examined for the very first time, firmly placing the Black Widow in the frame for a string of further murders – something of a cry for justice from beyond the grave. Based on this information, it is well and truly time to rewrite the history books.

Many intriguing questions are also examined in this gripping account. How did Martha develop such a chameleon-like character, which enabled her to continually reach for a box of rat poison to eliminate her troubles while simultaneously evoking the heartfelt sympathy of all those around her? How did she seduce naïve members of the medical profession into her trap? How did she manage to evade suspicion for so long, maintaining her reputation as a 'good little woman'? What role did her formative background play? Was she legally insane, or just unscrupulously evil? And how did her one error of judgement and an ensuing brilliant example of detective work finally bring her undone?

It is now time to answer these questions and for the astonishing story of Australia's ruthless Black Widow to finally be told.

CHAPTER 2

As the Twig is Bent –
A Miserable Early Existence

For an Australian woman destined to attract profound infamy throughout the world, Martha Needle had an inauspicious start to life. She was born on 9 April 1864 near the tiny South Australian town of Morgan, which borders the iconic Murray River. Her surname at the time of her birth was 'Charles', with her biological parents being Joseph Henry Charles and Mary Charles nee Newland.

A great deal more is now known about the social and environmental impacts of early childhood than was the case during the latter part of the 19th century. Decades of research in fields such as psychology and criminology have reliably identified several factors that can be triggers for later criminal atrocities.

Among those who have been studied most intensely are serial killers. Although not always applicable in every case, perpetrators of serial murder often have frightful early lives during which they endured family alienation and were bereft of normal levels of affection. As children, they are also most likely to have witnessed extreme violence and been personally exposed to cruelty, physical assaults and sexual abuse.

Martha was no exception. Her early existence was indeed utterly wretched and her childhood experiences could not have provided a more fitting template for her later misdeeds. And her 'family' of radiant relatives was an utterly feral mob of petty career criminals before she was even born.

Although both of her natural parents would remain mysterious figures to Martha for the duration of her life, it is now possible to sketch some tellingly accurate details about them from existing records. And it doesn't make pretty reading.

Her father was born in England in 1830 and he was 33 years of age at the time of Martha's birth. He died in 1870, when Martha was just about to turn six years of age. Martha's mother had married him in Adelaide in December 1853 when she was only 16 years old. But the couple's union was destined to be a pathetically unhappy one, punctuated by violence, spiteful separations, alcoholism, poverty and infant mortality.

They were also constantly on the move, rambling around the South Australian countryside from one shanty or sheep station to the next, as Joseph tried to procure work as a farm labourer. Such a peripatetic nature was not exclusively for sightseeing purposes. They would also pilfer anything they could get their mitts on and then routinely depart in the dead of night when the rent arrears finally became due.

In keeping with these harsh times, not all births were registered and although the untidy couple were to ultimately have six children, they did not officially record the births of any of them. Their first two babies were boys but they both perished while very young. Then Mary gave birth to four girls. A daughter, also named Mary, was born in 1857, followed by Ellen in 1860 and Dina in 1862. Although Martha became the last born of Joseph and Mary Charles' offspring in 1864, her parents were no longer actually living together when she arrived. Consequently, she would grow up completely unloved and unwanted.

A constant braggart, Joseph had first abandoned the unhappy marital home in 1862, leaving his alcoholic wife Mary destitute. She had resorted to drawing rations to survive and at one time she was forced to apply to a court for charitable funds to bury her 1-year-old baby, Dina. Mary, Ellen and Martha were therefore the only Charles children to survive to adulthood.

The miserable Mr and Mr Charles again parted company on very acrimonious terms at Julia Creek, near Anlaby in South Australia, when Mary accused her husband of attempting to poison her. After falling violently ill, she had noticed that some poison that was usually kept on the farm to destroy wild dogs was missing and she confronted her unloving husband with her suspicions that he had been lacing her food to try to do her in.

Significantly, he did not even bother to deny the allegation, only taking the time to remark that they were cohabitating so unhappily that she could expect nothing else.

The bitter separation lasted 12 months but then there was a brief reconciliation – presumably more for economic reasons than affairs of the heart. The couple shacked up again for a few months at the copper-mining township of Kapunda. It was during this small window of time that Martha was conceived. The unhappy couple separated forever seven months before Martha was born, with Joseph again demonstrating threatening behaviour towards his bedraggled wife.

The pregnant Mary made her way to the North-West Bend Sheep Station on the Murray River and offered to work for the owner, Mr Glen. It was at this rural property that Martha was ultimately delivered. Within four months, Mary had relocated again with her baby daughter and other children to the South Australian town of Port Lincoln.

An Incurable Romantic

By the time that Martha had turned two years of age, her mother had hooked up with another brutish man – 39-year-old Daniel Foran. Not just another unpretty face, Foran was a former foot soldier with a sordid past. He originally hailed from Limerick in Ireland before arriving in Australia with the 2nd Somerset Shire Regiment.

While shirking his duties as a soldier, the drink-addicted Foran had forged a deplorable service history. Military records indicate that he deserted at least three times. The British Army considered desertion to be the ultimate disgrace and perpetrators had the letter 'D' roughly tattooed on their arm using needles and gunpowder. In a time when tattoos were not utilised as a fashion accessory, Foran sported several of these 'D' tattoos.

After the death of her estranged first husband, Martha's mother quickly married Foran and adopted his surname. Their brief matrimonial ceremony took place in March 1870 at St Thomas' Church in Port Lincoln.

Once again, this matrimonial match-up was never destined to be a Mills and Boon romance. In between bouts of binge drinking and displays of temper, Daniel tried to eke out a precarious existence as a shepherd – but the household always remained dirt poor, often relying on handouts and charity. The couple also ultimately produced three more baby boys, stepbrothers to Martha and her two older sisters. Daniel Jnr was born in 1866, followed by John five year later. The last Foran child to enter the world was George in April 1875 but he died less than one hour later.

A Clear Cut Below The Rest

Giving discredit where it's due, Daniel and Mary Foran were appalling parents, as evidenced by their continual neglect, abusive behaviour and lawlessness. And while they may not have been individuals with personal conviction, they certainly had plenty of criminal convictions.

The primary Adelaide newspaper of the day, the *South Australian Register*, often devoted a column or two to some of the worst cases coming before the Adelaide Police Court. These daily snippets dealt with the morning's usual line-up of misery – drunks, vagabonds and riffraff arrested the night before.

Mary Foran was always among the most prolific of offenders, with a later police report showcasing her sparkling personality by simply summarising that she was 'addicted to drink' and had 'many convictions for drunkenness, indecent language and wilful damage'.[3]

In April 1875, the *South Australian Register* reported that 'Mary Foran, married woman, had been punished for uttering foul words in Sussex Street, North Adelaide' [where the Forans lived at the time]. This was followed by another article that appeared in July 1876, which dutifully informed the paper's readership: 'Mary Foran, married woman, was charged with leaving her son Daniel, aged ten, without means of support. Mrs Foran was ordered to be imprisoned for one calendar month with hard labour and her two children (the other a boy of five years) are to be sent to the Industrial School till they are 12 years of age'.

Such was the harshness of the times for Martha's younger stepbrothers, Daniel and John Foran. They would now spend the rest of their childhoods locked away in a draconian institution, performing menial labour. Their only 'crime' was having a mother who was a bellicose drunk. Unsurprisingly, both would grow up to be dysfunctional adults.

Their darling mama was back among the headlines in March 1877, with the *South Australian Register* simply stating: 'Mary Foran, an old offender, was fined 10 shillings and sent to prison and kept at hard labour for two calendar months for being a habitual drunkard'.

Trolling the streets while pickled in alcohol may have been socially unacceptable but it was the sinister side of her dearly beloved husband Daniel that proved to be most devastating for her youngest daughter, Martha. Before the neglected girl had reached her teens, her evil stepfather had settled into a furtive pattern of sexually molesting her.

On Tuesday, 4 April 1876, the *South Australian Advertiser* devoted a few lines to the disturbing case:

Daniel Foran, who was charged with indecently assaulting his stepdaughter, Martha Charles at Adelaide in December, 1875, and found guilty was next brought up for sentence. His honour alluded to the enormity of the crime of which prisoner had been found guilty, and sentenced him to the full term allowed by the Act, viz., two years with hard labour.

At the time of this ghastly offence, Daniel and Mary were residing in the South Australian hamlet of Brompton, along with their remaining clan of children.

A witness statement filed in the Criminal Sittings of the Supreme Court indicated that a neighbour had been attracted by a child's cries and rushed over to the Foran family's rented house to investigate. Upon looking through the window, the neighbour directly witnessed Foran attempting to 'carnally know' his young stepdaughter, Martha. ('Carnally know' is a staid euphemism often employed in the press during those times – today we simply refer to the crime as 'rape' or 'sexual assault').

The ferocity of the attack was such that Foran received the maximum penalty that the presiding judge could legally impose upon him. Even then, this was only a weak two years in the slammer. These were clearly different times and the sanctity of childhood was ranked cheaply.

An accompanying police report later noted that Martha's mother had been absent from the house at the time of the attack. Once Foran was released from the clink two years later, she refused to live with him ever again and the pair parted ways for good.

The case was so shocking that the editor of the *South Australian Advertiser* took the very unusual step of fully reviewing it. While re-emphasising that the fault rested with the law and not the hamstrung judge, the editor correctly concluded that most citizens would 'admit that the punishment was not sufficient for the crime'. What made it even worse – if that was indeed possible – was that the young child had been attacked by a man who should have been in a position of parental trust and doubly protective of her in the absence of her mother.[4]

This would not be the last time that Martha would feel betrayed by the male gender.

Mattie Charles

By the time that Martha Charles had reached this stage of her unfortunate life, she was known by the nickname 'Mattie'. Like all her barefoot brothers and sisters – and, for that matter, many youngsters of the era – 'Mattie' had only picked up some very disjointed free schooling along the way and any prospect of paying for further education was an impossibility.

Yet, despite her abbreviated tuition, young 'Mattie' had certainly learned the rudimentary basics of reading and writing and she was quite capable of scribing an emotional letter – albeit with a raft of spelling mistakes. Even though grammar was never one of her finest accomplishments and she would include capital letters and punctuation at regular intervals whether they were required or not, 'Mattie' would remain an enthusiastic letter writer for the rest of her life. The habit didn't always serve her well. Some of Martha's later and more passionate literary efforts would even help bring about her ultimate downfall.

One of Martha's best friends when she lived in Sussex Street, North Adelaide, was another young girl of a similar age named Eliza, whose married name in adulthood was Eliza Martin. About 20 years later, Eliza could still clearly recall witnessing Martha's mother severely hitting her youngest daughter with a stick. Martha had also explained to Eliza during these grim times that her mother regularly tied her up with rope and beat her.

According to Martha's later recollections, it was around this time that Mary Foran would sometimes refer to herself with the surname 'Kennedy' (presumably to stay one step ahead of the landlords she hadn't remembered to pay) and on one occasion she became so frustrated by Martha's behaviour, she threatened to cut her young daughter's throat. A local constable had to be called to break in through a window to quell the fracas, but he neglected to write a formal report, leaving the way open in the future for Mary to deny this incident had ever occurred.[5]

It was at this tender age that Martha formed the bizarre theory that Mary was not her real mother. This view had been fuelled by several snippets of information. Before his death, her boastful natural father Joseph had told so many whoppers that he resembled the reincarnation of Baron von Munchausen. One suggestion he made to anyone who would listen was that he was secretly a wealthy man who was the heir to a colossal £700 worth of property, held in trust in England.

As the last of the Charles children, Martha began to believe that she had been 'handed over' to Mary at birth simply for rearing purposes by Joseph after his *real* wife had died in an Adelaide hospital during childbirth. According to Martha's proposition, Mary and Daniel Foran had continued to conceal these facts from her to deprive her of her inheritance, while secretly plotting to somehow snatch the money themselves.

In Martha's mind, such thoughts made even more sense in light of the appalling way that Mary treated her. Surely a mother couldn't react to her own natural child that way? Even her friend Eliza noted that Mary appeared to be much harder on Martha than the other youngsters in her brood – and they were by no means spoiled with kindness.

But none of Martha's thoughts were logical. If Joseph Charles was such a wealthy man, why had he elected to anonymously live in miserable poverty in a far-off land? Nonetheless, Martha kept harbouring these notions as a form of mental escape. Her daily existence was so grim, surely there had to be something better out there to look forward to. She had already begun to plant the seeds of ambition for a much better life.

Given the circumstances of her upbringing, it's not surprising that 12-year-old Martha – a victim of sexual abuse, neglect, brutality and mental cruelty – had developed into a headstrong, rebellious and enraged young girl. Her mother – conveniently ignoring her own pitiful contributions to her daughter's foibles – would later complain that Martha had developed such a violent temper she could not control her. The pair remained at constant loggerheads and a hate-filled animosity developed between them that would never heal.

Servant Girl

The age of 12 was a significant milestone for Martha because it was effectively the end of her childhood. For most youngsters from poor families in this era, this was the age at which they commenced work. Every day the classifieds were full of advertisements for 'obedient' and 'willing' minors to take up positions as servants, messengers and trade apprentices. The initial reward for such roles was often little more than free board and keep and the youngsters involved were sometimes exposed to all forms of unpleasant exploitation. The hours were very long and the manual labour involved was extremely hard but a free bed and meal held a considerable amount of currency in the late 19th century for the hungry children of unskilled parents.

Martha was destined to become a servant girl, performing all the manual housework duties for a wealthy city family. Her first domestic job was working in the household of a Mrs Beresford, before she moved to the employ of a Mrs Drew in Port Adelaide. Her duties were exhausting and repetitive. Decked out in her maid's uniform, she spent a lot of time scrubbing floors, cooking on a wood-fired stove, cleaning up dishes and washing sheets.

Martha endured this tedious work, but a continuing health issue from her childhood interrupted her early employment. She suffered from an uncomfortable eye infection, which had been left untreated and allowed to fester. She was confined to Adelaide Hospital for 11 weeks and the resident physician, Dr Gardner, put a seton in her cheek – a thread drawn through an opening in the skin to allow infected matter to be discharged. In addition to the pain of the procedure, Martha was left with a permanent scar on her cheek – not the best of news for an ambitious, adolescent servant girl.

But this scar didn't detract too much from her appearance. Always a pretty child, over the next few years Martha would bloom into an alluringly attractive young woman, blessed with a trim and dainty figure. Most men in her presence would afford her an admiring second glance and she soon learned to always reward their attentions with an endearing smile. She came to learn that her charm was the only power she had.

Damaged Goods

Now that she had left the curse of her wretched family behind and commenced employment, an outside observer may have been excused for thinking that the young and attractive Martha was on the way to a happier life. But this would underestimate the deep psychological trauma and mental scarring that had already occurred.

The sexual assaults by her stepfather and criminal conduct of her mother only provided a brief glimpse of the totality of their behaviour during Martha's formative years, a small percentage of their actual offences and outrages. Their respective criminal records effectively only listed their failures – the times they were caught and dealt with. It is difficult to imagine just how many times Martha must have agonisingly endured the stench of alcohol and sour defeat as her stepfather pressed against her.

The maltreatment and detachment Martha had endured throughout her childhood had already sent her emotional and behavioural functioning haywire. Martha had already switched off and ceased to be a normal human being long before her teens. An emotional callousness had developed, in addition to a deep-seated distrust of men. Martha had learned that the world was a ruthless place, and her survival hinged upon looking after her own needs, not harbouring compassion for others.

Not only could she display outbursts of volcanic rage when things didn't go her way but she had also become masterful at suppressing her revengeful feelings with an inner, brooding menace. Her terrible temper could cool to an implacable hate.

We will never fully know how deeply these emotional demons lay beneath the surface of Martha's mind, or what exactly would later set them off. But in terms of the modern recipe for future behavioural catastrophe, the dreaded ingredients were all there – menacingly ticking away inside her head. The irreparable damage had already been done.

Martha's upbringing had also planted other subtle concepts into her psyche. She had observed her family living off handouts and come to understand the benefits of unashamedly exploiting charity. She had come to appreciate greed, grabbing what you could whenever you could.

And, most significantly of all, she had also undoubtedly heard her drunken, loud-mouthed mother repeat over and over again the family legend of her natural father Joseph trying to improve his personal lot in life by attempting to poison his unwanted wife. Although this incident had occurred before Martha was even born, Martha now made a mental note of this story.

The implied message it conveyed to Martha's impressionable young mind was that poison could lead to a solution. And whether they cared or not, the adults in Martha's life had provided her with the ideal apprenticeship for a criminal career.

She would ultimately graduate with honours.

CHAPTER 3

Early Marriage and Baby Carriage

Throughout her early teenage years, Martha maintained her mundane employment as a servant girl, but she had her sights set on a life away from performing housework for someone else. With her natural beauty and engaging nature, she looked like an ideal catch and was soon attracting plenty of attention from the young men in the district. Entering the workforce and then marrying at a young age was often the path taken by girls looking to escape a life of poverty.

She soon became acquainted with a hardworking carpenter living nearby – Henry Needle. Five years older than Martha, Henry had been born near Plymouth, England. The son of Thomas Needle and Hannah Brain, he had arrived in Australia with his parents and four siblings aboard the ship *Forfashire*. A short man, at around 5 ft 6 in (168 cm) in height, Henry, or simply 'Harry' to his closest friends, was presentably handsome and strongly built – the latter attribute making him well suited to the heavy labour involved in his carpentry trade.

It was around the time of meeting Henry that Martha spent too much time one afternoon sitting in the hot Adelaide sun. She was struck down with a severe case of sunstroke. Her health was severely impaired for a while, but with some thoughtful care from Henry's nurturing relatives, she eventually recovered. The previously neglected Martha had never known such kindness – either throughout her free-range upbringing, or during her time as a servant girl.

And it wasn't only the sun that was affecting her thinking. Martha was undoubtedly flattered by the attentions of a more mature man in Henry, a suitor who was soon destined to become her husband. As it turned out, she was to fall for his charms a bit too quickly, and their ultimate marital union was more the result of necessity than starry-eyed devotion.

While it has never been previously noted in any of the official reports dealing with Martha's sensational case, a close inspection of prevailing records clearly indicates that Martha fell pregnant to Henry when she was only 17 years of age – before they were married.

Having a child out of wedlock during this era was completely frowned upon as a social taboo. A 'bastard' child had no legal status whatsoever and a single mother was treated as an outcast without any means of financial or emotional support. If 'fortunate', her baby was destined to be whisked away to a church or charitable orphanage or be unofficially taken in by another family. Those who were not so lucky faced a dismal chance of survival at the hands of unscrupulous baby farmers.

During these times, the only solutions for most young couples faced with an unwanted pregnancy were seeking an illegal abortion (an extremely expensive and amateurish backyard procedure) or hastily organising a wedding. Like many before them, Henry and Martha opted for the latter. While it meant an extremely rocky start to matrimonial life, many couples facing the same predicament made the best of what they had. But in light of the truly tragic decade ahead, Henry and Martha's seemingly forced nuptials was not one of these situations.

Henry and Martha were hastily joined in holy matrimony at Christ Church, North Adelaide, in South Australia on 15 May 1882, with the Reverend Charles Marryat performing the ceremony. At the time of their wedding, the pregnant Martha had just turned 18 and Henry was 23.

In order for Henry to find work, the couple initially moved to the inner suburbs of Sydney and boarded in Elizabeth Street, Redfern. Their child, a little girl they named Mabel Hannah, was born at 440 Riley Street, Surry Hills, on 13 November 1882.

The informant listed on Mabel's birth certificate was proud father Henry but some of the information he provided suggests that his young wife had not fully briefed him about her background. He listed her place of birth as 'Darlinghurst NSW', even though she had been born in the backblocks of South Australia. Henry evidently did not know as much about his young wife as he thought he did.[6]

Like all of Martha's children – she would ultimately have three – little Mabel was not destined for a long and happy life. Tragically, she had been born in the wrong place at the wrong time. And she had also been born to the wrong woman.

After a short time in Sydney, the couple and their young bundle of joy relocated back to Adelaide. Despite their initial drawbacks, the newlyweds settled into domestic life together and, to the outside world at least, they looked just like any other battlers. Even though the building trade in South Australia was beginning to hit hard times, Henry was able to find just enough work to provide sufficiently for his wife and baby daughter.

The couple soon celebrated the arrival of another daughter, Elsie, born on 6 October 1884.[7]

The Needles spent some time living in the town of Birkenhead, about 14 km from Adelaide. Henry scrimped just enough money to buy two extremely cheap adjoining blocks of land there, with the intention that he may eventually build a family house. But this dream never came to fruition.

In the meantime, Martha forged some friendships with other local women about the same age, the most prominent being Miss Gallaty, who resided just up the road. At one point, Martha even managed to borrow £7 from her new friend but, as an example of an emerging tradition, never quite got around to paying it back.

Despite her budgetary miscalculations, Martha was now seemingly a devoted young mother of two baby girls and 'her Harry' toiled hard to provide for his family. Carpentry was then not a lucrative vocation but this didn't prevent the well-skilled Henry travelling around to pick up stints of employment wherever he could. Known as a capable workman, Henry was always well liked wherever he went.

But he was not always the fine pillar of society that most people perceived him to be. As time moved on in his marriage, a darker side to Henry was destined to emerge behind closed doors.

Tough Times: Surviving Inner-City Richmond

Around this time, many Australian tradesmen began to eye off the bountiful building opportunities springing up in Melbourne. In contrast to the shrinking South Australian economy, the Victorian capital was experiencing a so-called 'once-in-a-lifetime' building expansion funded by speculative borrowings. The city soon experienced an influx of workers, all wishing to be part of the prosperity.

At the beginning of 1885, Henry decided to take the plunge and try to make a better life for himself, his young wife and daughters. Temporarily leaving Martha, Mabel and Elsie in Adelaide, he travelled to Melbourne – settling into an inner-city boarding house in Bridge Road, Richmond. This establishment was run by Mrs Hannah Tutt, who offered food and lodgings for a weekly fee. Her clientele exclusively consisted of young interstate tradesmen like Henry, all seeking a more lucrative life in Victoria.

Since the gold rush years of the 1850s, the city of Melbourne had continued to prosper, famously earning the title of 'Marvellous Melbourne' from British writer George Sala. The city that greeted Henry had imposing public buildings, modern office blocks and even an elementary telephone system. A network of trams and trains was also being rapidly developed to link the inner and outlying suburbs.

Henry's plan was to procure employment as quickly as he could and then save sufficient funds to pay for his family to join him in Melbourne. And his scheme worked perfectly. After only three months, he had saved enough coin to pay for their passage to Victoria. He also knew that a boarding house was unsuitable for his family, so he began to rent a small, cottage-style house in the industrial municipality of Richmond. Towards the middle of 1885, Henry and his attractive young wife Martha shifted into 19 Wellington Street with their young daughters and belongings.

Located only 3 km east of the Melbourne CBD, the developing boundaries of Richmond were shaped by the Yarra River. Although some of the elevated areas on the eastern side had originally been the preserve of the gentry, the flatlands where the Needles settled were largely restricted to the needs of industry and were prominently lined with rows of cheap housing. 'Marvellous Melbourne', with all its Victorian splendour, had not yet reached this lowly part of town.

The dominance of industry and manufacturing was never more evident than near the swampy part of Richmond, where mud and sewage mixed with by-products from the abattoirs and soap works located along the riverbanks. The Richmond that Martha moved to supported at least 52 industrial establishments, including tanneries, breweries, boot factories, saddleries, electroplaters and furniture manufacturers. Other labour-intensive Richmond factories produced candles, clothing, rope and mattresses.

Surrounded by similar working-class families, the Needles settled in quickly to their new suburban life. With so many modest and compact workers' cottages built alongside each other, the local neighbourhood wasn't a wealthy one. Most of the financially challenged residents provided the employment fodder for the local factories and trudged off to work every day except Sunday, scrimping enough money to live week to week and to keep the landlord off their back.

They were often desperate, vulnerable people and most were never destined to turn into anything except their own gateway. The slightest economic downturn could see them unemployed and left destitute on the street. It was then common for families to have between five and ten children and the heavily populated Richmond area soon earned a moniker that would last for decades – 'Struggletown'.[8]

The day-to-day strain experienced by residents generated a sense of belonging among the 'Richmondites' and the community was always very closely knit. Everyone knew everyone else's business – or at least they thought they did – and sometimes the local gossip could be particularly scurrilous.

The Needles became popular and their neighbours began to view them as 'a comfortably situated and well-matched couple'.[9] When Henry was bringing in a healthy income, his beautiful young wife wore more fashionable and expensive clothes than were usually seen among the cobbled laneways of working-class Richmond. She liked to exude an exaggerated style, giving many people the impression that she hailed from a much more socially advanced station in life than was actually the case.

After working as a domestic servant for a number of years in much richer households, the fashionista Martha had certainly come to observe and appreciate the finer things in life. And she had also developed other alluring traits – one of which was the unmistakable capacity to effortlessly charm most men with whom she crossed paths.

Henry always struggled to keep up with Martha's demands. By its very nature, his work was casual in tenure and spasmodic on account of the weather. There was a stigma placed upon outdoor work among the breadwinners of Richmond, who recognised that an irregular income could disrupt family life. The most prized form of employment was the rarer 'government' or 'indoor' jobs, which usually provided a regular pay packet and more security.

The list of local social acquaintances known to the Needles continued to grow. Prominent among them were their immediate neighbours, Robert and Annie Robinson, who resided at 21 Wellington Street. Similar in age and socio-economic circumstances to the Needles (in other words, young and poor), the battling Robinsons would soon be rearing two baby daughters of their own – Florence and Isabella. But as a steadily employed railway worker, Robert was better off than Henry and wasn't usually impacted by the vagaries associated with a casual job.

Significantly, Robert was also a particularly talkative and ingratiating type of neighbour, who spent most of his spare time peering over the back fence and keeping tabs on everything that was going on. Because of this, he considered himself to know the Needles very well and had undoubtedly also offered the attractive Martha more than the occasional admiring glance.

Another prominent acquaintance of the couple was local man Owen Evans, who lived nearby at 66 Balmain Street, Richmond. A rather slippery character at best, who ended up working as a country prison warder, Evans had first got to know Henry while the pair boarded together at the residence of Hannah Tutt. He maintained his friendship with Henry and often visited the Needles at Wellington Street. 'I knew his wife and I was on intimate terms and was in the habit of seeing them frequently' he would later recall to a court hearing. It would be heavily implied at that time that the primary motivation of his visits was to not only make himself known to Henry's flirtatious wife, but also to explore their 'intimate' companionship in more depth.

Breaking Out

Similar to all other housewives, nearly all of Martha's daily requirements could at that time be supplied by the local hawkers, including bakers, milkmen and the 'rabbitohs', who moved around the local streets on a daily basis to sell their wares. But Martha preferred to amble away from the grimy, cluttered laneways whenever she could.

She liked nothing more than to dress in her finest clothes and stroll along the busy Richmond thoroughfares of Bridge Road, Swan Street and Victoria Street. The types of stores that lined these shopping strips were indicative of a rural past beginning to combine with a developing community. They included an array of hay and grain stores, grocers, hotels, butchers, shoemakers, chemists and doctors' surgeries. But there were also some that catered for the finer things in life – clothing stores, jewellers, milliners and hairdressers.

Martha became a familiar sight as she paraded along the shopping precincts on a regular basis – undoubtedly setting more than a few hearts fluttering among the dour shopkeepers. Even in harsh economic times, she never seemed to have any trouble procuring whatever goods she needed on credit. She formed a particular allegiance with the traders who sold clothing and other fineries, bestowing bracing levels of attention upon them.

One of Martha's favourite pastimes was visiting the local photographic galleries, which were popular at the time and dotted all around the main streets of the inner suburbs. For a small fee, Martha could briefly act like a princess, dressing in the most elegant clothes imaginable, and then have her photograph taken amid a range of theatrical scenes and props. Martha often included her children in these visits, although the invitation was never extended to her austere husband, Henry.

The proprietors of these Richmond galleries had no way of knowing at the time that their portraits of Martha and her children would later be worth a small fortune. Once Martha's infamy grew, newspaper editors from around the world would scramble to buy them. The most famous snapshot of all showed a staged Martha with a slightly satisfied grin, standing creepily next to some ornate iron gates. Some with fertile imaginations would later suggest that this portrait looked like Martha was standing at cemetery gates ready to welcome in her next victims.

Health Hazards

While things may have looked rather quaint around this time, the cramped living conditions and lack of effective sanitation practices meant that the threat of potentially fatal disease in this pre-vaccination era hovered menacingly over the entire Melbourne population.

As a capital city with open sewers, overflowing cesspits and heavily polluted creeks – not to mention the very careless emptying of bedpans – Melbourne was so pervaded with the odours associated with human excrement it attracted the mocking nickname of 'Smellbourne'.

The most consistent killer disease in early Melbourne was typhoid fever. A disease spread by consuming food or water contaminated by the faeces of an infected person, typhoid cases soared amid the primary risk factors of poor sanitation and unreliable hygiene.

The symptoms of typhoid would usually emerge within six to thirty days after exposure and could vary from mild to severe. The disease often started with a gradual onset of high fever over several days and a skin rash, weakness, abdominal pain, constipation and headaches.

The generalised nature of these typhoid indicators could be confused with those of other ailments by panicked Melbourne inhabitants and medicos. The disease was often referred to by other names, depending on the primary symptoms being displayed. Among the medical labels appearing on death certificates in this era were vague terms such as colonial fever, gastric fever and enteric fever.[10]

The fear of fatal diseases was never more acutely felt than in the slummy and densely populated areas of Richmond. The mere mention of the word 'typhoid' would send a shudder through the locals. At best, it was a very nasty disease that needed to be taken very seriously. At worst, it would mean a death sentence. And the by-product of all this was that most premature or sudden deaths were not investigated too much, with 'typhoid' often copping the blame.

CHAPTER 4

'Rough on Rats'… and Just as Harsh on Humans

Like most inner-city areas at this time, the underwhelming Richmond was not only heavily populated with battling local residents – it was also swarming with rats. Desperate measures – ranging from employing professional ratcatchers and fox-terrier handlers to the unregulated use of pea rifles – were all used to help keep the rat plague at bay. Another common killing method was the liberal use of rat poison, which was cheap and in wide circulation.

The most popular brand of rat toxin had the indelible name 'Rough on Rats'. Advertisements for its sale had begun appearing in Australian newspapers in the early 1880s and the graphically packaged product soon became a household name.

This rodent eliminator was an American invention, attributed to Jersey City manufacturer and part-time music publisher Ephraim Wells. The highly successfully product was promoted as a 'leading cause of cat unemployment' and even featured its own catchy 'Rough on Rats' jingle, which had been penned by Wells himself.

Guaranteed to 'clear out a whole house in a single application', 'Rough on Rats' purchases were eventually controlled by the various *Sale of Poisons Acts* around the country, although disturbingly it was still very easily obtainable at chemists. At most, a purchaser would need to be known to the pharmacist and be asked to sign a 'poison book' in front of a witness before leaving the store.

Despite its advertising hype, 'Rough on Rats' was a very simple product. It primarily consisted of the irritant poison arsenic, with some charcoal added to give the mixture a darker colour.

Although arsenic is a highly toxic substance, it has also been utilised by humanity in various ways since ancient times as a beauty product and colouring agent. But the secret has always been to ensure that exposure is limited to extremely miniscule amounts. Any ingestion beyond this level can lead to instant death in a human being.

A Murder Weapon

By the time 'Rough on Rats' hit the marketplace, arsenic had already forged a sinister history, being utilised for centuries as a means of committing murder. At one time, it was even referred to as the 'inheritance powder' – such was its popularity among impatient family members.

But a note for ambitious beginners: arsenic is a particularly stupid poison to use when trying to murder someone. The biggest practical problem with utilising arsenic to dispatch a non-essential member of the human race is that it remains easily detectable in the body long after death, even in tiny amounts. Unlike other chemical agents, arsenic does not deteriorate over time.[11]

The chemical longevity of arsenic presents a major threat to the would-be killer. If sufficient suspicions arise after death and the body is exhumed, a post-mortem will almost certainly reveal incriminating evidence. The extremely toxic nature of arsenic also compels a killer to administer small amounts over a period of time. Given that too much arsenic will cause instant death, the killer has to gauge how much to feed the victim to cause a gradual deterioration in health. But unexplainable long-term illnesses can also arouse suspicion, placing the suspect under further levels of scrutiny.

Although few people have volunteered to be subjected to the required taste-test experiments, it is known that arsenic can have an objectionable metallic flavour. This forces a would-be murderer to mix a powdered form of arsenic with food or to dilute it in liquid refreshments. The taste has to be disguised sufficiently so that the victim will actually swallow the intended dose.

How To Win Friends And Poison Them

It soon became clear that not everyone buying a box of 'Rough on Rats' in the late 1800s was content to follow the manufacturer's specifications. The product became a popular option for committing suicide and was also directly mentioned in a number of very prominent murder cases, both in Australia and abroad.

The most publicised Australian case up to that point involved Louisa Collins in New South Wales. During the 1880s, she endured four court trials before eventually being found guilty of poisoning two husbands with 'Rough on Rats'. Traces of arsenic were found in the remains of both men; Louisa's first husband had heavily insured his life.

Although the defence counsel for Collins suggested that arsenic may have been absorbed through exposure to the sheepskin tanning industry where both victims worked, or alternatively they may have been contaminated by impure bismuth used to treat their respective sicknesses, on 8 January 1889 Collins was executed for these murders. She therefore became enshrined in history as the 'Last Woman Hanged in New South Wales'.

But, as it turned out, Victoria still had a few more females to go.

All these arsenic cases featured heavily in the newspapers. And all the while, Martha undoubtedly kept up her professional reading.

Profile of a Poisoner

Although the world of serial killing has always been a landscape heavily dominated by men, the majority of serial poisoners in history have actually been women. It appears that when female serial murderers have taken the plunge, they have sought to kill in a *different,* more methodical way than their more violent male colleagues.

Women poisoners have also traditionally operated from the powerful position of caregiver, commonly adopting roles such as nurse, aged-care attendant or boarding home worker.

But the ghastliest female poisoner of all has historically been the one who seeks to take advantage of her own vulnerable family members, while convincingly playing out the day-to-day role of normal wife and mother. The media has often colourfully dubbed such women as 'Black Widows', named in honour of the deadly female spider that lures an unfortunate male in her direction and then consumes him after completing the mating act.

The motivations of human Black Widows can vary, but they are often centred on becoming the opportunistic beneficiary of their loved one's material possessions and insurance payouts. Others may have experienced domestic violence and, even though they have experienced some closeness with their partner for years, they finally snap and decide to rid the world of their cruel abuser. For others, it is simply a need to move on from a tiresome existence.

By their very nature, human Black Widows need to be organised, patient, longer-term planners. They must win the trust of their husband and those around them – which can take months or even years to achieve effectively – and all the while be hatching a manipulative plot. It is only when her unsuspecting husband or family members are sufficiently relaxed that the human Black Widow will finally expose her fangs and strike, most often by beginning to casually slip some poison into the foodstuffs and beverages she is conscientiously offering them.

Even upon the death of her victims, the act is not over for the effective Black Widow. To help evade suspicion even further, she will mourn heavily for her departed loved ones. And in the very unlikely event that over-troublesome officials such as the police or doctors rudely query any of the circumstances of what has occurred, she will be convincing enough to have the matter stamped 'cold case' forever. While this is all going on, the Black Widow may be spending the life insurance payout of her previous prey and will almost certainly be scanning the horizon and looking to seduce her next victim.[12]

Poisoning is often a particularly slow and agonising way to die, meaning that most human Black Widows need to be extremely cruel to serve up their venom on a platter. In addition to requiring a deft hand with the suitable doses, some unquestionably develop a sadistic streak. They begin to enjoy the secret power they have over human life and come to believe that they are smarter than the dullards around them and the clumsy authorities such as the police.

Some may even spend months nursing their victims back to health before poisoning them again – the ultimate cat-and-mouse game with human life. They begin to enjoy watching their victims suffer and may give them just enough poison to keep them in agony for months without killing them, all the while receiving community admiration for their sacrificial nursing skills. They may even enjoy watching their victims develop a spark of optimism before finally finishing the job and killing them off.[13]

Many of these personality traits would soon be evident in the compassion-impaired Martha and the much-hyped product 'Rough on Rats' was about to play a very significant role in her life.

CHAPTER 5

Mabel Needle –
The Loss of a Young Life

Among the day-to-day struggles, the Needles were soon to experience a family tragedy. Towards the end of 1885, their first year in Richmond, the health of their eldest daughter, Mabel, began to wane. The symptoms were vague but contrary to her previous good health, little three-year-old Mabel began to fade away before their eyes.

Despite the economic challenges that he faced and the variable nature of his employment, Henry had managed to join one of the local lodges of the Independent Order of Oddfellows (now simply known as IOOF), which was the equivalent of an insurance company today.[14] By paying a continuing subscription, members could receive benefits in the event of illness, including consultations with a local physician. So the lodge doctor, Dr Frederick Elsner, was now called upon to view the severely ailing Mabel.

While the physicians associated with lodges were usually sympathetic to their marginalised patients, they were not always the most astute examples of their profession. And this was the category to which Elsner belonged. In a professional sense, he was about as sharp as a bedpan. During the year leading up to Mabel's examination, Elsner had even been romantically distracted and subjected to a number of ethical dilemmas.

Early in 1885, Elsner had been practising in Woollahra, New South Wales, and was called to treat a vivacious 18-year-old named Annie Wild. This young woman was then betrothed to a wealthy older farmer named Stirling and had fallen pregnant out of wedlock. Stirling paid Elsner a whopping £1,000 to treat her, with a view to procuring an abortion. The primary condition that he placed on the practitioner was that he was to keep the matter quiet.

But somewhere along the line, Elsner took a fancy to the young patient himself. Soon he asked Annie to marry him instead of Stirling, with the added rider that should she refuse his request he would reveal all he knew to 'her people' and to those close to Stirling. Naturally, Stirling was somewhat dismayed upon hearing of this development but his reputation meant more to him than Annie so he gave Elsner another £2,000 to disappear to a different state.

Elsner married young Annie in July 1885 and used the additional £2,000 windfall to buy into the medical practice in Richmond. The unusually matched couple moved to Richmond soon after, where the young bride quickly noted that her husband had a short temper, drank heavily and liked to stay out at nights. He was particularly fond of music and even neglected his profession in preference to it.[15]

Mabel was one of Elsner's first patients in Richmond. He noted that the little girl had been suffering from fever, vomiting and spasms of the stomach for short periods of time but he could offer no long-term solutions.

On 28 December 1885, Mabel's short life came to an end, only seven weeks after her third birthday. Although she had displayed a number of generalised physical failings, Elsner could not nominate a specific diagnosis for her death. He preferred to suggest that she must have experienced 'cerebral' irritations, which had apparently led to a form of 'cardiac paralysis'. He officially certified that the little three-year-old had died from cerebral tumour (congenital) and respiratory and cardiac bronchitis.[16]

With fatal diseases such as typhoid raging throughout the squalid industrial areas, life was cheap and infants often withered away and died. There was no official autopsy or investigation into Mabel's death. With no questions being asked, the word of a medical practitioner – however peculiar – was the end of the matter and her passing became another inner-city statistic.

Like many people of this era, Mabel's heartbroken parents were now faced with the agonising task of burying one of their own children. This small ceremony was performed on New Year's Eve 1885 and the young girl was laid to rest at Boroondara General Cemetery in Melbourne's emerging north-eastern suburb of Kew. No-one knew it at the time, but due to Mabel's mother, the very name of this cemetery would later resonate around the world. And many secrets ended up being buried there.

Mabel's parents were able to scrimp together enough money to place a modest, heartfelt death notice in Melbourne's the *Age* newspaper on the very last day of 1885. It contained a few clumsy errors, but read:

> Needles – On the 28th December, at her parents' residence, 19 Wellington street Richmond, after a short illness, of tumor on the brain, Mabel Hannah, the eldest beloved daughter of Henry and Martha Needles, aged 3 years and 7 months.
>
> Little Mabel has gone to rest.

Of course, the notice should have referred to the surname 'Needle', not 'Needles', and Mabel had actually died at 3 years and 7 *weeks*, not 7 *months*. But the sentiment and depth of the advertisement's misery was unmistakable.

To add even further to the pain, Martha was five months pregnant with the couple's third child at the time of Mabel's death.

Upon the passing of her first child, Martha was inundated with the sympathy and attention of all those around her. The pity displayed by her neighbours, friends and even her husband all peaked at the same time.

Love and Other Bruises

But irrespective of this brief emotional interlude between husband and wife, the death of their eldest daughter put paid to any hope that Henry and Martha's relationship would successfully survive. It was now shattered forever.

Soon after the loss of Mabel, Henry also had another pressing burden. Local work in Melbourne had begun to dry up, partly because of the sudden oversupply of tradesmen. He was forced to seek work further afield and travelled to Sydney, where he stayed for several months.

Left to her own devices in Richmond, the lonely and disconsolate Martha began venturing out more at night on her own. The streetwise rumour-mongers had a free shot at goal, as the nocturnal Martha never seemed to be short of male admirers. A later newspaper report would reflect back on this time of Martha's unravelling life by explaining that she had become renowned locally for having 'a flighty disposition fond of company, and with a weakness for the admiration of the sterner sex, which was invariably accorded to her'.

Upon his return to Richmond, Henry remained extremely jealous and suspicious about his young wife's 'flighty' behaviour – apparently not without some justification. The tension in the marriage reached boiling point and, according to Martha's later accounts, Henry began to resort to acts of domestic violence against her. Others would also later support Martha's version of events.

By this time, Martha's sympathetic childhood friend, Eliza Martin, had also moved from South Australia and was living nearby at Crown Street, Richmond. She would continue to see Martha often. She later steadfastly testified in a courtroom that Martha frequently complained to her about Henry's unkindness and cruelty towards her. According to Martha, this alleged treatment had started with her husband distributing 'sly thumps' to her, eventually culminating in a beating in their Richmond home that caused her to give birth prematurely.

Such observations provided some strong corroboration – albeit from a partisan source – to the claims about domestic violence that Martha would later make.

Having come from a childhood background of unrestrained violence and poverty, Martha now found herself well and truly trapped in a stifling, financially drained, loveless matrimonial situation. She firmly believed that she had pinned the tail on the wrong donkey – the man of her dreams had not only become her worst nightmare but he was also evidently prone to dispensing physical abuse against her.

This was not the life Martha had dreamed of as a miserable young girl growing up around the backblocks of South Australia. And residing in the poor part of Richmond had also begun to grate on her. She now much preferred dressing up and going out; she yearned for the attentions of men. She also liked money and the things she could buy with it, in addition to the power, prestige and security such capital could provide. She had seen a glimpse of the good life and now gained little satisfaction from the drudgery of performing domestic chores for a man she did not love. And so, unburdened by normal conscience, her personality profile was about to warp irretrievably.

'Rough on Rats' was not the only questionable product readily available for purchase from the local chemist during this era. 'Patent medicines' and elixirs could also be cheaply purchased across the counter without any form of prescription. With very few laws then relating to drug sales and usage, these substances were marketed extensively in newspaper advertisements, offering all sorts of health claims and promising to deal with myriad unrelated ailments.

These tonics routinely adopted reassuring names, such as 'Dr Haines' Golden Specific', which only served to camouflage their actual ingredients – including later-discovered nasties such as cannabis and morphine. These commercial products were consumed on a mass scale by a population ignorant of their possible side effects and addictive potential.

One of the most popular patent medicines of all was the potentially dangerous painkiller 'Dr J. Collis Browne's Chlorodyne'. As its name implied, this brew was said to have been 'invented' by Dr John Collis Browne, a doctor in the British Indian army, and had originally been intended to treat cholera. Browne later sold his dicey formula to a pharmacist, who began to patent the product and advertise it widely throughout the British Isles, not only to assist with cholera symptoms, but also to allegedly address an impressive array of other conditions, such as insomnia, neuralgia, epilepsy, hysteria, asthma, consumption, diphtheria, palpitations, rheumatism, gout, toothache, meningitis and even cancer.

With an endless stream of questionable 'testimonials', the spectacular advertising for chlorodyne was far from modest in nature. It extolled the product as 'the most wonderful and valuable remedy ever discovered' and 'the wonder drug of the 19th century'.

The actual ingredients of the compound help to explain why it became such a big hit. Effectively, chlorodyne was a mixture of laudanum (a powerful alcoholic solution of morphine), cannabis and chloroform. Such ingredients not only helped the 'medicine' live up to some of its outlandish claims but also made it highly addictive and a potential poison. Deaths from overdoses of chlorodyne, either deliberate or accidental, became a frequent occurrence. Coroners' reports of the day would often tell the tale of a body being found in a room littered with empty chlorodyne bottles.

As the popularity of Browne's legendary chlorodyne grew, generic imitations began to spring up and be sold locally. The active ingredients of the product were well known and chemists could easily make up their own cheaper versions. These rivals often replaced the laudanum with morphine hydrochloride, making them even more addictive and dangerous in larger doses.

If misused, chlorodyne could cause adverse side effects, similar to those listed for morphine abuse. These included psychiatric disorders, such as hallucinations, euphoria, confusion, restlessness, agitation, delirium and disorientation; and nervous system disorders, such as dizziness, sleep disturbances, headache, vertigo, raised intracranial pressure and seizures. It was also likely to lead to the eye disorder miosis, an excessive constriction of the pupils.

Relevantly, it was around this time that Martha became a regular consumer of chlorodyne, originally telling some of her acquaintances that this was to treat 'a pain in her side'. In all likelihood she was also seeking to eliminate a lot of other pain in her life, including in her 'backside', given the stresses associated with her strained marriage and tedious daily existence.

Unquestionably lured by the flashy hyperbole appearing in the advertisements, Martha's medication of choice became chlorodyne. From then on, Martha would rarely return from her local shops without a purchased bottle of chlorodyne stashed in her purse.

Although she was something of a closet user, Martha's chronic chlorodyne consumption increased with every passing year. Like many other forlorn housewives, as her pain intensified she would turn to the product for solace, oblivious to the fact that its overuse was probably the cause of the pain itself. Her world full of hopes and dreams had mostly been replaced by empty bottles of chlorodyne spread around her rented house.

With little or no information available about the possible effects of chlorodyne, the link between Martha's future behaviours and use of the product was certainly never made during her day. Neither has it been properly understood since, with some pundits simply content to label her as showing signs of 'insanity' rather than examining further the impacts of her chlorodyne usage. But in reality, Martha's emerging addiction to chlorodyne would go a long way to explain some of her ongoing behaviours.

With an increased awareness evolving during the 20th century, the cannabis and opiate components of Martha's favourite potion were removed. While these days chlorodyne is confined to the history books, the updated 'Dr J. Collis Browne's Mixture' is still available in Britain as a harmless treatment for coughs and upset stomachs.

Doctor Shopping

As her health and demeanour became more erratic, Martha extended the circle of doctors with whom she consulted, both in Richmond and beyond. Not restricting herself to the lodge doctors, she was soon well known to an assortment of medical men, none of who were particularly aware that she was also consulting with other members of their brethren. In addition to Dr Elsner, over the next few years she would soon be fully acquainted with Drs Hodgson, McColl, Burton, Payne, Singleton and Snowball.

Likewise, she began to visit at least four different chemist shops around the Richmond area, which included three in close proximity to each other in Bridge Road. All of these establishments produced their own generic versions of chlorodyne. In these circumstances, Martha never struggled to procure any drugs, prescriptions or potions she needed – no questions asked.

Of course, even though she flitted around, Martha still had her favourites. She always found Bridge Road chemist James Stiles particularly amenable. Stiles was also a speculative investor on the side and knew the value of a pound. He would unhesitatingly provide whatever was requested once the correct money was produced.

And Martha's favourite medical man of all was the ageing Dr John Singleton – a legendary physician and philanthropist in early Melbourne. Singleton had been the founding doctor of the newly established children's hospital and he also wrote a regular column in the *Age* newspaper under the title 'Singleton Cures'. And even though Singleton operated in the neighbouring suburb of Collingwood, Martha always found the trip to his clinic to be very worthwhile because it came with extra benefits.

Singleton's greatest achievement had been the establishment of a range of charitable outlets and missions, which included a number for 'fallen, friendless and destitute' women. He also provided many free services at his clinic for those desperate down-and-outs who could not afford to pay. This was the type of arrangement Martha liked and she was soon unashamedly receiving any charitable handouts she could procure, even though strictly speaking she was being supported by a dreary husband and was not sufficiently 'fallen' or 'destitute' at all, and only rarely felt 'friendless'.

And the good news didn't end there. In the Christian spirit, Singleton also operated a free dispensary next to his clinic, to provide drugs and medicines to those who could not afford such necessaries, and Martha was often in the front of the queue.

The dispensary was operated by Singleton's eldest son, John Jnr, who in contrast to his esteemed father was a particularly unprincipled type of individual. Even though he had no recognised medical training, John Jnr was inclined to provide unqualified treatment when offered money to do so. On one occasion, he was even fined in court for scandalously masquerading as an eye specialist and unsuccessfully attempting to remedy a patient's fading vision by putting a camel hair brush up his nostrils.

But Martha was willing to overlook such indiscretions, because he would always hand over any items she requested without delay or discussion. And this included his own generic brand of chlorodyne.

CHAPTER 6

A Bit of Flightiness

While the birth of the couple's third child on 28 April 1886 – a daughter the Needles named 'May'– brought some joy, the addition of another mouth to feed at 19 Wellington Street was now a particularly pressing issue. Henry was struggling to find work and other income sources were needed. Among the domestic tensions, the Needles decided that they could make up their economic shortfall by taking in some boarders. Although this was scarcely a lucrative option, it would utilise the only money-making skills that Martha had developed in her youth – namely cooking and cleaning for other people.

Boarding was an extremely popular form of housing during this era and was often facilitated by women who had been widowed and left with no other income-producing options. While very few of the transient young men seeking employment in the big towns could afford to rent a whole property, most could scrape up a few shillings to rent a room and pay a little more to have 'the woman' of the house cook their meals and wash their clothes.

To support their new venture, the Needles moved out of their small cottage in Wellington Street and rented a larger residence nearby. They shifted to a two-storey house at 110 Cubitt Street, Richmond, which was located on the corner of Balmain Street. While the extra rooms in this house could accommodate the intended boarders, the entire venture would only add further to Martha's dismal domestic commitments.

From a matrimonial point of view, the thought of the distractible Martha taking in boarders was also a relationship disaster. Already known to have at least a roving eye, she now found herself surrounded by eager young men living at the same address, while her grumpy husband was often away searching for work.

The new address at Cubitt Street also seemed to be cursed in other ways. In what was initially thought to be an extraordinary run of misfortune, all surviving members of the Needle family (except Martha herself) would soon leave this unhappy house in coffins.

A Creature of the Night

After men began to respond to the advertisement offering cheap lodgings at Cubitt Street, the Needles' social circle naturally continued to expand. Although they had no way of knowing this at the time, many of those who became acquainted with Martha would later be scrutinised in the most public way imaginable. Some would even have their daily lives altered forever.

One of the boarders who ended up being flagrantly named and shamed – both in court and in the newspapers – was routinely referred to as a 'man named Mercer'. It was said that he had become closer to his landlady than was customarily expected to be the case and he had been abruptly shown the door by the furiously jealous Henry. This man was Harry Mercer, an aspiring young bootmaker who had left his home town of Bendigo to seek better opportunities in the Big Smoke. Once away from the influence of Martha, he would settle into life as a solid family man and would eventually become the manager of the Victoria Boot Company. But the shame of his association with the Black Widow would never totally leave him.

Martha's favourite boarder of all turned out to be Archibald 'Arch' Martin, who, in between his dalliances with Martha, plied his trade as a tobacconist in nearby Swan Street. Before Martha came along, he was considered an 'unknown' – a status he richly deserved – although she was soon all over him like a cheap suit. The pair became sufficiently close that she confided in him stories about her earlier years. She even went as far as to tell him about the severe bout of sunstroke she had endured in Adelaide. Henry had good reason to be jealous of Martin, who was not only kicked out of Cubitt Street in a hurry but later went even further afield and immigrated to New Zealand.[17]

Another man who later found himself in the public spotlight for igniting extreme jealousy in Henry was the ill-fated Ernst Altmann, who at that time conducted a thriving jewellery business with shops in both Swan Street, Richmond, and Elizabeth Street, Melbourne. His private interactions with Martha were not only exposed in the newspapers a number of years after they occurred – they also helped set his life on a path to ruin.

A highly skilled jeweller and engraver, Altmann was a married man and considerably older than Martha, having been born in Melbourne to German parents in circa 1850. Altmann had married 25-year-old Maria Scherell in 1879 and the couple had moved to 16 Gipps Street, Richmond, where Maria also established a boarding house. The marital and age drawbacks associated with Altmann probably meant little to open-minded Martha, who would have been bedazzled into her older-man crush by the fine jewellery that he could give her.

Altmann's downfall started when he began to engage in private visits to Martha at her Richmond address while Henry was away. Henry ultimately received an anonymous letter that outlined the nature of these activities; after a considerable amount of delving, he formed the view that this letter had been sent by Mrs Maria Altmann.

Mrs Altmann conceded her authorship and insisted that her statements were true. After Henry confronted Martha about the accusations, she tamely admitted that Altmann had been visiting her but denied any actual impropriety, even though she would have had more chance of persuading him of the existence of the tooth fairy.

Altmann's previously promising life soon started to unravel. He separated from his wife and went bankrupt about 1896 – two years after being unreservedly named as a potential philanderer at Martha's sensational murder trial. He shifted interstate but he was unable to recapture any of his past success and died a broken man.

Thomas Gilroy

From 1888 onwards, Martha spent an inordinate amount of time frequenting the drapery store of Mr James Moloney at 160 Swan Street, Richmond. Not all of this effort was to exclusively attend to her urgent drapery needs – she had also taken a fancy to the young shop assistant working there, 28-year-old Irishman Thomas Gilroy. And the attentions were clearly mutual.

After marrying Sophia Luxon in Dublin at the beginning of 1887, Gilroy and his new wife had moved to Melbourne to try their luck shortly after. The couple had a son, James William, born in Richmond in October that year. But this would not prevent the smitten Gilroy falling under Martha's spell. While each of them was married to someone else, they would still seek to relieve some of their marital tensions and flirt shamelessly with each other.

Whenever the easily flattered Martha entered the shop, Gilroy would announce loudly that if ever Martha's husband died, he would gladly become 'husband No. 2'. Such comments lost some of their jocular impact after Gilroy's 27-year-old wife died in April 1889. And in any event, Martha was still married to the ever-grouchy Henry. But the pair's attraction to each other remained undeniable.[18]

Brotherly Love

In 1888, Martha first laid eyes on three dashing young brothers – Herman, Louis and Otto Juncken. They instantly had something in common, because the Junckens also hailed from South Australia.

Yet, in contrast to Martha's background, the Junckens were part of a well-regarded family who, for many years, had made their mark while residing in Lyndoch, a German settlement district about 14 km from Gawler. Their late father had been a successful builder, while their mother was the highly protective Irish-born Margaret. She was a blunt woman who ruled her family with a rod of iron.[19]

The Juncken family was a big and healthy brood and they all survived the ravages of childhood to grow up into fine adults. There were ten offspring in the family – seven of them strong, active working men and three of them said to be girls of high refinement.[20]

At 26 years of age, Herman was the oldest in the family and had first ventured to Melbourne about the same time as the Needles made a similar trek from South Australia. Herman was followed the next year by his brothers, Louis and Otto.

Like Henry Needle, Herman and Otto worked as carpenters in South Australia and he had first known them through his profession in that state. Otto in particular was an intelligent and ambitious young man. He started working for Clements Langford, one of Melbourne's major builders at the time, and would later successfully study architectural drawing and carpentry at the local Working Men's College.

While the majority of the Juncken boys had followed their father's footsteps into the building trade, Louis had trod a different path. He had undertaken an apprenticeship in saddlery. In this pre-car age when equine-drawn transportation dominated the needs of the community, the world of saddlery was a thriving business, with retailers sometimes struggling to keep up with demand.

Louis was quick to notice these opportunities and, in March 1890, he opened his own saddlery shop in rented premises located in busy Bridge Road, Richmond. Another Juncken brother, Charles, later made the move from South Australia to join Otto and Louis living in Richmond.[21]

Although a close friendship had not then developed between the Needles and Junckens, they were clearly on very convivial terms. Otto could later recall the first time in 1888 he had been fleetingly introduced to Martha – it was at a boarding house in Richmond Terrace where he and Herman were then staying with a local family called Nicholson. It was a very brief formal introduction lasting only a few minutes and it took place during a party being held at the Nicholson residence. He spoke to her again at this location a few weeks later.

Both Herman and Otto were later invited into the Needles' own home on at least three occasions, two of these times being to attend parties the Needles had organised. The social contact between Martha and the Junckens may only have been a passing one at this stage but she had obviously taken more than a quick glance at young Otto – and she must have liked what she saw. This was the start of some very bad news not only for Otto but ultimately for the entire Juncken family.

Another significant acquaintance forged by the Needles at this time was with the electrician Thomas Smith, who resided with his family at 3 Sherwood Street, Richmond. Smith knew the Junckens well through the building trade and had also met Henry the same way. Smith had managed to build up a healthier bank balance than most tradesmen in Richmond and his house was furnished accordingly. But there was also less to him than met the eye, because such capital had been raised through a dubious mixture of business acumen and not always settling his debts on time. Even more significantly, members of the Smith family had heard some of the rumours concerning Martha and considered her to be a bit of an ordinary unit with delusions of adequacy.

Insurance Planning

Throughout the first half of 1889, Henry was forced to travel far afield throughout the Gippsland region of Victoria in search of work. While he traipsed from one small town to another, his convivial wife remained at Cubitt Street, attending to the needs of her boarders. Henry still firmly believed that she was probably attending to their needs in more ways than one.

On 1 June 1889, Henry was stationed at Warragul, the Gippsland town some 100 km south-east of Melbourne. While there, he filled out and signed a proposal to insure his life for a whopping £200 and forwarded the applicable paperwork to the office of the Australian Widow's Fund Life Insurance Society in Melbourne.

For Henry, this policy would be akin to his death warrant. Despite the massive £200 bounty on his head, he curiously didn't go to the trouble of writing a will, even though it would later be revealed in a courtroom that Martha had been imploring him to do so. Martha could see great benefits in documenting his intentions and she was undoubtedly anxious to be his sole beneficiary. But Henry remained unmoved. He may have suspected that, as the saying goes, 'Where there's a will, there's a way'.

Insurance-wise, 1889 had already been an active year for Martha. Four months before her husband saw fit to take out a policy on his life, she had insured the lives of both her surviving children, Elsie and May.

Like most forms of peddling, selling insurance from door to door was a common practice at that time. When an agent for the Temperance and General Mutual Life Assurance Society Limited, John Holt, knocked on the door at Cubitt Street and presented his well-rehearsed pitch, Martha became very interested in the policies he was flogging. It was then possible to take out 'penny a week' life insurance and endowment policies, with the premiums deliberately kept as low as possible and collected at the door on a weekly basis so that the very poor could still consider the proposition.

Martha took out separate 'penny a week' policies for both Elsie and May and conscientiously kept up the payments every week.[22] With such security behind her, Martha could at least feel cautiously optimistic about her future.

CHAPTER 7

Untimely Demise of a Husband

Within four months of taking out his life insurance policy, the previously healthy Henry was struck down by a sudden illness. He was attended to by Dr George Hodgson, who was by then the resident lodge practitioner for the Richmond area.

The 35-year-old Hodgson, a native of Dublin, had arrived in Richmond with a seemingly impressive although mixed background. After being trained in his home country, he had been appointed as an assistant surgeon at an Irish infirmary, a position he held for six years. He had then entered the service of a shipping company as an onboard physician and visited various parts of the world before finally settling in rather unglamorous Richmond.

Hodgson noted that Henry had always been a robust man but that he was now suffering from acute vomiting. The symptoms puzzled Hodgson. At first, he suspected that Henry may have been suffering from lead poisoning – but then again, perhaps he was also showing some of the early signs of typhoid.

As his physical condition steadily worsened, Henry also demonstrated some unusual behavioural traits. Most notable of all was his obstinate refusal to take any food handed to him by his wife. Anything she offered to him he would wave aside – and if she continued to press the issue, he would throw the food over the floor or dash it against the bedroom wall rather than accept it. Some of Martha's acquaintances helped her to nurse Henry during his illness and remarked how peculiar this behaviour was. Henry would take food when they offered it but adamantly refused to do so whenever his lovely wife entered the room holding the tray.

On one of his visits, Hodgson noted that Henry had left untouched some chicken broth and jelly that Martha had served him. This led to Hodgson remonstrating with Henry, lecturing to him that if he did not take sufficient nourishment, he would surely die. Hodgson even went as far as berating Henry about the cruel position and dire financial mess in which he would leave his loving wife and children if he passed on.

The taciturn Henry never provided any explanation about this behaviour, leaving Hodgson and Martha's friends alike to conclude that it must have simply been a display of irritability from a dying man. Its effect was certainly disastrous to the rapidly waning Henry, because he was not allowing himself to be sufficiently fed.

All told, Henry's illness lasted 17 days and his condition was so critical at one point that Hodgson visited him three times within a few hours. In contrast to Henry's stubbornness, Hodgson found Martha a delight to deal with. No only had she remained in rude health the whole time, but he later wistfully described her as 'tender and thoughtful' throughout the entire ordeal.[23]

As a last act of desperation, Henry insisted on being seen by another doctor. And not just any doctor – he asked to receive a home visit from the famous physician from Collingwood, John Singleton. Martha knew Singleton well enough to organise this quickly but Singleton was not able to offer any miracle cures. After examining Henry, the extremely concerned Singleton could only tell the stricken patient that he would surely die within a day or two and encouraged him to prepare for the afterlife.

Singleton's diagnosis proved to be correct. Henry died on 4 October 1889, with his vigilant wife hovering by his side. The extraordinary death certificate originally provided by Hodgson expressly cited the official cause of death as 'sub-acute hepatitis, persistent vomiting, enteric fever, and exhaustion, due to obstinacy in not taking nourishment'. In other words – according to Hodgson at the time – Henry had died from inflammation of the liver and intestines, and from exhaustion due to a lack of nourishment. The last cause of death listed – 'exhaustion, due to obstinacy in not taking nourishment' – had never been seen by Hodgson before, let alone written on a death certificate.

Yet, despite the mysterious nature and sudden onset of the illness, the bizarre behaviour shown by the deceased and the fact that the first three maladies mentioned in the death certificate were consistent with symptoms of arsenic poisoning, no post-mortem was performed. This meant that Henry's burial could quickly take place without any impediment.

Hodgson's diagnosis would later be exposed as bunkum. Another worrying development emerged, namely that different copies of the original death certificate were later uncovered, with some copies conveniently omitting the reference to 'persistent vomiting'.[24]

A Melodramatic Moment

Martha was now quite literally a Black Widow, dressing in dark mourning clothes – although she carefully maintained her sense of style. She played the role of widow with a considerable degree of pathos, gratefully receiving the abundant sympathy of friends and neighbours.

Martha duly contacted the local funeral director, Herbert King, from nearby Lennox Street in Richmond, to quickly organise Henry's funeral. She must have been satisfied with the service offered, because this first contact would ultimately mark the start of a sequence of repeat business opportunities for the local undertaker.

Martha also contacted the *Age* newspaper to ensure a death notice was placed in the classifieds the very next day. The wording of the notice was brief and bland. It not only lacked the emotional feel that had recorded the passing of three-year-old Mabel four years earlier, but it was also far from typical of the type of death notices that heartbroken young widows were then inclined to write while farewelling their much-loved spouses:

> NEEDLE – On the 4th October, after a short illness, at 110 Cubitt-street, Richmond, Henry, the husband of Martha Needle, late of Exeter, South Australia, aged 30 years.

> South Australian and Sydney papers please copy.

The dispassionate, matter-of-fact tone of this advertisement soon became the topic of conversation among the Richmond gossips. They were quick to scurrilously comment that Martha had not described Henry as her 'beloved' husband, or used the classifieds to refer to him with any particular degree of affection. This time, the scandalmongers were right on the money.

Henry's funeral was held on 7 October 1889 – only three days after his death. The funeral notice that morning in the *Age* stated:

> The Friends of the late Mr HENRY NEEDLE are respectfully invited to follow his remains to the place of interment, the Boroondara Cemetery, Kew. The funeral to move from his late residence, No. 110 Cubitt-street, South Richmond, THIS DAY (Monday the 7th inst. At 2 o'clock pm)

> HERBERT KING, Undertaker, 18 Lennox-street Richmond

As anticipated, the funeral of the outwardly popular Henry was heavily attended. He was buried in his own plot – B2477 – in the Church of

England Section of the Boroondara General Cemetery, not all that far away from where his young daughter, Mabel, had been earlier laid to rest. The centre of attention throughout the entire proceedings was his mourning widow, Martha. Those present continually expressed their sympathy to her, as the brave young woman with two infant daughters in tow had now lost her husband and eldest child within a short space of time.

Apparently adding to Martha's woes, there were no social security payments to fall back on in those days. With the rent and other living expenses still due, many widows were forced down the path of destitution. Although Martha continued to take in boarders, many locals now wondered how she would raise her remaining two daughters without the steady financial support of a husband. They need not have worried.

Although she had never mentioned to anyone else about Henry's life insurance, Martha was secretly way ahead of the game and was already applying with enthusiasm to access her new-found income source. Before Henry had scarcely turned cold, Martha sent a letter to his insurance company to hasten the payment of his policy. This happened the very day after his death and two days before his funeral. It starkly read:

The Australian WIDOWS' FUND Life Assurance Sty
Melbourne, 5 Oct. 1889

Mr Donaldson
Secty A.W.F. Society —

Dear Sir —
I have to inform you of the death of my husband under Policy No 36627 [Henry Needle] who died yesterday 5 inst. [cause Hepatitis vomiting, Entric (sic) fever and obstinacy

in refusing food]. Kindly forward me with necessary papers and oblige.

MARTHA NEEDLE

For Martha, Henry's death was like winning a small lottery. After all, she now believed that she was due to personally pocket at least £200, a colossal amount of money in the late 1880s. But while Martha was incredibly streetwise in some areas, she was not particularly well versed in the fine print associated with the often-counterintuitive world of insurance policies. Not only did she discover that the payment process would take much longer than she had anticipated, but her plans for an immediate financial windfall did not fully fall into place either.

It wasn't until the 29 November 1889 that the insurance company paid over the amount of the claim to the Trustees Executors and Agency Company, which was then charged with the responsibility of acting as administrators of Henry's estate.

The executors first insisted that all of Henry's carpentry tools, books and clothing be sold, which Martha did by holding a raffle in the local community. The sight of Martha raffling off Henry's possessions only confirmed to many that she was indeed a widow in financial distress, heightening the sympathy for her even further. She openly pushed the sale of the raffle tickets among her friends by telling them that the death of her husband had left her 'entirely without means' and she regularly complained to acquaintances about her poverty.

Martha's primary miscalculation was to overlook the fact that she had not been Henry's only dependant. There were also his daughters to consider – the company handling his estate determined that their shares should be held in trust, not simply handed over to their mother.

The value of Henry's estate was ultimately calculated at a gross figure of £211 and 15 shillings. The bulk of this amount was the £200 life insurance policy, while the remaining money was what had been

raised by selling Henry's tools and clothes. The two allotments of land
he had once diligently purchased for his growing family at Birkenhead
were deemed to be of such little value that they didn't even rate a
financial consideration in his estate.

Only one-third of the final calculated amount was ultimately paid
to Martha and even this was made available to her in instalments.
She received £30 on 18 December 1889, £21 on 20 February 1890
and she was able to retain the £11 and 15 shillings raised through the
local raffle.

The remaining two-thirds of the estate – a considerable £127
– remained in the hands of the company, being the joint share of
Martha's two children. This money was held in trust and invested on
behalf of the youngsters. It would be made available to them when
they reached an age of maturity. Unless of course, heaven forbid, they
failed to reach this age. In the unlikely event that this tragedy occurred,
each share would be passed on to their grieving mother.[25] Effectively,
two more death warrants came into being.

It was indeed remarkable that the insurance company involved did
not more robustly investigate Henry's death. While it remains easy to
imagine Martha heavily mesmerising hen-pecked lodge doctors, her
capacity to do likewise to insurance men spoke volumes about her
subtle methods of control.

After all, the insurance company had big money on the line with a
policy that had only run for a short time. Yet nothing was seemingly
made by the guardians of the company of the 'causes' of Henry's death,
which even included the extraordinary medical symptom 'obstinacy'
in refusing food. It appears that the insurance company had been left
to consider the altered death certificate of Henry, which had somehow
omitted 'persistent vomiting' from the original one issued by Hodgson.

A Cash-Strapped Widow

Martha's acting skills were also being constantly put to good use throughout her local community. Although with two boarders in her house paying their weekly fees she was by no means broke, she continually liked to portray herself as being financially barren – readily accepting any handouts, gifts, free loans, charity and sympathy being offered.

Such impressions of borderline distress were easier for her to maintain as Melbourne began to plunge further into the depths of one of the most severe economic Depressions ever recorded. As the early 1890s approached, the speculative finance that had underpinned the local land boom was rapidly withdrawn, leading to the collapse of land prices, banks and businesses.

These hardships had a particularly devastating effect on Richmond, with local workers facing mass unemployment and untold poverty. The prospect of being thrown out onto the street, and even the thought of facing starvation, were constant threats for all in the community. As the Depression deepened and the realities of survival hit, crime rates soared and the fear of uncontrolled lawlessness intensified.

And all of this was occurring in an era when those operating the justice system were clearly fuelled by the belief that criminal tendencies were hereditary. In such a light, those residing comfortably in the grand boulevards of the affluent leafy suburbs could view those in the inner-city slums, lanes and alleys with maximum suspicion. It was always more convenient to blame genetic factors than to address the environmental deficiencies in the community that led to increased criminal activity.

From Woeful to Wonderful

Martha had privately evaded the economic woes affecting her neighbours. She also began to relax a little and open up to well wishers about her beloved Henry. Now that he was securely planted in the ground and his estate had been settled, she dropped her guard. And she was in no mood to provide Henry with a glowing character reference.

When Henry's old boarding-house keeper, Hannah Tutt, tried to console the young widow about losing her husband, Martha surprised her by immediately exclaiming that she was 'not sorry' that he was dead. According to Martha, Henry had never been good to her, had always been stubborn and would not take food when he was ill. He even refused to make a will, despite her requests for him to do so.

Martha's old neighbour from Wellington Street, Robert Robinson, had always remained disarmingly close to the Needles, even after they had shifted to Cubitt Street. As an indication of the extent of this relationship, he had visited Henry regularly during his entire illness and was constantly at his bedside.

In an extraordinary move, Robinson and his family would leave Richmond and relocate to the distant country town of Morwell, some 150 km east of Melbourne. This might not sound significant, until it is realised that this major upheaval occurred on the very first day after Henry passed away.

For some reason or other, the recently widowed Martha would regularly make the arduous journey to visit the Robinsons in far-flung Morwell, often staying for several weeks at a time. During one such visit, Robinson's increasingly wary wife Annie made the mistake of asking Martha if she would be glad if Henry was still alive. Martha replied without hesitation, 'No I would not. If he walked in through that door I wouldn't speak to him'.

A slightly less reliable yet equally damning summation was provided by the shifty contact Owen Evans. He would later suggest to a court that Martha had engaged in a *private* conversation with him about her marriage woes well over a year *before* Henry's untimely death. According to Evans, Martha had told him that she had made a mistake marrying Henry and insisted that she should have married someone else.

About a fortnight after Henry's funeral, Evans and Martha allegedly returned to similar themes during another overly 'intimate' conversation. This time Evans said he had sympathised with Martha about the loss of her husband before she told him, 'I am not sorry that he is dead. He left marks and bruises on me when he died. The people in the neighbourhood are talking about me for not having advertised Henry as my beloved husband in the death notice – I have not done so as he was not my beloved husband. He treated me as an old woman of sixty, by not allowing me to attend dances, and the people of the neighbourhood have also said that I will marry again. So I would if I had an offer.'

Evans was determined to maintain some sense of self-righteousness while declaring all this in court. He also wanted to sit so firmly on the fence that he probably had numerous splinters lodged in his backside. He publicly declared, 'I was never aware that Henry knocked her about. I did not believe her statement at the time about the marks and bruises on her. Henry as far as I know was always kind to her.'

Unfinished Business

It wasn't long after Henry's death that Martha decided to keep a man to his word. That man was none other than the overly romantic widower Thomas Gilroy. To the shop assistant's surprise, Martha entered Moloney's Drapery Store one day and boldly announced to him, 'Now, you have always said that if my husband died, you would be No. 2. He is dead now and I intend keeping you to your promise'.

Gilroy was a little disconcerted by Martha's directness and he mentioned this initial trepidation to some of his fellow employees, but they attached little importance to it. The drapery expert nonetheless remained attracted to the charms of the widow and for some months at least, in the prudish phraseology of the times, he 'paid her marked attentions'. He visited her constantly at Cubitt Street and was said to spend many Sunday afternoons there.

Eventually, the pair became rather loosely engaged to be married and Gilroy spoke about the engagement to some of his friends. One of these buddies was an old schoolmate, the well-known police constable Joseph Robinson, who was stationed at Richmond. This wily policeman knew enough about Martha's reputation to try to dissuade Gilroy from going on with his marriage plans.

But in the end, it was not Robinson's advice that ended the talk about the 'engagement'. The relationship between Martha and Gilroy began to become very strained and frequently erupted into disagreements. Thoughts of marriage stalled but Gilroy nonetheless continued his visits to Cubitt Street and the pair undeniably remained in contact.[26]

A Fateful Reunion

Although Otto Juncken and Martha had once had a passing social contact, neither had seen each other for a considerable amount of time until a chance encounter in central Melbourne.

Nine months after Henry's death, Martha was journeying down the busy thoroughfare of Swanston Street when she ventured upon the handsome Otto casually walking in the opposite direction. After a brief exchange of pleasantries, Martha began to complain to Otto that while she had once fraternised with him and several members of his family, none had bothered to visit her since her husband's death and the commencement of 'her troubles' as a widow. Squirming with embarrassment, the polite Otto promised that he would start going to see her. Otto had unwittingly fallen into the Black Widow's web and the ramifications for both himself and his large family would ultimately be devastating.

It all started innocently enough. At her request, Otto began visiting Martha at her house in Cubitt Street. In the beginning, he would drop by casually about once every three weeks. As was the case with all visitors to her house, he quickly noted the care and attention she offered to her two children, Elsie and May. For these children, however, this observation was about to be severely tested.

CHAPTER 8

Mummy Dearest – Elsie and May Needle

'Can a mother's tender care
Cease towards the child she bare?'
— William Cowper

About a year after the untimely death of her father, six-year-old Elsie Needle began to fall ill with peculiar symptoms. Trusty local quack George Hodgson treated her in the same Richmond house where he had unsuccessfully tended to the ailing Henry. He later vaguely recalled that he first suggested Elsie was suffering from a debilitating dose of measles; although his memory remained hazy, he believed the young child had been vomiting. The one clear memory that the doctor retained from this time was of Elsie's appealing mother; he later told a courtroom she had never appeared 'inattentive or unkind', nor had she ever obstructed his attendance.

A similar version of events was later recalled by Otto, who, much to Martha's delight, had visited the widow more often to console her about her second daughter's illness. At least, it seemed, Martha had derived some secondary gain from the unpleasant situation.

Despite the cutting-edge medical expertise of Hodgson and the valiant nursing efforts of her mother, Elsie languished for nearly two months before finally passing away on 9 December 1890. The death certificate issued by Hodgson certainly provided an unusual combination of ailments, recording that she had died from 'exhaustion and gangrenous stomatitis' – the latter a disease of the mouth and gums. This clumsy diagnosis could mercifully be described as inadequate.

Martha was again quick to announce the tragedy in the classifieds, ensuring that the following tear-jerking insertion appeared in the *Age* newspaper the very next day:

> NEEDLE – On the 9th December, at her mother's residence, 110 Cubitt-street Richmond, Victoria, after seven weeks of patient suffering, Elsie the eldest beloved surviving daughter of Martha and the late Henry Needle. Aged 6 years 2 months 3 days.
>
> Now all but has gone ere the sin knew or sorrow felt.
> – Inserted by her loving mother
> Adelaide papers please copy

It was obvious from this advertisement that Martha was becoming more 'poetic' over time. The notification displayed an enhanced emotional tone, in comparison to her other bereavements. Although while Henry was alive, the couple had not advertised the funeral of their eldest daughter Mabel, Martha now ensured that this was done for Elsie. The Black Widow wanted as many people there as possible to help share her distress. While busily organising another job for the undertaker, Herbert King, she ensured that the following appeared in the *Age* on the very same day as the death notice:

> The Friends of Mrs. MARTHA NEEDLE are respectfully invited to follow the remains of her late beloved daughter,

Elsie, to the place of interment, the Boroondara Cemetery, Kew. The funeral to move from her residence, No. 110 Cubitt-street, Richmond, on Thursday, the 11th inst. At 11 o'clock a.m.

Herbert King, Undertaker, Lennox-street, Richmond

And so, amid her mother's attention-seeking grief, little Elsie was buried at Boroondara General Cemetery's plot B2477 – the same plot where her father had been laid to rest the preceding year. This occurred only two days after the little girl's untimely death. The only consolation for Martha was that she was now entitled to claim Elsie's share of Henry's estate. A short time later, the Black Widow placed a little more than £60 in her purse – all in good time for a spot of Christmas shopping.

Farrell's Flat

Martha had never restricted her complaints about her late husband to close acquaintances such as Hannah Tutt, Robert Robinson and Owen Evans. She had even been known to unexpectedly spill the beans about her former marital woes to passing strangers. However, with a few ugly rumours starting to circulate around the alleys of Richmond, this behaviour was beginning to be more than a little unwise.

The most publicised example occurred shortly after the death of Elsie. Martha decided to take her surviving daughter, May, and travel through the backblocks of South Australia to visit one of her sisters. But Martha inadvertently caught the wrong train and ended up incorrectly arriving at the remote Farrell's Flat Railway Station.

Local stationmaster Alfred Clayer quickly realised that the pretty stranger had made the mistake of coming to the wrong station and would now have to wait many hours to catch a return train, so he generously invited her to his private house for some refreshments.[27] Although their guest was an affable young woman, the stationmaster and his wife were soon stunned when she began to speak freely of her past married life and her apparently improved status as a widow.

Long after Martha had been delivered back to the station to continue her interrupted journey, Mr and Mrs Clayer remained stunned that a stranger could speak so candidly with them. And the world's press would later seize upon their recollections.[28]

An Early Feminist

Martha didn't just spend 1890 denouncing her dead spouse and burying her second-born child. Like many other women, she was also becoming more aware of the prevailing political and social landscape. The women's suffrage movement at that time was not only agitating for the right for women to vote, but the members were also seeking a range of other measures to bring about equality in the community.

Martha lived in an era when women were not expected to play any type of role in public life. There were no women parliamentarians, nor could women hold any position in the court system.

During 1891, a Women's Suffrage Petition was organised, which came to be seen as a landmark in the fledgling women's movement in Australia. Nearly 30,000 'ordinary' women signed the petition, with 26 of these signatures belonging to residents of Cubitt Street, Richmond – and prominent among them was the signature of Martha Needle.

One of the objectives of the suffragists was to gain full legal equality for women. Martha would soon be putting this concept under intense scrutiny.

Little Maysie

Martha's only surviving daughter, May, was a great favourite with the boarders living in the house and her mother also apparently worshipped her. But only seven months after the death of her older sister, Elsie, four-year-old May's health also slowly deteriorated. The previously healthy child began to display peculiar and worrying symptoms, the most notable of which was constant vomiting.

By this time, elite medical practitioner George Hodgson had left the lodge practice in shabby Richmond to set up business in the more affluent suburb of Windsor. He had been replaced at the lodge by Dr Charles Payne, a younger medico. Having previously practised in Hobart, Payne and his young wife had only just moved to the municipality of Richmond and were still finding their feet.

Payne first visited May at Martha's request on 20 August 1891 and was immediately puzzled by the symptoms that he witnessed, recording them loosely as 'obstinate vomiting and brain irritation'. The inopportunely named Dr Payne was so concerned with what he was seeing that he began visiting every day and then agreed to seek a second opinion.

These were very tough times and most Richmond citizens were forced to avoid using doctors and medicines at all, due to their scant financial resources. Calling upon another practitioner would involve some extra charge. But Martha had no concern about this at all – she would spare no expense for her only surviving child, May – and the experienced Dr Burton was called to Cubitt Street to examine the ailing youngster.

Martha would later suggest that she had also been keen to pay to have Dr Elsner and Dr Snowball in attendance, although Payne could not directly recall this. In any event, she was particularly keen to have Dr Elsner back on the case – after all, he had not asked too many uncomfortable questions while treating her first child, Mabel.

It was during May's illness that the 'friendship' developing between Martha and Otto began to intensify. The honourable Otto saw May frequently during her illness, his sympathies were aroused and his visits became more frequent. Martha was undoubtedly relieved to know that she still had the shoulder of a handsome young man to cry on in such a moment of motherly distress. Just for practise, she even borrowed some money from him.

In an effort to cheer up her ailing daughter, Martha bought her a pet bird in a cage and placed it in her room. Yet, irrespective of how many doctors were in attendance or how many supportive friends came to visit, nothing could save May. The pet bird would ultimately outlive its owner.

The little girl died on 27 August 1891, within one week of Payne first seeing her. Although no autopsy was conducted, Payne was confident enough to write out the child's death certificate, citing the official cause of death as 'tubercular meningitis', specifically noting that the constant vomiting was pointing to irritation of the brain. These 'causes' bore a striking resemblance to the symptoms that had claimed the life of Martha's first child, Mabel, six years earlier.

Payne didn't just lose his young patient. As it turned out, Martha never paid his full bill either. The account of £1 and 11 shillings remained on the lodge's books for several years before being written off.

Untold Grief

Martha's apparent distress escalated with each family death she was forced to endure. But she went right over the top upon the death of her last child, May. The death notice appearing in the *Age* the very next day was a sentiment-charged tribute from a shattered young woman. While her poetic endeavours were never likely to rival the combined works of Shelley and Keats, Martha went to considerable effort to publicly express her heartbreak:

> Needle – On the 27th August, at her mother's residence, 110 Cubitt-street, Richmond May (dear little Maysie), the only surviving child of Martha and the late Henry Needle, aged 4 years 11 months and 11 days

> Adelaide and Sydney papers please copy.

I had three little treasures once,
They were my joy and pride,
But one by one they all have gone.
They all have early drooped and died.
All is dark within my dwelling,
Lonely is my heart today,
Now unheard, unpitied, unrelieved,
I must bear alone my load of care.

– Inserted by their loving mother

All of the previous Needle funerals had drawn heavy attendances. As was now a publishing tradition, Martha again used the classified pages of the *Age* to draw the biggest crowd of all to May's funeral:

> The Friends of Mrs. MARTHA NEEDLE are respectfully invited to follow the remains of her beloved and only daughter, May, to the place of interment, the Boroondara Cemetery, Kew. The funeral to move from her residence, No. 110 Cubitt-street, Richmond, on SATURDAY, the 29th inst. at half-past 2 o'clock p.m.
>
> HERBERT KING, Undertaker

Aware that this was now the fourth funeral that Martha had been required to pay for in recent times, Herbert King suggested to Martha that she may like to save on some of the costs on this particular occasion. He presented a plan that would minimise most of the usual expenses.

But Martha would not hear of it – nothing was too good for her 'Maysie'. Instead of cutting costs, Martha insisted that no expense be spared – giving the impression that she was sacrificing everything she had to preserve the memory of her last child.

As Martha hoped, May's funeral drew an extremely large number of mourners. The sympathy that they felt for Martha was difficult to describe. This poor woman had now suffered the ultimate misery of not only losing her husband, but also laying to rest all of her three children. And all of this had occurred within an incredibly short space of time.

The B2477 family gravesite at Boroondara General Cemetery was again reopened and four-year-old May was buried there, joining her father and older sister, Elsie. And once again Martha pocketed more than £60, May's share from the late Henry's life insurance policy.

To Martha, these insurance payouts must have seemed like money for old rope – but she was yet to realise just how true this cliché would become.

CHAPTER 9

A Fresh Beginning and a Besotted New Man

To the people she encountered around the laneways of Richmond, Martha now cut a lonely, subdued figure. While always draped in her customary black mourning clothes, she continued tending to a few boarders at Cubitt Street for a month or so after May's death. Now completely unencumbered, she also took the opportunity to travel extensively, at least by the standards of the 1890s.

Several times she paid the fare to ride along the rough railway tracks of Gippsland to stay a couple of weeks with her former neighbours, Robert and Annie Robinson, at Morwell – undoubtedly enlivening the former's heartstrings and annoying his wife during her visits.

She also made a long journey to the little town of Hilton in South Australia to visit her mother, who was residing there at the time. In light of the deep hatred that had developed between the pair, the motivation for such a trip was curious indeed. Her mother had never seen any of Martha's children while they were alive, nor met Henry or any of his family.

Although Martha managed to stay at Hilton for two weeks, the attempt at a workable reunion was an utter disaster as the pair fought furiously the whole time. Martha's mother was then destitute, surviving on government rations, and renting a tiny two-roomed house from the local farrier, Mr M. Wilkes.

Years later, Wilkes could still clearly recall meeting Martha during her stay, as she looked somewhat out of place in the tiny backwater. 'She was a fine-looking woman and always dressed well' he would tell a newspaper reporter. 'Judging from appearances, I would say that she was in prosperous circumstances ... Her mother and she did not live happily together and the former used some very strong language at times with respect to her daughter ... I noticed nothing peculiar about Mrs Needle except that she did not appear to be on good terms with her mother.'

Towards the end of this unhappy holiday, Martha's mother fell drastically ill. She was so sick that many believed she was about to die – but the old girl just managed to pull through. The final straw for Martha's trip came when her mother began broadcasting around town her belief that Martha was so evil she must have poisoned her in an attempt to procure some insurance money (she then had a small £15 life insurance policy) and, what's more, she must have done likewise to her husband and all her own children.

Once this uncomfortable suggestion was made, Martha quickly did a runner and caught the next train back to Melbourne.

It was shortly after this time that Martha's mother took the extraordinarily bitter step of suing two of her own children – namely Martha and her stepbrother, John – for allegedly failing to provide her with adequate means of support. In the days before the availability of age pensions, the onus often rested with the offspring to support their elderly parents, if they could afford to do so. Martha and John were both forced to attend an Adelaide Court. They managed to convince the presiding magistrates that they did not have any financial means to assist and their pitiable mother's application was quickly dismissed.

From that point, Martha would never have the pleasure of seeing her mother again, although this did not prevent the old woman publicly and enthusiastically denouncing her daughter's 'terrible nature' at every possible opportunity.

An Anguished Mother

To many outsiders, the tormented Martha never recovered from the untimely deaths of her three children. Her melancholy was such that she was virtually inconsolable. On most weekends, she would journey the considerable distance from Richmond to Boroondara General Cemetery, taking almost a full day to visit the gravesites of 'her babies'. She also went to substantial expense to have an elaborate memorial constructed at the gravesite of Elsie and May, in the form of a large metal shield. Inscribed on the shield was a touching poetic composition, penned by the budding Poet Laureate Martha herself:

In loving memory

Of

My dear children

MABEL,

Who died Decr. 28th, 1885, aged 3 years and seven weeks

ELSIE	MAY
Who died Decr. 9th 1890	Who died Aug. 27th, 1891
Aged 6 years & 2 months	Aged 4 years & 11 months

Little lips that murmured mumma
Still and silent now they are;
Tiny feet no longer patter,
Hushed forever 'neath the clay.
One by one they wandered from me,
And I linger here alone;
But their sweet and loving mem'ries

Blossom through the loving years.

By their loving mother – M. Needle

At the foot of the grave was a black box with a glass front. In this box were an artificial floral wreath and a photograph of Elsie and May – a studio portrait in which Elsie is shown holding a hoop. In a corner of this photograph was stuck a likeness of the other Needle child, Mabel, who was buried about 50 m away.

There was no mention of Henry anywhere on the inscription, nor was there any memorial for him, even though he was buried in the same grave as two of his children.

In keeping with the harsh economic times, most of the gravesites surrounding the Needle plot were either unmarked or adorned with a very basic headstone, making the Needle memorial even more stunning in contrast. The expense of such a memorial was also a talking point, although no-one was aware of the insurance payouts the grieving mother had pocketed.

On the Move

The death of her last child would soon see the restless Martha sever her connection with the Cubitt Street residence. She told neighbours that she felt compelled to leave the dwelling because the tragic deaths of her husband and children had caused her to look upon the house as being unhealthy.

But, owing to her friendship with the Juncken brothers, she was not destined to go far.

By this time, the saddlery shop that Louis was operating at 137 Bridge Road, Richmond, had developed into a thriving business – certainly not surprisingly in this pre-car age. Before long, Louis' younger brother, Otto, had started working in the shop. While the front part of the two-storey dwelling was rented by the Junckens and occupied by the saddlery shop, the rear section of the building had been sublet to a local widow to utilise as a boarding house. The Junckens even boarded there themselves.

Towards the end of 1891, the Junckens' housekeeper left to take up another job. Even though the brothers were aware that Martha commonly suffered from 'hysteria', they decided to ask her if she would like to join them as the new boarding house keeper. Martha had previously declined a similar offer they had made (on account of concerns over her own health and her need to be devoted to her ailing daughter, May), so Louis now took it upon himself to make the request personally.

This time Martha accepted the offer, which had been made through a mixture of necessity and pity for the grieving widow. She moved to 137 Bridge Road in January 1892 with her belongings – and a considerable amount of emotional baggage – to commence her new life. But, as had been the case with 110 Cubitt Street, this address would soon be associated with tragedy and untimely death.

This housekeeping position offered attractive terms. Although Martha was required to rent the back portion of the premises for 18 shillings per week, each boarder agreed to pay her 16 shillings per week for her cooking, cleaning and other housework. When she first moved in, there were five boarders – Louis, Otto and Charles Juncken and the brothers James and Frank Winwood. All up, a potentially tidy profit for Martha.

Of course, there were also other benefits, not the least of which was the opportunity to live close to Otto, a man she was becoming deeply obsessed about. Prior to moving into Bridge Road, Martha had maintained some measure of formality, referring to both Otto and Louis as 'Mr Juncken'. Now it was simply 'Otto' or 'Louis'. Collectively, she always liked referring to the boarders as 'her boys'.

Martha's tenure as housekeeper got off to a rocky start. Although her domestic skills were sufficient, she never appeared to be in good health and constantly complained of the terrible loss she had suffered because of the untimely death of her children. On several occasions, Martha's health was so poor that the benevolent Junckens were forced to employ another woman, Georgina Lillis, for lengthy stints to do her duties.

On the first occasion, Lillis lived at Bridge Road for almost two months. Martha was ill in bed for a lot of this time and Lillis observed her regularly having fainting fits. During the second stay by Lillis, Martha remained in bed for a full two months after having a 'slight operation' for haemorrhoids. Once again, Lillis observed Martha constantly fainting and having fits throughout this entire time. [29]

Martha continued to consult with a multitude of doctors. Among their number were some familiar faces from the times when her children were being treated, namely Drs Elsner, Burton and Hodgson. None appeared to link Martha's increasing use of chlorodyne with her ordeals.[30]

The other problem for Martha was that her 'romance' with Otto was beginning to look like a one-sided infatuation. Flirt as she might, she could not get Otto to take the hint. As the consummate 1890s gentlemen and apparent romantic idealist, he would later go to great pains to proudly declare to a court that there had been absolutely 'no lovemaking' and 'no impropriety' whatsoever between Martha and himself around this time.

By April 1892, Martha found herself being attended to by the medical man who was destined to become her most favoured doctor of all – trusted local lodge practitioner Dr Donald McColl. There is a saying that the secret of medical science is to placate the patient while waiting for nature to take its course. This was a school of thought generally subscribed to by Donald McColl. There is another saying that doctors bury their mistakes. In this respect, McColl was probably also well represented. As an easily side-tracked 30-year-old medical man who was not prone to asking too many awkward questions, McColl was the type of practitioner Martha liked.

While McColl could not make out anything physically wrong with Martha during his numerous consultations, he noted her 'mental worry'. He concluded that this anxiety was because her affection for Otto was not being reciprocated. The interfering doctor even took it upon himself to play Cupid and mentioned this privately to Otto. Still, Otto remained emotionally unmoved.[31]

It soon became clear to the manipulating Martha that she would need to hatch a melodramatic plot if she was to finally capture Otto's heart. Unlike most men, he appeared to be blind to her charms. She would need to hasten the course of true love and would try to do so through sympathy.

Good Friday fell on 15 April 1892. Otto, Louis and Charles Juncken, along with James Winwood, used this holiday to travel to the Yarra Valley town of Healesville for an overnight stay. On their return to Bridge Road the next day, Frank Winwood greeted them with the unhappy news that Martha was again ailing badly in bed. He also passed to Otto a private letter that Martha had penned for him. Complete with spelling mistakes, the woeful letter read:

> Richmond, Friday night,
> April 15th/92
>
> My dear friend,
>
> You will be shocked you know when you get this note, but you must not think that I have been ungratful for your kindness, I know that you have [all] tried to make me forget my tribels but I cannot forget for instead of forgetting I feel my loss more every day. If only one of my little ones had been speared I would not feel life so hard but as it is I have nothing [all my life] I have known nothing but trubel I am so tired of so much trubel I have tried hard to fight against fate, but I now give

it up. Dear Otto you must not think that I am doing this without thought for I have been thinking of it for a long time. Dear Otto it is sweet to know that you have been my friend for I have had so few and I hope dear that you will forgive me and not think too unkindly of me for I am so tired of a life of suffering and sorrow wich has ever been my fate. I am going away but should my body be found I would like to bee buried with my children. dear Otto there more than enuf money in the bank to pay you what I owe you also Mr King and will you kindly send seven pounds to Miss Gillaty [sic] in Birkenhead that I owe her − to you I give the photos of elsie and may that are framed and hanging over the mantelpiece in my room and will you please take care of Maysie bird while it lives. As you know I would like my sisters to have what I leave in the house not that it matters very much what becomes of them − only I would not like the Needles to have anything that was ever mine for they have never tried to make my life any happier for me but I am glad to think that it will soon be ended and I will bee free from so much sorrow and pain you can never know the sad heart that I have had ever since all my dear little ones have been so crully taken from me, forever with kind regards to all the boys and to you dear Otto a fond and last good by from your unhappy friend.

Martha Needle[32]

It was evident from this letter that Martha still owed money to a number of past acquaintances, namely the funeral director King and her old friend Miss Gallaty from Birkenhead. It was also clear that she was no longer on good terms with members of the Needle family. But the biggest revelation of all was her implication that she wanted to end her life.

This time, Martha's plot to gain Otto's attention was highly successful. The alarmed Otto immediately interpreted Martha's writings as a suicide note and his sympathies were aroused. Finding Martha sitting up in bed, Otto suspected that poison might be her selected means of self-destruction. He made an urgent search of the premises and, in addition to finding the customary bottles of chlorodyne, he located a box of 'Rough on Rats'. As a consequence of Otto's discovery, the spotlight fell on this deadly rat poison for the first time during this whole drama.

Otto threw out the box of 'Rough on Rats' and then had a heart-to-heart talk with Martha. After expressing his personal concern for her, he made her promise that she would abandon all her suicidal thoughts. As the pair talked, the topics of romance, obligation and their future together entered the conversation. The pair agreed to be married.

Aided by the previous counselling of McColl, Otto had eventually been convinced that matrimony would provide Martha with the best prospects of moving away from her dark times.[33] So even though her engagement had been rather tenuously founded on the dim prospects of a suicide note, Martha apparently had her man. The Black Widow's trap had worked spectacularly.[34]

The newly betrothed couple formalised their arrangement by publicly announcing their engagement a few weeks later. But at this stage the 'engagement' remained on vague terms, with an actual marriage date yet to be set. While Otto was prepared to marry Martha straightaway, Martha did not want to set a date while her health was still so poor. As it turned out, the proposed marriage was the subject of continual delays and was ultimately destined never to occur.

But Martha began to have plenty of fun in the meantime. For a woman who was no stranger to unhappiness, the romantic Otto was a breath of fresh air; she greatly enjoyed being spoiled by her new fiancé. While her previous long-term partner – the sulky Henry – had 'refused to take her to dances' and in her mind 'treated her like a woman of sixty', Otto first took her to a dance at Richmond Town Hall and quickly followed this up by tripping the light fantastic at two more dance nights. He also began to take her out to the theatre.

Her 'engagement' also did no harm to Martha's bank balance, as Otto now began to pay all her personal and medical accounts. Of course, this was not the first time that Otto had dipped deeply into his pocket for the Black Widow. He had already 'lent' her £2 when her child, May, had died and had also sent her a further £7 when she was travelling in Adelaide in 1891 (none of which he got back). While he was being taken to the cleaners, he had been led to believe that Martha only had a few pounds to her impoverished name; he was also left in the dark about her insurance windfalls.[35]

In a number of other respects, it was also becoming an unusual courtship for Otto. In between keeping up with a vibrant social calendar and being ripped off in the process, he was fully expected to travel with Martha to Boroondara General Cemetery on most weekends to witness her publicly mourn over the graves of her children. This became one of their regular dates.

When the courtship was at its strongest, the accomplished wordsmith Otto even took the time to write to his beloved Martha while she was travelling in South Australia. Addressing her as 'My darling pet', he sought to cheer her up by alluding to the 'time not then far distant' when they would be married and living happily together. Through his love, care and attention, he vowed to make her life one of perfect pleasure. Waxing lyrical, he continued, 'When we have the happy, quiet, peaceful home, as I know we will have, when you have the kind husband that I will try to be, to care for you, to love you, and to share your every little trouble; when you have the blessing which I trust providence will give us – then you will recover your lost strength which those miserable years with that miserable wretch robbed of you'.[36]

A Negative Development

As a proud family man, Otto had promptly informed his brother, Louis, and the rest of the Juncken tribe in both Victoria and South Australia of his matrimonial intentions. In an era of parental deference, he needed to gain the approval of his elderly mother. Without such an ongoing blessing, Otto was unlikely to ever do anything.

At first, Louis (a very influential figure in Otto's life) was agreeable to the union. He even expressed his view to Otto that Martha appeared to be 'a good and virtuous woman'. But over the next 15 months, he saw enough displays of Martha's erratic health, recurring fits and, worse still, her frightful temper to form the view that she was not the sort of woman he would want to marry his younger brother.

In turn, the vain Martha became dismayed with Louis' declining attitude towards her and complained bitterly about him to the increasingly hassled Otto – and, for that matter, to anyone else within earshot. Martha would not only fly right off the handle at the slightest infraction, but she would also hold sullen grudges. She also had a decent dose of paranoia thrown in for bad measure.[37]

Not only did Louis' opposition to the marriage grow by the day, but also he was ultimately the conduit for a family move against it. He was in the position to observe Martha at close range on a daily basis and began 'writing home', most particularly to his mother, to express his concerns about the inappropriateness of the proposed nuptials.

This only served to increase the tense 'coolness' that had developed between Martha and Louis. She viewed him as spearheading an attack against her intended marriage and jeopardising her entire future happiness. Martha was equally unimpressed with the rest of the Juncken clan – particularly the old matriarch – who appeared to accept whatever negative views Louis saw fit to express about her. In Martha's mind, the members of the Juncken family had now become her bitter opponents.

At first, Otto seemingly stuck to his romantic guns. He wrote to his mother, saying that he had made up his mind to marry Martha. He even proudly showed Martha the letter before he sent it. He was less enthused to reveal to Martha his mother's reply, which flatly advised him not to marry Martha on account of her continued ill health. This was the type of reaction to an upcoming marriage that was apt to make a young woman feel a tad unwelcome – and all the while, Martha thoroughly seethed.

Although she wasn't the first or last person in history to have diverging opinions with a future mother-in-law, she eventually picked up her trusted fountain pen and wrote a particularly bitter letter to Otto's mother. While the diplomatic Otto did his best to dissuade her from sending it, she forwarded it anyway.

The result was predictable. Otto's mother sent him a terse reply. This time she not only advised him again not to marry Martha on account of her continued ill health, but she also added another reason – in her view, Martha was also an ill-tempered woman.

An Increasingly Unconventional Engagement

Since agreeing to marry Martha, Otto had not only been required to routinely trek to Boroondara General Cemetery and endure the ongoing disapproval of his family, he was also fully expected to embrace Martha's misguided obsession about her 'real' parentage and 'rightful' inheritance. This was all tenuously based on some of the whoppers her inebriated father, Joseph, had seen fit to tell while well refreshed with alcohol.

Although privately Otto did not see any merit in Martha's outlandish claims, he agreed to draft a business letter to the Chief Registrar of Probate in London to make the necessary inquiries. But this did not happen until Martha had written at least three pitiful – and rather underhand – dispatches of her own as part of her passionate yet pointless crusade.

In her first letter, Martha covertly adopted the formal-sounding pseudonym 'A.F. Delbroke' and sent her correspondence to her stepfather, Daniel Foran, in a crude attempt to 'trick' him into telling her all he knew. A quick glance at its contents would have alerted even the boozing blockhead Foran that the letter was unlikely to have emanated from an official source:

Melbourne, December 4, 1893, 'To Mr foran:

'Sir,- It will be grately to your advantage if you will kindly send me all pertuclers and informashion concerning that little girl you had living with you and your wife when you lived in Port Lincoln and north Adelaide. She was known as Martha Charles when she grew up, and I want you to tell me whos Child she was, for I know that you will know all about her. Was she Mrs. Forans own child. If not, who is her mother and father, and wher did your wif get her frome, for we do not think that any mother could be as crewl to her one child as she was to that little girl. Please tell me if you now wher Martha Charles is now, and if she has got any brothers or sisters, and wher she was born, and how old she is. It will be to your agvantge to give all the information that you know concerning that child.

'Yours,
'A.F. Delbroke
'G.P.O., Melbourne'.

Foran did not respond to this fine correspondence.[38]

A short time later, Martha was at it again – this time writing to a Mr Bartlett, the owner of one of the sheep stations where her 'family' – then using the surname 'Kennedy' – had once briefly called home when she was a child. This time she felt no need for subterfuge, citing her own name and address:

'137 bridge-roade,
'richmond' to Mr barklet.

'Sir,

'I hope you will excuse the liberty, but it is a matter of grat im portince to me. I wish to ask you If you can recoll to memery a family that worked for you about 16 or 02 years ago cald foran or latter known as kindy – thy had a little girl with them cauld Marther, do you remember she was left to look after foran or kindy and 2 little boys when he kineday worked for you cutting hay at a palce cauled peroper one sume such name whilke Mrs kineady was In Adelaide hospitable with a bad leug. Well sir can you tell me wither that Child Martha was her onne child, as I fell very doubtful about it and Mrs. Foran will not tell me wher the child was boran nor the name of anyone that kew the girl wile she was very young: so knowing that you know them If you can only recall them to memory the also lived on a station named lake hamaltion, but I can not rightly re-member the name of the overseare or I could write to him. The kinadys also lived at the little swampe, and I think they worked for a gentleman named allright, but I am not sure about his nam, hoping this will not put you to too much truble if you Can give me eny information Concarning that girl Martha you will be doing a kindness to one that has sufferd very much frome Mrs. Kinadys unwomanly treatment.

'yours

'sincerely

M. NEEDLE

Again, Martha's written inquiry went unanswered.

Still resolute, Martha's next literary effort was directed to a private detective working in Melbourne:

> 137 Bridge road, Richmond
>
> Dear Sir, - I wish to know If you think my case worth Investigation, While I was a child I was brought up by a woman who sad she was my mother, but I do not bleave that she is. In the first place she was allways to crule to me, more crule than anny mother could be to her own child, but as I got older she would tell me nothing to throw a true light on the past and now she will not tell me anything that I wish to know. I will tell you the story as I know it. A man wich was soposed to be my father left his wife with thre Children. Two girls and a boy – sevem months befor I was born thouse Children wear put In the destutet [Destitute Asylum] in south Australia, and were never claimed by their pearints, and the allways thought they had nether fother nor mothor until thy wear woman and then theur father turned up, and his excuse was that he alwas sent money to his sister in port Lincoln to pay for their keep but she never paied It in. so then he heard that ther was a warnt out for him for the money and he Said he had none, so he cleared out and neglected them altogether he told my sister than he never knew what became of his wife but that this woman was not her, My sister thinks that our mother went to the Adelaide hospital and died giving bearth to me and that this woman took charge of me. I remember when I was a child haring her and the man she cald my stepfather talking a lot about sevin houndred pounds that they wear goin to get, but I was not old enough to understand that there was anything wrong, and It was then that she stured my sisters up, and told them that she was their mother, but all she and this man wanted was to find out how they could get the money, but It seams she cannot get It, and

she will not tell me the true state of things. My sister saw a lawyer, and he told her that this was money thouse people wear keeping from them, and that if she had money to pay him he would find all the rights of the Caise, but of corse she had no money, so if you think the case Is worth taking up you would get so much per cent, when our money is restored to us. I must tell you that this woman told (her son) a short time ago that there was seven houded pounds laying in wast, and she sad It shall rot wher It Is for they shall never have it, she must have lived with this man for years as his mistress, for she had two or three children by him befor they wear married, and I have just found out that she married him in the name she always told me was her maiden name, and how could she do that If she was my father's wife. I cannot tell you all In writing, but if you think It wirth taking up please let me know and I will Come and see you. If I could make this woman tell me truthfully who I am it would be a grate relefe to Me. Hoping to hear from you soon.

I remain yours resptfuly

MARTHA NEEDLE.

Once more, the letter never received a reply.[39]

More in exasperation than anything else, Otto eventually sat with Martha and put together a properly drafted letter to the most appropriate source of information available. It stood in sharp contrast to Martha's previous literary efforts:

137 Bridge-road, Richmond,
Victoria, Australia.

To the Chief Registrar, Court and Probate,
Doctor's Commons, London

I, Martha Needle, maiden name Charles, hereby put in my claim as heir to the moneys and estate of William Charles. As far as I can learn my father, the said William Charles, left me, when a child, in charge of a woman in South Australia. This woman kept me in total ignorance of my parentage, or, I should say, misled me in making me believe that she was my mother by a former husband. This I have always had good reason to doubt, and it is only lately that I have become possessed of reliable information which proves conclusively to me that my doubts were well founded, and that she is no relation to me whatever. I have ascertained that I was given in her charge whilst my father went to England, and that he never returned, but died about the year 1873, leaving his money and property to his only child. This child I claim to be, and trust that I will be enabled to prove so to your satisfaction and the satisfaction of the executors of the estate. I only ask that you will put me in possession of whatever information lieu in your power to assist me in proving my claim.

Trusting that this will receive your early attention.

– I am, respectfully yours. (no signature)

In answer to this particular letter, the registrar actually wrote back, giving formal particulars about the searches that could be conducted. But life was about to get so hectic for both Martha and Otto that the matter then went no further. And the mystery – if one actually existed – was never solved.[40]

Health Issues

Not only had manic Martha become obsessed about money she would never receive, she also alarmed those around her with her weirdly declining health and behaviour. Always partial to having a tipple or three of chlorodyne when feeling a trifle stressed, she was now guzzling this concoction like never before. And her alarming 'fainting fits' had moved into overdrive.

The fits would generally occur in the evening – coincidentally after a day of heavy chlorodyne consumption – and she would occasionally have several in succession, lasting hours at a time. Otto believed that she often fell into unconsciousness during these fits and was insensitive to pain and temperature. On one occasion, she was lying in a marble-like state with her eyes fully open and Otto touched her eyeball – but she didn't flinch or exhibit any feeling whatsoever.

At other times, Martha would fall into a state of hallucination and replay an incident from her past life while failing to recognise those around her. During one of these occurrences, she addressed Otto as if he was her late husband, Henry, and acted out a scene by raising her hands as if to ward off a blow, exclaiming words to the effect of 'One day you will strike me once too often Henry Needle'. While in this state, she would also go searching for her dead children, all the while issuing them with instructions such as 'Elsie, make sure you hold May's hand when crossing the road'.

Martha would also get the wanders late at night – venturing several times in a trance-like state to the nearby house of her childhood friend, Eliza Martin, with the protective Otto trailing a short distance behind. On the first occasion, the disorientated Martha sat herself down on Eliza's sofa and, when asked 'Mattie, what's the matter?', could only answer 'Oh, my head, I'm silly' before falling into a full-blown stupor. Another time, she moved from room to room, wildly looking for her deceased children. She caressed a pillow as if it was a child and declared that she needed to visit her dead babies at their grave at Kew Cemetery.

In light of such behaviours, it may seem that Martha was losing her grip on reality. However, in between her 'fainting fits', she continued to cope with a normal (albeit tragedy-laden) life in a strong-willed and self-assured way. She also continued to display an intelligent manner and an extremely sharp mind, which bordered on conniving and manipulative. But her life was clearly on a slippery slope.

CHAPTER 10

An Obstacle No More – The Destruction of Louis Juncken

'Hell hath no fury like a woman scorned.'
– William Congreve

History now tells us that it was never a good move to treat Martha offhandedly or stand in the way of something she wanted. Louis Juncken did both. And, what's more, he had confronted her while he was in a vulnerable position. He was the most easily accessible of all of Martha's opponents in the Juncken family. The pair not only resided in the same premises, but she also cooked for him every day.

Although Martha may have been somewhat careless with settling her financial debts, if she perceived someone had crossed her she would always pay back with interest.

In August 1893, the usually healthy Louis fell ill. The primary symptoms were persistent vomiting and a putrid discharge of pus from his gums. Louis' condition was serious enough for a doctor to be consulted and so Martha's favoured lodge practitioner, Donald McColl, came to visit him. McColl expressed concerns that the patient had been vomiting over a two-day period and formed the view that the pus from his gums was poisoning his stomach.

Louis remained ill for a considerable period of time but after seven or eight days he slowly recovered – and the shining light throughout the ordeal proved to be Martha. Despite the previous antagonism between the pair, she tended to him with considerable sympathy. Such was her devotion that Louis began to view her from a changed perspective. He realised that she could indeed display such a kindly and nurturing side that this more than compensated for her volatile temper. He even changed his mind about her intended marriage, now believing that she was a suitable catch for his younger brother. But this revised enthusiasm for Martha was not reciprocated by his mother.

The Star Boarder

Throughout these dramas, there had been a few changes to 'the boys' Martha was looking after at Bridge Road. Frank Winwood had moved out in July 1892, followed by his brother, James, during April 1893.

In August 1893, local 20-year-old carpenter Howard Percival Stanley Setford (always known as Stanley) arrived. Stanley Setford's life would soon be set on a tumultuous path. The following year, his financially ruined 64-year-old father James would be involved in a sensational murder trial after he slashed the throat of his two-year-old son, Frank. Following a heavily publicised case, Setford's father would be found insane and sent to Ararat asylum.

Meanwhile, Stanley would be boarding at Bridge Road. He would be there throughout all the evolving dramas and have a front-row seat to see the developments unfold. He would also become a close confidant of Martha and a sounding board for her, all of which became evident with the protective testimony he would later give in court.[41]

A Sinister Turn for the Worse

In April 1894, some eight months after his first illness, Louis became sick again with the same symptoms – vomiting and sore gums. He had also been complaining of a horrible taste in all the foods he was served and his tongue was swollen and sore. On 25 April, Louis called on Dr McColl at his home. He explained that he was feeling so poorly he feared he might have caught the dreaded typhoid. A quick check of Louis' temperature convinced McColl that typhoid was not the culprit. He prescribed a quinine mixture, told Louis to keep on light food and asked him to return in a few days if he wasn't any better.

By 30 April, Louis' condition had deteriorated so much that he could not even visit the doctor. Instead, McColl made a house call to Bridge Road. He found Louis in bed, complaining that his gums felt the same way they had last August. A closer examination by McColl found an abundant discharge of pus exuding from beneath Louis' gums. Louis was also still vomiting.

Hardly a cutting-edge medical researcher at the best of times, the usually conservative McColl would make an extremely unusual diagnosis from left field. After noting the copious discharge of pus coming from Louis' gums, he concluded that Louis was suffering from Riggs' disease of the jaw – nowadays more likely to be referred to as 'pyorrhoea'.

Riggs' disease – named after John Riggs, the American dentist who first described it – was at that time a relatively new addition to the medical textbooks and considered a very rare disease in its aggravated form. Although McColl had not formally studied Riggs' disease at university, only two months earlier he had read an article about it in the revered medical journal *The Lancet* and he had obviously been suitably impressed.

McColl further presumed that the pus caused by the disease was being swallowed and irritating Louis' stomach. In addition to prescribing a stomach sedative, McColl ordered Louis to use a cleansing lotion for his mouth and to take care not to swallow any of the 'poisonous' pus.

As McColl continued visiting Louis over the next few days, his patient's health steadily improved. And McColl had also been continually impressed by the manner of Martha towards Louis. As far as he could observe, she was not only very kind but she also 'gave him every attention' during his illness.[42]

By this time, Martha had also changed her strategy with Louis in an attempt to get what she wanted. She began to secretly win his affections by flirting with him as well. Unknown to Otto, his older brother had started to fall under the spell of the attractive landlady and was now having private conversations with Martha about their 'love' for each other. Whenever the opportunity arose, the pair would steal a quick kiss. The previously oppositional Louis began to act like a smitten teenager.

Stirred on by Martha and her sweet talk, by 10 May Louis' strength had sufficiently returned for him to finally get out of bed. Anxious to also get back to his now-neglected saddlery business, he even spent the morning sitting at his desk and attending to his accounting books.

The satisfied McColl now felt sufficiently confident to tell Louis that he did not need to call again, unless of course there was an unforeseen relapse. The practitioner undoubtedly felt professionally vindicated. His rare diagnosis of Riggs' disease and accompanying treatment had led to an extremely sick man regaining his previous good health.[43]

But there was another factor that McColl had not accounted for during Louis' recuperation. Throughout the majority of his 1894 illness, which commenced on 24 April, Louis had been attended to by his devoted housekeeper, Martha. She had taken full responsibility for providing Louis with all his meals and drinks, in addition to dispensing any of his medications.

This had changed on 30 April, when Mrs Emma Jones, the mother-in-law of Louis' sister, arrived from Sydney and stayed with her relatives at Bridge Road before leaving for Adelaide on 8 May. Throughout her stay, Jones had helped Martha care for the ailing Louis and, strikingly, this time frame had coincided with Louis' steady recovery.[44]

But now that Jones had left, there was about to be a sudden turn for the worse.

An Urgent Shopping Trip

There was a proliferation of pharmacies situated along the strip shops of Richmond. As a regular purchaser of medications, Martha was well known at all of them. On 10 May, just before 7 p.m., Martha left her residence at Bridge Road and walked down to the pharmacy shop of Mr James Stiles.

Curiously, she had gone to this establishment, even though there were other chemist shops closer to where she lived. The pharmacy of Benjamin Baker was only a few doors down at 100 Bridge Road and the walk would have only taken about a minute. Likewise, the store of Mr Nicholas was only a quick three-minute stroll away on the same side of Bridge Road and the chemist shop of Mr Richards at 84 Swan Street, Richmond, was also nearby.

Once she arrived at her intended location, Martha asked pharmacist Stiles for a box of 'Rough on Rats'. For once, the usually very accommodating Stiles hesitated, pointing out that in accordance with the prevailing *Poisons Act*, Martha would not only need to sign the store's 'poisons book' prior to making such a purchase but she would also need to bring along an independent witness. Leaving the store empty-handed, Martha then made her way to the pharmacy of Mr Richards in Swan Street. Same story – Richards could only sell her a box of 'Rough on Rats' if she provided an independent witness.

Departing into the night, it did not take Martha long to find a volunteer – namely Thomas Brittain, the long-time boot salesman at the Exhibition Boot Company at 130 Swan Street. Martha had first become acquainted with Brittain over seven years earlier when she had been a regular purchaser of his shoes. Even though he hadn't seen Martha since she moved away from Cubitt Street 18 months previously, the pair quickly reignited their friendship.

Martha explained to Brittain that she urgently needed something with which to poison rats and that Mr Richards, the chemist, had stated that he would not sell it to her without a witness. The ever-obliging Brittain later recalled, 'I asked her what use she was going to make of it. She stated that they were troubled very much with rats. I advised her to try Phosphate Paste as I had used it with very good results. She replied that she had tried it with very little effect.'

Brittain then agreed to accompany Martha to a chemist shop to witness her purchase. While she initially moved in the direction of the Stiles shop, Brittain had previously had some disagreements with Stiles and convinced her to go to the shop of Mr Richards instead.

Mr Richards was no longer in attendance when the pair entered his shop at approximately 7.30 p.m., so Martha spoke to his able assistant, George Miller. After she requested some 'Rough on Rats', Miller ensured that Martha and Brittain signed the appropriate book and the purchase was completed. Leaving the store with her precious wrapped-up parcel of 'Rough on Rats', Martha allowed Brittain to walk with her a short distance before they parted and she headed back to Bridge Road. The next time the unfortunate Brittain would see Martha would be in a court of law.[45]

A Sudden Relapse

Immediately following Martha's purchase of 'Rough on Rats' on the evening of 10 May, and only a short time after the departure of Emma Jones, Louis again fell violently ill despite having previously regained most of his normal health. At 8 a.m. on 11 May, Dr McColl received an emergency message to come to Bridge Road immediately.

When McColl arrived, he found Louis much worse than before. He was vomiting again and his mouth condition had seriously deteriorated. The bewildered McColl decided that he needed to rest the mouth and stomach of the patient altogether for a few days and ordered that he only use suppositories. This treatment continued with some slight success right up to 14 May. On 15 May, McColl allowed Louis to be fed by mouth again but on examining him the same day he now discovered a supposed abnormality with his heart. This led to

McColl presuming that some of the pus from Louis' gums had been absorbed by a raw patch in the stomach and then been carried by the circulatory system to the heart, causing the rare but extremely serious ulcerated endocarditis.

With such a diagnosis, McColl now believed that the life of the previously healthy Louis was in serious danger. This time he insisted that a trained nurse be engaged. Even though Louis had refused this request before – preferring the exclusive attentions of Martha – McColl went personally to the residence of nurse Clara Stevens and organised for her immediate move to Bridge Road. She arrived around noon. Martha had done such a good job attending to Louis that Nurse Stevens fell into her duties without any trouble.

McColl had instructed Stevens that the only nourishment the patient should receive was tepid milk and brandy given every half hour. He also left a bottle of mixture to be given as prescribed. Martha would respectfully prepare the milk and brandy and bring it to the nurse every half hour. Stevens remained most impressed by the quality of Martha's care towards Louis, later recalling, 'Mrs Needle was in and out of the room assisting me. It seemed to me to be in a very kind manner that she helped.'[46]

At 9.30 p.m., McColl received another urgent call to immediately attend the bedridden Louis. This time, he found Louis in a state of semi-collapse. An examination of his heart appeared to show that the condition noted that morning had further developed. McColl now knew that Louis was dying. He called for the attendance of another doctor to provide some extra assistance. The highly credentialed Dr Grant (a medical gold medallist from Edinburgh University, no less) arrived just as Louis was taking his last breath.

The doctors tried to resuscitate the stricken patient but there was nothing they could do. Louis died just before 10 p.m., with McColl, Grant, Stevens and, of course, the ever-present little ray of sunshine, Martha, mournfully standing by his deathbed.

McColl discussed the symptoms he had observed with Grant, a doctor he revered as 'not second to any man in Melbourne'.[47] Extraordinarily, both medical men momentarily entertained the possibility of poisoning but, on account of McColl's purported Riggs' disease diagnosis, they convinced themselves that the absorbed pus had caused the uncommon condition of endocarditis of the heart.

McColl mentioned to Otto that, in light of the unusual cause of death, a post-mortem could be conducted to examine Louis' damaged heart. While Otto had no personal objections to this occurring, he believed that such a thought would be distressing for his elderly mother. Upon hearing this, McColl did not bother to press the matter further and simply let the suggestion slide. McColl duly produced a death certificate indicating that 30-year-old Louis had died from 'gastritis and endocarditis'.[48] The diagnosis would later prove to be a glaring howler.

Another Job for Herbert King

As a fellow local business owner in Richmond, busy funeral director Herbert King had known Louis quite well while he was alive. Now he found himself engaged by Louis' devastated family to bury him. Not only was Louis the first of the ten Juncken offspring to die, but at only 30 years of age he had tragically done so well before his time.

Upon hearing of Louis' death, his mother and his oldest brother, Herman, immediately travelled by the all-night train to Melbourne from South Australia and went to stay at 137 Bridge Road. Mrs Juncken had already received numerous floral tributes and letters of condolence. This included a wreath of artificial roses and jessamine in the form of a cross, sent by Martha; a card bearing a verse and her signature was attached.

Given that Martha had devotedly been Louis' main caregiver, Herman appreciated any conversation he could have with her about his brother's last days. While shedding some tears, she told Herman that Louis had died 'from his heart being affected'. She gently explained that she was in the room when he passed away and was talking to him shortly before his death.[49]

Martha's approach to Louis' grieving mother was nowhere near as cordial. The pair briefly spoke, with Louis' mother taking the time to thank Martha for her kindness to Louis during his illness and expressing her view that any ill feeling between them should be forgotten at such a time. Nonetheless, Martha immediately formed the view – somewhat illogically – that she had been snubbed and overlooked. She even went as far as believing that Louis' mother was being maliciously cruel towards her. Martha now hated the matriarch Mrs Juncken more than ever.[50]

It was decided by Louis' family that they would take the expensive step of laying him to rest at his family's spiritual home in Lyndoch. King loaded Louis' body into a leaden coffin at Bridge Road and soldered it down the same evening. The coffin included a glass window in the front so that the deceased could be seen – a request made by his distraught mother, who wanted to see his face one last time.

On the morning of 17 May, King had the coffin moved to his funeral parlour and loaded it into an outer shell. The body remained there until 9 a.m. the next day, when it was taken to Spencer Street Railway Station and loaded upon a train. From there, Louis made his last journey back home to South Australia, accompanied by his grieving mother and brother Otto. Louis' funeral, which attracted a large number of mourners, was conducted on 19 May at the small and picturesque Lyndoch Cemetery, on the outskirts of the settlement.[51]

Whether or not she was welcome remains unrecorded, although Martha did not travel to Lyndoch for Louis' funeral – remaining at Bridge Road to attend to the daily needs of her remaining boarder, Stanley Setford. By the time that her 'fiancé' Otto boarded the train to South Australia, Martha was not on good terms with him because the pair had argued repeatedly about Otto's mother. Martha was still insisting in merciless terms that Otto's mother had treated her coldly.

Worse still, she believed that Otto was now siding with his mother.

A Ranting Letter

While still temporarily in South Australia, Otto received an extraordinarily bitter letter from Martha. Although he did not know it at the time, this single item of correspondence was to play a key role in the future story of Richmond's Black Widow. It was Martha's most spiteful literary effort to date – and that covered a lot of ground.

Even though Otto was disgusted with what he read and promptly destroyed the letter, Martha had maintained her habit of keeping a copy of everything she sent. Martha's 'copy' was later found, before being leaked and published in various forms in the world press. It revealed her unhinged inner rage and was certainly not one for her time capsule.[52]

Martha's furious words were destined to be used heavily against her. In light of the comment in the court of public opinion that this letter would later receive, it was routinely quoted in full. Although many editors of the day later saw fit to make alterations to the punctuation, grammar and spelling, meaning there were differing versions in circulation, these were Martha's original words the exact way she wrote them, complete with the underlining:

> Richmond,
> May 22nd/94.
> ~~To Mr Yuncken~~
> To Otto
>
> You could leave your greifstricken Mother long enough to write to me in this manner well this is as I expected for I knew your dear Mother would make <u>you</u> see things with <u>her</u> eyes as she has done befor you try to excuse her by saying she wanted to see me on Friday morning to thank me for my kindness to

your brother, well that she could have done while she was here If she so wished one would have thought that as soon as she came over here she could never rested until she talked to me about her dead child, knowing as <u>she</u> did that I was with him through all his illness she made the excuse to me in the evening that she could not talk and laught with me, well do you or her think I expected that she could laught but I did expect that she would spake to me in a friendly way if only concerning her dead son. She could thank Mrs Gray for coming out but me that had done so much for her children she could not speak to. You know that I tried to be friendly with her when she cane and befor <u>she</u> left but she would not let me surly Otto you knew in your heart that I did not deserve such treatment you know that she left this house in the morning without one <u>word</u> to me and yet <u>you</u> blame me for my cold manner. In the evening after she had been in my house for over 4 hours and never opend her lips to me all that time but she could talk to the old lady about Mr Smiths grand home <u>very</u> nice talk for a heart broken mother I must say she ought never to have left this house until she left with her sons body for Adelaide. I can tell you that your Mothers conduct in going from here is the talk of all the road another prof of her grief and to show what aheard hearted old thing she is to tell me she never brought her cap when I asked her to take off her bonnet did she for one moment think I expected she had done so if she had come withought any thing on her head, people would not have been so surprised as they were to see her bring lougge with her but it must be as pepel say she came for a trip did she sit all day and all the evening at Mr Smiths with her bonnit on her head. <u>No</u> of course you think <u>your</u> dear Mother is heartbroken but she cannot pas that off on a woman who has lost all her children why I would never have gone out visation befor your brother was in his grave as his loving Mother did while his poore body was lying at the railway station why did your wicked Mother come over her for to mak us more unhappy than we were befor for if she is the good loving Mother that you think she is why did she not come to see her child befor he died the doctor over there told her that her son might not get over his illness yet she never came to see him in life and neither would she you If you were diying for she is like the one that is gone all self when I asked her if she would like to go up and see her boy after Mrs Gray had gone she sade that stairs are too trying for her so she did not forget her owne self even at such a time when you told her the poore dog was not Lous but mine she would not look at it and you say that she entered my house with all ill fellings buried of corse Otto I bleave you that she told you so but could you not see how bitter she was to me when she came and left. No you cannot see anything wrong that your Mother dose your poore fool to say you thought this sad event would cause a reconsilition between her and I Friday was no day for such talk and even if she wished to make you happy she could have spoken to you alone about that. It was her and you between you that has caused me so much missirey and therefor it was for you two to settle it all. I wonder bouth you and she are not afrade that god will strike you bouth dead when you are planning my ruin betwen you are you so blind as not to see that if your dear Mother did want to speak to me on Friday morning that she should have come to the house early and not waite for you to fele the way and again what time would she have had with me at the late hours she wanted to bring her you silley man she only tells you this knowing as she does that she can make you belive whatever she likes. Fridays weeks is right into her hands to poison you against me wich is a very easy matter for any one to do when you would alow your Mother to part _us_ in the first place as _you_ did you would have let her do it if we had been married by all the Ministers in the world for you know then that nothing would have parted us. If you had been a honnerable man or if you wished to make a honnerable woman of me, but No men like you had had your turn and I could be throwen aside, but remember this the day you cast me off for your Mother you will soon be Motherls for I shall _kill her_. If I have to walk every mile from here to Lyndoch I have vowed to my god to do this and I shall keep that vow, bouth you and she shall see what it is to try a woman as I have been tried by you and yours you accuse me of my treatment to you on Friday if you wanted me to be kind and loving to you why when you saw how your dear Mother treted me when first she came to my house did you not show me a little symthy to make up for her unkindness but No unsted of you speaking kindly to me and asking me to try to bear it for your sake you could come and tell me your Mother had not been very curle to me thereby acknogting That she was curle to me and another porfe of _your_ _love_ for _me_ you could surlay tell me that night that you _might_ not be any _longer_ then a fortnight remember that was all made up in the afternoon befor I offended your dear Mother do you think that was right to go and leave me in this death stricken house for so long would I have left you so long by yourself at a time like this I would not say one word about you staying so long. If your mother had not got her family with her or if you had been the only boy but as it is I do not know how Otto _you_ could think of leaving me so long by myself you never from the first of your brothers death expressed one word of sorrow for me do you think that all this has not been hard on me in itself without your curel treatment to me why did you not stay home so long when your father died but then your dear Mother had no one to poison your mind against me at the time. It seems she was not as heart-broken but that she could not worke her plans with you before you ever got home she was afraid if she left you to yourself that you might have wreting to me in a kindlay manner and that would upset her work of corse <u>you</u> and <u>she</u> magnife my faults <u>but</u> <u>you</u> cannot see what your dear mother is working for while you are telling her all your plans and truble and she trying so hard to part us. I hope you will be <u>man</u> enough to tell her <u>all</u> She and you have been the cause of doing for me and you can tell me why your mother came Over for No it was a excuse to see me and to work her wicked ways for after she came there was no respect whatever paid to your brothers memory nor no kindness showed to any of his friends here. She made the excuse to study the expenses why did <u>she</u> not think of that befor she came and why does she not think of yours while she is keeping you away so long or why did she not think of all the expenses and truble she put you to twels months ago dear loving Mother. Your dear friends the Smiths have never been near since you left, you did not know that it was all made up for dear Mother to say with them a week before she came. Otto but for that I do not blame you for I am sure that you did not know anything about that arrangement for they all looked out that you did not know they got the letter the day that Aggie should have come home old Smith said what he did to you about asking your Mother to his grand house to put you of your gard so as far as that goes I knew you were not to blame but you are to blame for allowing him to dectate to me like he did the old sneak that he is, you will think I am saying a lot but I never entend to say one word to you again concerning your old

Mother but for all that you think that I shall not keep my word and kill her if she parts us for I have quite made up my mind for that she shall never cause another woman all the sin and missery <u>she</u> has brought on me. No you can do whatever you like while you are over home you say Herman is coming with you What a wonder you can both leave her at once please tell Charles that he must have his boxes take away for I shall have them no longer in my house as this is not <u>your</u> <u>brothers</u> <u>home</u> now. I want you to write at once and let me know whether you intend to still bord with me or are you going to do as your mother wishes you to do, if so let me know at wonce as I will only need a small house for Stanly and myself.

Your cast off landlady
P. S. Don't forget to tell your Mother confesser all I have done to you.

As it turned out, Martha had done herself no favours by choosing to underline the words 'kill her' and, once discovered, the contents of this letter would haunt her for the rest of her days. A quick temper will always make a fool of a person soon enough – and now Martha had transformed her anger into an art form.[53]

CHAPTER 11

More Dreadful Misfortune

A couple of weeks after Louis' funeral, his brothers Herman and Otto arrived back in Melbourne. This time, Herman was in Melbourne for business reasons. As the oldest brother, he took responsibility for winding up the saddlery shop previously conducted by the deceased Louis.

Herman slept in a spare room at 137 Bridge Road and Martha prepared most of his meals, in much the same way that she had always attended to the dietary needs of the other occupants. To that point, Herman had never openly objected to Martha's engagement to Otto and, unlike his mother, had remained on reasonably good terms with her. Nonetheless, as a prominent member of the Juncken family, he sensed a simmering tension brewing.

He could smell the pungent odour of carbolic acid in his room because Martha was in the habit of lighting up a 'Carbolic Smoke Ball' to fumigate the house – not that this action ever had much effect. The Carbolic Smoke Ball – the main ingredient of which was carbolic acid – was an ineffective and fraudulent device marketed in the late 19th century. It supposedly protected the inhabitants of a residence from influenza and other ailments but about the only thing it actually disposed of was money from the purchaser's pockets.

And despite her exposure to carbolic fumes, within three days of Herman's arrival Martha was ill in bed. Herman took the opportunity to tell her he was sorry she was unwell and the pair continued their conversation. The discussion inevitably turned to the topic of Herman's mother. Martha again complained bitterly of what she said was his mother's 'cruel' conduct towards her.

Herman then delivered a few home truths to Martha, something that Otto had always been too weak to do. Herman told Martha that she was greatly to blame for the situation because she had not treated his mother in the same spirit that his mother had showed to her. She should also make every allowance for the condition his elderly mother had been in – she had been greatly distressed by Louis' untimely death and had been travelling all night to get to Melbourne. Martha wasn't listening, preferring to persist in her claims that she had been treated very unkindly.

The next topic of the awkward conversation was even more pressing. They spoke about winding up Louis' former business. Herman indicated that he intended to sell the saddlery and give up the adjoining house. Given that Martha would be unable to reside there much longer, he suggested that she apply for a housekeeping position elsewhere. He also indicated that it would not be suitable for her and Otto to reside together at another house, because as an unmarried couple, such behaviour would be 'injurious to their reputations'.

If Martha had expected any form of protest from the virtuous Otto, she would have been mistaken. Otto had already thought the same thing, telling Martha that they should live apart for a time on moral grounds and also to allow time for matters to heal between herself and 'his people'.

On hearing Herman's news, Martha appeared to faint. It would later be a matter of considerable conjecture as to how genuine this condition was. Herman formed the view that a sophisticated degree of acting was involved. Nonetheless, he waited about five minutes for Martha to recover before he left the room.[54]

Although to all outside appearances Martha still apparently got on well with Herman, he had now delivered to her some information she didn't want to hear – a very bad move. The conversation Herman had with Martha appeared to confirm that the threats she had made about his mother were secretly being laughed at and also that her intended marriage plans, if still contemplated by Otto, remained bitterly opposed by his family.

Martha then repeated her customary action when feeling under duress. She picked up her pen and began writing a letter. In this one to Otto, she not only suggested a short separation but also again hinted at suicide. A newspaper editor later helpfully corrected the spelling and punctuation. The published version of the letter read:

> To Otto
>
> I once thought I won your unalienated heart. Pride sternly sets foot upon this spark of hope with cruel insistence. Your love has never been mine, and defrauded of the diamond can I accept and patiently wear the paste. Dear, I propose at least a temporary change in our relations … When you asked me to become your wife neither of us contemplated this cruel separation your unkind and heartless mother has involved upon us. And for your sake, and hers, I am willing to fetter you by an engagement, and want you to be entirely free, bound by no promises, your heart shall no longer be burdened by bonds which I can loosen, because your peace and happiness are more to me than my own. I grant you complete release for twelve months. If after that you consider me necessary to you, then you can have a renewal of your bonds.
> Martha
> P.S. – Dear Otto, I feel very ill, and I sincerely hope this will be my last illness, as I am so tired of life, as you know I have no happiness to look back upon and none to look forward to.

If it was not for the fear that I would not meet my dear little ones and yours in the spirit-land I would pass away this night, and you please remember if I am tempted to do away with my miserable life, on your hands and your wicked mother's rests the sin. If I get worse please don't bring a doctor, for I will not see him.

Martha

As it turned out, Martha did not 'do away' her 'miserable life' that night. Instead, she lay awake in bed, her mind churning over other solutions.[55]

Breakfast Time

The very next morning – 6 June 1894 – Martha prepared Herman some breakfast. The pair was alone in the house and they sat and chatted while Herman consumed the fried eggs, bread and cup of tea she had provided. Like his now deceased brother, Louis, Herman had always enjoyed extremely good health but immediately after he finished his breakfast he felt ill and went outside to vomit. Martha remarked that this was very strange, as he had previously appeared to be so well. She advised him to go upstairs and lie down. Once upstairs, Herman vomited twice more.

Martha came upstairs and asked if she could do anything for him. He asked for another cup of good, strong tea, which she duly went downstairs to prepare. Upon drinking the beverage, Herman felt a little better. He then decided to leave the house and walk to see his acquaintances, the Smith family, at nearby Sherwood Street. The walk only took about three or four minutes and he consumed nothing else on the way there. Shortly after arriving at Sherwood Street, Herman was again taken ill and was soon vomiting repeatedly.[56]

Herman's condition was deteriorating so quickly that he asked members of the Smith family to call for a doctor. Although they were spendthrifts, the Smiths could afford a private practitioner and were not reliant on the lodge doctors. Crucially, they called their own regular physician, the vigilant Dr William Boyd.

Although he was also a medical man practising in Richmond, the energetic Boyd stood in stark contrast to the slapdash lodge doctors. Martha was not one of Boyd's patients, which also allowed him to be more objective. Whereas the lodge doctors relied on keeping their clients happy to maintain their living, Boyd had no such concerns. And he was not in a position to be influenced by Martha.

Boyd immediately noted that Herman was suffering from violent retching and great weakness. Herman was also complaining of a sensation of emptiness in the pit of his stomach. At first Herman expressed his concerns that his younger brother had just died unexpectedly and he feared that whatever his brother had might have been contagious. When Boyd learned that Dr McColl had listed Louis' cause of death as 'endocarditis', he not only reassured Herman that this was not contagious, but he also scoffed that this was an extremely rare condition and a very unusual cause of death.

Boyd prescribed Herman some medication – a bismuth mixture to act as a stomach sedative. Although Herman took what he had been prescribed, he was still too ill to leave the Smiths' residence. He stayed there that night and all of the next day. While at Sherwood Street, Herman's vomiting eventually ceased. On Friday 8 June, Herman remained at the house until Boyd had called and said that he was now making pleasing progress. Finally feeling much better and reassured that he had now recovered, Herman had breakfast at Sherwood Street before leaving the house to go back to Martha at Bridge Road.

He arrived there at midday and had eaten nothing since breakfast. Martha was just about to prepare lunch and asked him if he would like some. After replying 'yes', he was given bread and butter and the customary cup of tea. Immediately after Herman had finished the tea, he again felt very sick. Martha remarked that this was very strange –

she couldn't understand how Herman had been taken so ill upon his arrival in Melbourne. She once again advised him to go upstairs and lie down. Herman declined to do so, primarily because he was finding the smell of carbolic acid in his room to be overpowering. The kind Martha went as far as offering him the opportunity to rest in her room instead, where she was even willing to make him more comfortable by lighting a fire in the fireplace.

Herman said he would prefer to get some fresh air and again left the house and went down the road to the Smiths. Although he had not vomited at Bridge Road, he vomited violently upon arrival at Sherwood Street and Boyd was again called. Even though Boyd prescribed Herman some more medication, by now his suspicion about the patient's unusual condition was fully aroused. He gave one further instruction to members of the Smith family – if Herman vomited again, they were to preserve the vomit in a clean chamber pot. Boyd had privately begun to believe that Herman might have been the subject of some form of irritant poisoning. If the vomit could be properly preserved, he could organise a proper analysis of its contents. Boyd's decision to move down this path was destined to immortalise him in legal history.

There was no need to wait long. Herman vomited into the chamber pot almost straightaway and it remained at the side of his bed until Thomas Smith came home from work that evening. As instructed, Smith put the contents of the chamber pot into a rinsed bottle and delivered the bottle to Boyd.

Although Boyd had no practical experience in analysis, he knew where to get it done. The Government Analyst in Victoria at that time was the world-renowned 63-year-old Cuthbert Blackett.

Known as a man with fine principles, Blackett was the twin son of an English minister and had been apprenticed to a pharmacist in the British county of Norfolk. He had first arrived in Melbourne in 1853 but would later travel to Europe to complete further pharmaceutical studies. In 1871, he had returned to Melbourne and established a pharmacy, where he remained until 1887, when he was appointed to the Crown Law Department. Blackett had already appeared as an expert witness in many prominent criminal trials and was universally respected by judges and lawyers alike.[57]

The next morning, Boyd ventured with the sample of vomit to Blackett's office in Melbourne's Swanston Street. Blackett was not there, so Boyd passed the bottle over to the caretaker of the School of Pharmacy, Joseph Lowry, instead. Lowry kept the bottle under lock and key before handing it to Blackett's assistant, William Wilkinson. He also kept the bottle in a locked cabinet for two days before handing it to Blackett on 11 June.

Blackett removed the vomit from the bottle and did the necessary analytical tests. He then soberly reported back to Boyd some staggering news. 'I have made an analysis of the contents of the stomach which you submitted,' he wrote, 'and I find that it contains a considerable quantity of arsenic. Your diagnosis is therefore abundantly supported.'

So, Boyd was right – the vomit of Herman showed the presence of the deadly poison arsenic. When Boyd relayed this news back to Herman, the pair didn't take long to conclude that Herman was being systematically poisoned. By a quick process of deduction, they also centred on the likely, yet surprise suspect – the ever-obliging Martha Needle.

They further noted that throughout the entire ordeal, the Smiths at Sherwood Street had an interstate guest staying with them, namely Emma Jones – Herman's relative, who at one stage had helped Martha nurse his ailing brother, Louis. While Emma was there, Martha had issued her with a number of urgent invitations to go for tea at Bridge Road but Herman now advised her against it. Martha was very disappointed that Emma did not take up her invitations and even felt offended by the refusals.

After fully discussing the surprising developments, both Dr Boyd and Herman agreed it was time to talk to the police.[58]

CHAPTER 12

Setting a Trap for the Black Widow

The next day was 13 June 1894 – a Wednesday. Early that morning, Herman and Dr Boyd attended the central police branch in Melbourne and were referred to Superintendent Joseph Brown. The potential seriousness of their allegations saw the matter immediately handed over to two of the force's most highly regarded detectives – Alfred Edward Whitney and Robert Fryer. They had no way of knowing it at the time, but this case would be career changing for them. It would even lead to both becoming highly recognised faces in the community, akin to modern-day celebrities.

Whitney was a 44-year-old officer with over 20 years of experience in the criminal department in Victoria and he had been connected with many significant cases. In the preceding few years alone, he had undertaken a prominent role in several complex trials that had required him follow up 'very delicate threads of evidence' to bring criminals to justice.[59] But none of these cases would prove to be as prominent or compelling as that now confronting him with Martha Needle.

Fryer had only recently joined the detective ranks, after a fine stint in uniform. The only detective tuition available at that time was on-the-job training and Fryer had been appointed after an impressive interview with senior officers. He was very much seen as the understudy to the more experienced Whitney.

Desperate Times

As the economic Depression began to bite, this had already been a very active time for Victoria's much-maligned police force, with a number of highly publicised cases hitting the recent headlines. Prominent among them were two trials that ended with the accused dangling from the end of a rope.

In 1892, the notorious swindler Frederick Deeming was hanged at Melbourne Gaol for the heartless murder of his young wife, after her decomposing body was found buried in the fireplace of a rented house in Windsor. As fate would have it, the bodies of Deeming's previous wife and four children were also later found in England, buried beneath the floor of a rented property.

A few years after Deeming, baby farmer Frances Knorr had been hanged at the beginning of 1894 for the ruthless killing of two babies left in her care. Knorr had become only the second woman executed in Victoria, after the first had occurred some 31 years previously – an ominous sign of the tougher approach to crime likely to be adopted in such harsh times.

And now, as Whitney and Fryer were hearing the allegations about Martha, they realised that her case could turn into the biggest of the lot. Bad stories didn't get much better than this.

Crime Stoppers

In many respects, this was a different era in policing and detective work to what is practised today. With an absence of forensic indicators such as DNA analysis (and not even fingerprints could be reliably traced for several more years), the better detectives were required to live off their wits and 'hunches' while they displayed advanced skills in questioning and deduction. Eyewitness accounts, whether reliable or not, became a vital tool in any investigation. And the detectives needed to be all-rounders. While upon a major crime being reported today an entire squad of investigators may be assembled, in the 1890s only two detectives would be provided with the assignment.

It was also not totally out of the question for some of the less reputable upholders of the law to be irresistibly tempted to take a few short cuts – verballing witnesses, manufacturing evidence, copping bribes and even resorting to the occasional clip across the ear to help make a potential witness see the value in 'assisting' them with their inquiries. More than once it had been half-jokingly suggested that the members of Victoria Police in that era were the best police that money could buy.

Another common trait among the very poorly paid detectives at that time was the propensity to leak as much information as possible to the newspapers, including any self-congratulatory pieces and portrait photographs. As well as helping to flush out more witnesses, the resulting publicity would later do the detective no harm when seeking an extra pound or two via promotion. The police also often worked on a reward system – receiving a bonus if they solved a complex crime. This approach would later be heavily criticised at a Royal Commission, it then being believed that such efforts to uphold the law should not just revolve around a scheme of randomly allocated benefits.

But, having said all this, Whitney and Fryer were very good at their craft. As Herman and Boyd related the known facts to them, they began to recognise that this whole scenario could potentially turn into a monster case.

After hearing from the two witnesses, Whitney and Fryer surreptitiously began to gather as much information as possible about this mysterious person of interest, Martha Needle, and her 'domestic history'. They soon came to understand from her dirt file what an unlucky person she appeared to be – not only had Louis Juncken recently died under her watch but, in recent years, her whole family had also perished while in her loving care.

With a positive result for arsenic now confirmed in Herman's vomit, the circumstantial evidence that she had tried to poison him was very strong. But being a bit unusual and desperately unlucky did not necessarily make her a killer. Was this apparently sociable young woman really capable of being a 'Black Widow'? Had her family members simply caught a bad case of death or had she given them all a helping hand on their journey to the afterlife? Was she a misunderstood and tragic widow or a cunning and devious mass murderer?

Whitney and Fryer knew that the sensational nature of this investigation meant it would initially need to be kept very quiet. The pressmen of the daily broadsheets would quickly seize upon any titbit of information and this would subsequently ruin the course of the investigation.

They also felt compelled to act very quickly. For all they knew, the woman involved could be planning to poison others or may be already doing so.

And to make the case really 'stick', it would also be best to catch her in the act. Normally, in poisoning-related cases, they would be looking at a dead body but Herman had evidently escaped from the plot and was now sitting eagerly in front of them. They still had the element of surprise in their favour. All they needed now was for Herman to cooperate.

Whitney and Fryer formulated a plan to catch Martha the very next day, a move that would go down in the annals of Australian police history as one of the most famous examples of detective work. To make it happen, these experienced officers were relying on the fact that Martha would follow a predictable routine.

If their 'hunch' was right, Martha had been a master manipulator of others, an evil architect of wrongdoings and a compulsive planner for most of her life. This time, however, the roles would be reversed and the Black Widow would find herself caught in a well-planned trap.

The Plot

Herman now found himself being given heavy riding instructions by the detectives. He was set to become the volunteer guinea pig in the whole operation.

Herman had previously told the detectives that whenever he entered 137 Bridge Road, Martha would habitually offer him a cup of tea. This habit was so ingrained in Martha's behaviour that she was probably at risk of contracting her own case of tannin poisoning. The detectives saw an opportunity to exploit this established behaviour, while avoiding outright entrapment.

Herman and the detectives travelled together to 137 Bridge Road, arriving just before 1 p.m. This time had been deliberately chosen – it was usually when Martha was having lunch and getting ready to boil the billy. Herman was told to enter the building in the normal manner while the detectives concealed themselves outside. Whitney told Herman that he was to act as naturally as possible and if Martha offered him a cup of tea, he was to accept it.

Despite their restricted time frame, the detectives had obtained the necessary warrant and were planning to storm the house and seize the cup of tea before Herman drank it. They would then organise for its contents and any other suspicious foodstuffs in the house to be tested by Blackett. But pivotal to the whole plot was the need for an unsuspecting Martha to take the bait.

As planned, Herman entered the house at 1 p.m. and ventured to the kitchen. There he saw Martha alone and, as predicted, she was just washing up things that were left from lunch. Martha greeted him in a friendly manner. She had a brief conversation with him, indicating that in keeping with his earlier advice, she had been to see someone about another housekeeping position.[60] Martha then asked the crucial question that would change the course of the entire investigation – 'Would you like a cup of tea?'

When Herman agreed, Martha needed to rekindle the fire to begin making the tea for him. After sitting patiently for a short time, Herman found himself becoming nervous. He stood up and briefly left the room several times, but never at Martha's request.

It proved to be an agonising wait for the detectives outside. After about six minutes had passed, they feared something might have gone wrong. But during Herman's last absence, he quickly went outside and told them what was happening – Martha was preparing a cup of tea for him and she had to light the fire.

Herman went back to the kitchen and waited another ten minutes. Becoming restless again, he moved to leave the room. Upon seeing this, Martha unassumingly asked him, 'As you are going out, will you mind going to Miss Howell's next door to get a glass of milk?' Herman agreed to do this and, upon his return, he was soon handed his cup of tea. Martha had even prepared a cup for herself.

Warily, Herman stole a quick glance at the contents of his cup. He would later recall that it did not appear to differ in colour from a normal cup of tea, 'only that there was sort of dust floating about on the top of it that looked a dark colour'. Extraordinarily, Herman was even brave enough to have a quick sip, only to have his tastebuds immediately detect a metallic, coppery flavour.

After he received his cup of tea, Herman took it and left the room. He placed it on a table at the foot of the stairs. By this time, he was out of Martha's sight and had left her sitting on a chair near the fireplace. He then went outside and called in Whitney and Fryer. As they charged into the house, Herman picked up the cup of tea and indicated to Whitney that this was the one poured by Martha.

With Herman still gripping the precious brew, Whitney led the trio towards the kitchen. As they entered the room, they quickly noticed that no-one was there. Momentarily feeling that their quarry may have taken flight, Fryer urgently ventured into the yard and Whitney also peered out the back window.

Whitney then directly cast his eyes on Martha for the first time, as she strode up the yard in the direction of the kitchen door. A curious Martha entered the kitchen, which was now inhabited by two strangers and Herman. Whitney wasted no time explaining the situation. 'We are detective police. My name is Whitney and this is Detective Fryer. I have a warrant for your arrest for poisoning this man' he informed her, pointing his finger at the sheepish Herman.

Martha appeared dumbfounded. While she was destined to look a little hazy for the rest of the afternoon, this didn't prevent her turning to Herman and snapping, 'Did you put them up to this?' He admitted he had. Even in a crisis, Martha still knew how to make a man feel bad.

With two hefty police officers now standing in her kitchen, making outrageous allegations, Martha would need to think on her feet. Luckily, this was a skill that had been one of her trademarks throughout her young life. She acquitted herself well.

All conversations and actions during this brief window of time were destined to be recited, critiqued and studied at length in future years. In this era devoid of recordings, and with a lower threshold of legal rights for accused people, detectives would be routinely required to commit conversations to memory or scrawl a few rough notes for later reference in court. Their versions of events would often be conveniently slanted in favour of their case and therefore heavily questioned.

Although the *exact* words that were exchanged between Martha and the detectives at this crucial point came to be disputed, it was reasonably established that after Whitney read the contents of the warrant, he said to Martha words to the effect of 'This is a very serious charge and be very careful what you say, for anything you say may be used for or against you in this case'.[61] He then pointed to the cup that had been brought into the room by Herman. 'Did you supply this man with this cup of tea?' Martha simply said, 'Yes'. 'Where did you get the water from?' Whitney inquired. Martha pointed to the fireplace where the kettle was standing. 'From there' was the terse reply. 'Where did you get the sugar and tea from?' continued Whitney. Martha pointed to the various receptacles in the kitchen where these items were stored. Whitney's attention then turned to the second cup of tea sitting on the table, the one from which Martha had been drinking. 'Did you get that from the same place as the other?' Martha had no hesitation in saying she did.

Whitney explained to Martha that he intended to take possession of all these articles and then curiously asked her, 'Have you any jars in the house?' Although the police plan appeared to be working to this point, they had not thought ahead enough to bring their own means of storage. Martha pointed to the bottom of a cupboard in the kitchen, where Whitney found four large, corked jars. He washed out the jars using the kitchen tap. He then poured Herman's cup of tea into one of the jars, sealed it with the cork and labelled, dated and initialled it as an exhibit. Using different jars, he then followed the same process with Martha's cup of tea, the remaining tea in the teapot and the water still in the kettle.

Whitney then asked Martha the crucial question, 'Do you have any poison in the house?' She immediately replied, 'Yes, I have Chlorodyne'. When he asked her if she had any poison on her person, she was just as quick to answer 'No'. In Martha's presence, and with Fryer and Herman looking on, Whitney then began searching the house. Martha seemed unfazed. 'It is no use looking, you will find nothing,' she offered.[62]

Whitney began with the cupboard from where he had procured the jars. In the bottom of that cupboard he found a few inconsequential items not needed for the investigation but the top of the cupboard revealed much more.

In the top of that cupboard, Whitney found a coke box iron, an old-fashioned household contraption with a hinged lid into which hot coals were dropped to warm the base. He brought it down and placed it on the kitchen table.

Martha was quick to add, 'You can search away – you will find nothing in the iron'. Whitney nonetheless decided to test Martha's theory. He opened the top of the iron and found a wooden box inside with its label removed. Its contents were about three-quarters full. 'What is this?' he asked, before adding, 'It looks like 'Rough on Rats'.' Martha didn't respond directly to these comments but, upon Whitney eagerly continuing this line of questioning, she openly volunteered that she had purchased the product at 'Richards – the chemist in Swan Street, Richmond' in the company of Mr Brittain.

Whitney then asked a loaded question, 'What did you have it for?' – only for Martha to answer in a slightly sarcastic tone, 'For rats'. She later thought it wise to add, 'I have not used it for some time'.

Whitney took his prized 'Rough on Rats' exhibit and quickly labelled and initialled it on the outer woodwork.

After thoroughly searching the kitchen, Whitney asked Martha if he could see her room. Martha led the detectives up the stairs but, as she approached her room, she quickened her pace in its direction. She quickly grabbed a bottle of chlorodyne sitting on some shelving and looked like she was about to consume it, before Fryer intervened and grabbed the bottle from her grasp. Whitney observed that Martha looked very agitated and he asked her, 'Were you going to poison yourself?' She replied defiantly, 'I would be more likely to poison myself than any other person'.

While searching Martha's room, the detectives made more discoveries than Captain Cook, including a stash of hundreds of poison-pen letters. The detectives quickly noted that Martha's correspondence had embraced all types of people, including lawyers, doctors, policemen, private detectives, clergymen, tradesmen and 'admirers'. Among the correspondence were dozens of letters of condolence from unknown and anonymous sympathisers with her in her bereavements – all of which had been thoughtfully retained.

Some of Martha's own compositions were highly personal – mostly love letters to Otto. Others were threatening missives to people she felt

had wronged her. There were also the letters to a number of parties
with Martha's inquiries about her seemingly imagined inheritance in
Britain, plus the letter from Louis Juncken arranging for the interview
at which Martha would agree to running the lodging house at the rear
of his saddlery shop.

Disturbingly, the detectives also found stored away in various old
envelopes some pieces of paper on which were written the medical
names for various diseases, including those from which her late
husband and daughters had been certified to have met their deaths.
Martha was clearly a woman who liked to keep her professional library
and medical research up to date.

It was Martha's correspondence with Otto that drew the most
attention. The detectives found it curious that the pair had continually
chosen to exchange letters, even though they had usually lived
in the same house and saw each other frequently during the day.
They concluded that they either did not want to attract attention to
themselves by being seen in constant communication, or remained
filled with the romanticism of young lovers.

And Martha had been halfway through writing another verse of
poetry to Otto. Her unfinished sorrowful work read:

> TO A DEAR ONE OTTO.
> They would give thee to another,
> They would break thy vow.
> They would give thee to another,
> And my heart is lonely now.
> They remember not my sorrow,
> They remember not my tears.
> They would sever in one fatal hour,
> The tenderness of years.
> But it is well to leave me,
> Wouldst thou so deceive me ...

Martha's habit of retaining letters, ingrained from a young age, had now left trails of evidence against her and also embarrassingly implicated others in a number of uncomfortable ways. Many of these items of correspondence were destined to appear at trial; the more salacious ones would also be systematically divulged to the press.

Throughout the house, the detectives also found numerous photographs of Martha's late children, items of children's clothing and other mementos of her dearly departed 'little ones'. All of these were carefully preserved. Whenever the detectives touched these items, Martha would burst into tears and tell them not to touch them as they belonged to her dead children. Watching on, Herman believed Martha's distress to be genuine – so much so that he pitied her.[63]

An Uncommon Criminal

Satisfied with their work, Whitney and Fryer then transported Martha and their gathered exhibits back to Melbourne. There were 15 exhibits in all, which – apart from the 'Rough on Rats' and chlorodyne – included such day-to-day substances as iodine and liniment.[64] Martha was placed in a dank holding cell at the city watch house, which was then connected to the Melbourne Gaol through a small passageway between the two buildings.

She would later be transferred to the prison itself, which consisted of a row of imposing bluestone buildings designed to accommodate the single cell design favoured at Pentonville Prison in London. This prison system imposed long periods of isolation, silence and continual surveillance in an environment dominated by the clanging of bells – and Martha would soon experience all of these factors.

Meanwhile, the exhibits that had been collected were placed in the strongroom at the detective office. The following morning, they were handed to Blackett in the same condition they were collected. Blackett anticipated that he would be able to provide a preliminary report by the end of that day.

With their prized accused safely held in the lockup, Whitney and Fryer were so enthused they ventured back to Bridge Road that evening to conduct another search of the premises, mostly by candlelight. They also took the time to grill Otto Juncken and confiscate a number of Martha's letters that he had in his possession. At one point, they even prevented him trying to destroy one of the letters.[65]

On Media Street

As part of the prison processing procedures, Martha was soon required to stand alongside a rough wall and have two quick mugshots taken. Her days of glamour photographs being taken in local studios were now nothing more than a memory. The mugshot photos would not only be attached to her well-thumbed prison file, but they would also be ultimately leaked and circulated among eager newspaper editors.

In comparison to hundreds of other mugshots from that time that featured scowling women with hard-worn faces and limited dental arrangements, these photographs of Martha showed a relatively attractive, classy, well-groomed and well-dressed young woman, who looked completely out of place in a smelly cell. Glancing to her left for one of the photographs, Martha may have looked a little flustered and apprehensive but her expression gave no impression of a woman capable of the devious crimes of which she was now being suspected. The second mugshot showed her glaring straight down the barrel of the camera lens. She had an indignant stare that gave a mixed impression of ambivalence and defiance.

An Ugly Transition - From Sharing Cups of Tea to Eating Porridge

Martha's reasonably comfortable existence and enjoyment of the finer things in life were over forever. Within the space of one day, her life had gone base over apex. She was now facing an attempted murder charge – and even the possibility of execution. The remainder of her days would be dominated by bluestone walls and barred windows – and the company one was forced to keep in the loathsome prison environment was also sometimes less than ideal.

Any skerrick of her personal privacy was also gone. Martha's shocking story would be quickly relayed throughout the world and her every move would be reported on dramatically. And, as her infamy spread, she would find herself at the centre of intense scrutiny and speculation each and every day.

CHAPTER 13

A Public Frenzy

The detectives were required to bring Martha before a court within 24 hours of her arrest to briefly outline the case against her and seek approval to keep her in custody. The police initially laid only one charge against her – 'feloniously causing to be taken by Herman Juncken poison, with intent to murder'. In the meantime, their investigations and the analyses by Blackett would continue. If something else was found, they could later amend the charge or add further charges.

The police then contacted newspaper reporters, providing all the necessary details and even a few photographs as well. In an age before radio, television and computers, the newspapers were not only in abundant supply, but they were also the primary form of information, gossip, scandal, speculation and entertainment for people in the community. In Melbourne alone, there were three major publications – the *Herald*, *Age* and *Argus* – in fierce competition with each other and sometimes producing multiple editions each day.

When covering major criminal matters, enthusiastic reporters would engage in a different journalistic style to that usually encountered today, often putting forth theories about what had occurred, tracking down their own 'evidence' and embarking on personal crusades. Their stories were always eagerly awaited, in the same way that a modern viewer might look forward to the next episode of a dramatic soap opera.

Martha first went to the Police City Court (the equivalent of the Magistrate's Court today) on the morning of Thursday 14 June. By the time that she appeared at the courthouse, the newspaper editors had been fully briefed about the entire sensational story. Their reporters were waiting with their pencils poised and were scrambling to find out as much as they possibly could about this apparently sinister and intriguing woman, Martha Needle.

And the reporters' activities were not restricted to the courthouse – they were soon speaking to any of her associates, neighbours and relatives they could track down. Article after article began to appear across all the front pages, most of which were then duplicated in other newspapers and distributed throughout Australia and the world, via a sophisticated cable system.

The reporters were particularly anxious to find Martha's mother. As is often curiously the case when people can attract notoriety through criminal sensations and are offered money to talk, at least *two* women claimed this honour. The first was an aged woman living in Birkenhead but, after further investigations, the reporters dismissed her as an oddball.

Then they found the real deal, Mary Foran, who was only too happy to offer her thoughts. By this time, Mary was living in West Thebarton, an area in South Australia primarily devoted to the brick-making industry. She refused to provide her daughter with a glowing testimonial, bitterly telling the world that Martha was most 'undutiful, cruel and headstrong'. She also said that Martha was possessed by 'a fierce temper', and had even tried to kill her.[66]

The Much-scrutinised Cameo

From her very first appearance in court, the attractive Martha became an object of extreme fascination. The courtroom would be overflowing each and every time she appeared, not only with reporters but also with voyeuristic members of the public – many needing to queue for hours to be among those fortunate enough to gain admission.

To complete the picture, newspaper artists would clamour around the courtroom, their heads bobbing up and down while they quickly sketched likenesses of Martha, the lawyers, the judge and all the witnesses. While these artistic efforts often barely resembled their intended subjects, it didn't seem to matter. Most of these sketches would readily find their way into the next available newspaper edition.

Frocks and Shocks

During all of Martha's court appearances, a great deal of the commentary centred on her fresh good looks, her reaction to the proceedings as they unfolded and her choice of wardrobe. In the latter respect, she became something of a fashion barometer. Her propensity to still wear dark mourning clothes seemed to galvanise the sobriquet now being bandied around in the headlines about her – namely, the 'Black Widow'. None of this was relevant to the proceedings. If this sort of attention occurred today, it would invariably be labelled as sexism and harassment.

Every time Martha appeared in court, she would also be subjected to intent stares from those in the public gallery. On numerous occasions this behaviour would become so pronounced that the presiding judge would be required to intervene and warn those in court to refrain from such actions.

As reporters tried to gauge Martha's reaction to the evidence being outlined, many of the conclusions they drew were contradictory. In this game, Martha could not win. If she sat passively, she could be labelled 'cold' or 'heartless'; if she displayed emotion or shed a tear, she risked being called an 'hysterical' or 'anxious' member of the fairer sex. In many cases, different people viewing the same scene interpreted it differently. Where one person thought that Martha seemed 'uncaring', another person would label her emotions as 'keenly felt'.

Martha's first court appearance set the scene for what was to come. Despite the horrific nature of the allegations being outlined, it appeared to surprise some that Martha did not look like the embodiment of a she-devil at all. Even though she was suspected of crimes that would make the most hardened social misfit blush, those seeing her in the flesh could attest to the fact that she looked like many a young woman one would encounter in the street. She did not have little horns sprouting from her head, nor did she carry a pitchfork. Some reporters were pleased to note that she had an hourglass figure, with most of the 'sand' still resting up the top.

The *Herald* newspaper's main subheading informed its readership that this now notorious woman was actually 'A Pleasant-Looking Person', 'Smiling, But Silent'. The paper went on to explain that she was also 'well dressed in half mourning, and wore a jacket of material resembling sheepskin'.

The primary South Australian paper, the *Advertiser*, cut straight to the chase by saying, 'The accused has rather pleasant features … she walked steadily, and seemed to have nerved herself for the ordeal, as she showed no signs of emotion while in court, in spite of her grave position. She looks about 30 years of age, and is of medium height and slim build. The face is thin and white, while her hair is fair and was worn in short curls'.

The *Australasian* was the least subtle of all, quickly treating its readers to a pictorial display and informing them at the same time that the accused had a 'neat figure'.[67]

At this initial brief hearing, it fell to Whitney to explain why Martha had been arrested and why she should stay in custody. Among those in court to hear his evidence was Martha's conflicted fiancé, Otto, who would publicly hear for the first time the stories about the woman he had fallen in love with trying to murder one of his own brothers.

Once Whitney had entered the witness box, he spoke in rather exacting terms, as police officers have always been inclined to do when outlining their handiwork. According to him, Martha had made 'a desperate effort to get possession' of a chlorodyne bottle and was only prevented from doing so by Fryer.

At this very first stage of court proceedings, Whitney was implying that Martha wanted to use the contents of the bottle for the purpose of self-harm. This was a very convenient point for the police to make when trying to keep the accused in custody. Most relevant of all, the police were still waiting for Blackett's analytical reports. In the circumstances, Whitney asked that the matter be adjourned for seven days and that Martha be remanded in custody.

The magistrate granted Whitney's requests.

Although under the intense gaze of everyone in court, Martha was not asked to speak at all during this court appearance. She was whisked back to Melbourne Gaol the moment it was concluded.

A Fatal Draught

Late that very afternoon, news first broke that Blackett's preliminary testing had been completed and that his eagerly awaited interim report was now available. The *Argus* newspaper told its readership that the results were 'sensational'.

It was also very bad news for Martha. While Blackett had hypothesised that the consumption of two grains of arsenic would be sufficient to kill a normal adult, in the brew of tea poured by Martha into Herman's cup, Blackett had detected a whopping *ten* grains of arsenic.

Reporters quickly did some simple mathematical calculations and then rather loosely wrote that this had been enough arsenic to kill Herman Juncken 'five times over'. Blackett's language was a little more subdued but it conveyed the same message. He just blandly said, 'It would be a fatal draught for any human being'.

More damning still, Blackett found no arsenic whatsoever in the cup of tea from which Martha had been drinking. This clear result was hardly surprising, given that Martha had been sipping from it with no ill effects, but equally incriminating because she had agreed that it came from the same pot as Herman's cup.[68]

In typical prejudicial fashion, the abundant newspaper reports about the case had already jumped well ahead of the actual proceedings, with most articles now openly querying the untimely deaths of Louis Juncken and members of the Needle family. Many articles had even gone so far as to suggest that Louis' recently buried body be exhumed from its plot in South Australia for analytical testing. The airing of Blackett's results sent these calls into overdrive.

The extensively read *Argus* was leading the charge by explaining to its readers that 'there were many other items of information gleaned by the detectives in connection with Mrs Needle's history' and that 'these constitute such a remarkable story that it may be accepted as certain that the body of Louis will be exhumed, and not at all improbable that the bodies of Mrs Needle's husband and three children may also be disinterred'.[69]

While it was never made clear how the *Argus* reporters had gained enough inspired confidence to speculate that these potential actions 'may be accepted as certain', it could have been useful to glance in the direction of the police. Victoria's upholders of law enforcement were never averse to navigating a story in the direction they were seeking.

But by this stage, such subtleties didn't matter. The entire Martha Needle story was the type of saga that all newspaper editors and reporters dreamed about. There was nothing better to boost circulation in the fiercely competitive newspaper world than a lusty murder case and this one had everything – an attractive woman in the dock, dastardly betrayal, manipulating seduction, wretched treachery, unfettered greed, an intriguing police investigation, some misguided love and romance and even implied sexual scandal. Readers all around the world were collectively holding their breath waiting for the next instalment.

In such circumstances, there was now absolutely no going back.

The Brief

With her prospects rapidly sinking, the time had clearly arrived for Martha to delve into her previously guarded insurance money to engage the best defence lawyer she could afford. And, as it turned out, she was destined to hire a really well known, sharp, argumentative and opinionated one. While such personality traits might be disadvantageous in normal circumstances, Martha was no longer facing normal circumstances – in fact, the world was diabolically closing in on her.

Even though she had already squandered much of her insurance windfall, including through the construction of the expensive gravesite memorial for her children, Martha engaged 48-year-old David Gaunson from the Melbourne law firm Gaunson and Wallace to defend her. Despite all his foibles, she could hardly have chosen a better man to fight on her behalf.

A controversial politician as well as a lawyer, Gaunson had shot to prominence (or some would have said 'infamy') long before he answered Martha's call for help. Born in Sydney, Gaunson had been admitted as a lawyer for 25 years and was already accustomed to representing extremely famous and desperate clients.

As a bright young man, 14 years earlier, he had conducted the initial defence of legendary Australian bushranger Ned Kelly and was convinced that he had found a loophole in the prosecution case – namely that Kelly could not be found guilty of murdering members of the pursuing police posse because they were out to kill him. In Gaunson's optimistic eyes, this meant that Kelly could only be found to have fired his gun in self-defence.

Gaunson later handed over the reins as Kelly's defence lawyer to the inexperienced Henry Bindon and was dismayed that this argument was not continued. Of course, Kelly was ultimately found guilty of murder and hanged in 1880 – but in an effort to spare his life, Gaunson had even been prominent in arranging a mass meeting and petition in support of clemency.

Even though Gaunson was a fierce opponent of the death penalty and had forged a highly publicised career as a fearless defender of colourful clients, his reputation had also taken a battering and history does not remember him kindly. He has since been described as 'a criminal lawyer in both senses of the word'. Gaunson tended to see this differently, boasting in his later life that he had cheated the local prison of more deserving tenants than anyone else.

Among Gaunson's clients over the years was Madame Brussels, keeper of Melbourne's most notorious brothel. Some of Gaunson's detractors – and there were plenty – were quick to suggest that part of his arrangement as the Madame's 'legal adviser' involved freely sampling the wares offered at her establishment. Gaunson also became the spokesman for the Australian liquor industry, developing a maxim that a man should get drunk once a month for his health's sake. It was noted that he tended to overdo this maxim in his personal life.

Most controversial of all, around the dawn of the 20th century, Gaunson represented notorious illegal starting-price bookmaker John Wren. Operating out of the working-class suburb of Collingwood, Wren eventually came to the attention of police and turned to Gaunson for help. Exactly what happened next is not clear but Gaunson managed to get the police well and truly off Wren's back, allowing Wren to operate with relative immunity. He also advised Wren of the best ways to cover up his numerous illegal betting activities. Author Frank Hardy later controversially depicted Wren's life story in the epic Australian novel, *Power Without Glory*. The association between Wren and Gaunson in this novel can be quickly ascertained through the shifty character 'Garside', who was clearly based on Gaunson.

As a politician, Gaunson made a good criminal lawyer. After three vain attempts to enter the Legislative Assembly of Victoria, he was ultimately elected as the member for Ararat in a by-election held in May 1875. As a good-looking young man with considerable personality, Gaunson looked to have a bright political future. But his reputation soon plummeted.

He at once assumed a prominent position as a hard-hitter and wasn't just a thorn in the side of his adversaries – he upset members of his own party. Many secretly rejoiced when he sustained a bitter defeat and was ousted after a ministerial election in 1881.

Gaunson returned to parliament from 1883 to 1889 but only made an appalling reputation for himself as the unruliest member of the House, conspicuous for constant obstructionism. In 1887 alone, Gaunson rose to speak a colossal 308 times, delivering diatribes often lasting for several hours. Throughout his parliamentary tenure, he also made powerful enemies, not the least of whom was the prominent editor of the *Age* newspaper, David Syme – a bad move for any citizen wishing to be well treated in the press.

Despite his acute intelligence, it was clear that Gaunson had always struggled to cultivate the requisite diplomacy to thrive long-term in political ranks. The future Prime Minister of Australia, Alfred Deakin, probably summed up Gaunson's political career best by declaring, 'he was only disqualified from marked successes by his utter instability, egregious egotism, want of consistency and violence of temper'.

Several personality traits fashioned during his life experience were now obvious as Gaunson prepared to defend Martha. He had forged a deep hatred of the power of the press and bemoaned their propensity to speculate about unproven facts. For very good reason, he was also dubious of the police. From personal experience, he knew that they could not always be totally relied upon to tell the whole truth and nothing but the truth. In turn, neither the press nor the police were well disposed to Gaunson.[70]

Trying To Bail Out

During his first court appearance for Martha, Gaunson immediately lodged an application for her to be granted bail. The urgent bail hearing was held on Saturday, 16 June 1894, before Police Magistrate Keogh and a large number of Justices of the Peace, namely Messrs Cooke, Lancashire, Learmonth, Cherry and Bowley. Although the bail decision would rest with Keogh alone, the JPs could volunteer their services as observers. While this opportunity was rarely taken up, this time the bench was crowded with those wanting a front-row seat to the biggest show in town. As the official dealing with the city's louts and ruffians on a daily basis, Keogh was not known for being a particularly sentimental man.

While Gaunson was doing his best to get Martha out of prison – at least temporarily – the police opposed the application, primarily on the grounds that they feared she may commit suicide if liberated.

Gaunson conceded the seriousness of the attempted murder charge against the accused but held that it was aggravated by the sensational way in which the accounts of the alleged crime were given in the newspapers – heavily implying that such actions could prevent his client from getting a fair trial. He said it looked as if the newspapers had already engaged in a conspiracy to hang Martha and it would be unfair to deny her bail. With an unfortunate pun, he accused journalists of making statements that 'poisoned' the community against her.

To Gaunson, there was a dividing line between what was and was not acceptable – and this line had well and truly been crossed. Martha was being presented in many of the press reports as not only appearing before the court for attempted murder but also on charges not yet levelled at her, such as having murdered her husband, children and Louis Juncken.

Despite his customary abrasiveness, Gaunson's point was well made. Any potential juror in Melbourne who read the newspaper articles being written about Martha would have readily presumed that she had committed these crimes. And these articles weren't just being produced in Melbourne. They were appearing constantly in every corner of Australia and all throughout the world.

Gaunson then turned to the circumstances leading up to Martha's arrest. He vowed that 'when the time came' he would 'have something to say of the horrible plot – some persons might call it a ruse – laid for the accused at her house to arrest her'.

Gaunson also stated that the accused was in 'delicate health' and required care different from that allowed under prison regulations. Unless she had access to proper food, medical assistance and the common necessaries of life, she might break down completely and be unable to sustain her health sufficiently to meet the charge.

In these cost-conscious times, prisoners on remand were usually allowed to have food supplied by friends outside the prison. Martha had been denied this privilege, even though Otto had indicated his willingness to provide the necessary meals. The only reason that Gaunson could think of to justify this decision was the fear that poison would be smuggled to Martha from outside and 'she might just do away with herself'. Gaunson scoffed at the likelihood of this. He had never heard of such an argument being used against the granting of bail.

As pre-empted by Gaunson, the 'suicide' card was the exact one played by the police. Whitney explained the particulars of Martha's arrest, again telling the now well-known tales of how she had attempted to gain possession of a bottle of chlorodyne; how another poison, 'Rough on Rats', was found in her possession; and how she had made a number of veiled suicide threats in the past. This led him to reiterate that if Martha were released, 'she would probably poison herself'.

This comment riled Gaunson. He began to allude to the type of defences he may seek to raise later – but on this occasion, his efforts were unrewarded and bail was refused. Keogh was brief in summing up the case and gave very little away. He simply stated that he was of the opinion 'the accused should not be allowed out on bail under the circumstances mentioned'.[71]

For now, Martha would stay in the dirty lockup.

CHAPTER 14

Digging Up the Truth

K eenly urged on by the press, the detectives working on Martha's case had already commenced a rare application to exhume human remains. They were looking to unearth the body of Louis from its resting place at Lyndoch. 'Though the body has been more than a month buried there should be no difficulty in ascertaining whether arsenic had any connection with the death or not', the *Argus* newspaper proudly announced, before further informing its readership that 'arsenic is a mineral poison, and does not pass away as vegetable poisons do'.[72]

But with the investigation now extending to South Australia, there was a new set of local regulations and bureaucratic red tape to negotiate first. Whitney and Fryer prepared a report to justify why Louis' body should be dug up and this was relayed through official channels. An important feature they emphasised was the fact that Martha had evidently purchased a box of 'Rough on Rats' only *five* days before Louis' death.[73]

In full anticipation that the request to exhume Louis' body would be favourably met, the detectives began to put the preliminary arrangements in place. The man chosen to supervise the disinterment of the body and perform the post-mortem examination was well regarded and eccentric surgeon Dr James Neild. Although to this time the 70-year-old Neild had not been connected with this case, for some years previously he had been engaged by the Victorian government to perform 'special post-mortems' and to act as the official coroner, including for the Deeming case two years earlier.

A short and natty man, Neild was once described as 'keen-eyed and beetle browed'. Indeed, during his own court proceedings, Deeming had privately whispered words to the effect that Neild was the funniest man he had ever seen.[74]

As a Melbourne resident for nearly half a century, Neild was not only a lecturer in anatomy at the local university but also a renowned journalist. For many years, he had been the dramatic critic for the *Australian* newspaper and, in that capacity, his name was known throughout the English-speaking world. Although Neild was the type of person who seemed to delight in controversy, the public was assured that he was 'a man of very large ability, and the utmost confidence is placed in his skill'.[75]

It was planned that Neild would travel to Lyndoch with Whitney, Herman Juncken and undertaker Herbert King – the latter pair hopefully able to provide evidence of identification. After the body was disinterred and identified, the autopsy examination would take place in a tent erected near the cemetery.

Whitney and Fryer were fully aware that a later point of opposition likely to be raised by Gaunson was that any bodily samples collected had somehow been contaminated. Special care therefore needed to be taken to eliminate this suggestion being made. New jars were procured by Whitney and submitted to Blackett for chemical cleaning. The mouths of the jars were covered with impervious material and sealed. They were then placed in a specially constructed box that would not be opened until required at Lyndoch.[76]

Permission to exhume Louis' body was granted by the South Australian authorities on 20 June 1894, only a day after the Victorian request was received. The Victorian contingent, with their necessary equipment in tow, then left Melbourne by rail the very next day ultimately bound for Lyndoch.

Prior to leaving for South Australia, Whitney and Fryer attended Melbourne Gaol and served Martha with a copy of the South Australian order for the exhumation. Martha asked Whitney to read it to her, which he promptly did. She then made no remark of any kind. According to Whitney, he also told her that if she wished she could have a representative at the disinterment but she only took this news with apparent indifference. Whitney further ensured that a copy of the same order was served upon Martha's lawyer, Gaunson.[77]

The Victorian contingent's arrival in Adelaide was treated as a cause célèbre and their every move was reported. The press had joined in on the fervour of the moment and, even before a clod of earth had been disturbed or a single analysis of Louis' remains had been commenced, no regard at all was being paid to Martha's rights – particularly the accused's presumption of innocence.

The *Brisbane Courier* stated that the late Louis was 'supposed to have been poisoned by Mrs Needle', whereas South Australia's prime newspaper, the *Advertiser*, also simply referred to Louis as 'one of the supposed victims of Mrs Needle'. The latter publication even described Whitney as 'one of the best-known members of the Victoria police, who is in charge of the case' and quoted the beaming – and prejudicial – detective with the blurb, 'He described Mrs Needle as being of a cold, callous disposition, and says she accepts her position with equanimity'.[78]

The newspapers were also openly racing ahead and speculating that Martha's family members would also be disinterred. After all, the detectives had already received information that indicated Martha's husband and three children had all exhibited symptoms very similar to those noticed in the case of Louis and Herman Juncken. 'It is probable that the bodies of all four will now be exhumed, despite the length of time they have been in the ground' confidently announced the *Advertiser*.[79]

The 'Expedition' to Lyndoch

Exhuming a body and conducting a belated autopsy is a grisly business and the party undertaking the task wasted no time in getting the job done. They left Adelaide by train bound for Gawler early on Saturday, 23 June 1894. The size of the group had also increased. In addition to Neild, Whitney, Herman Juncken and Herbert King, there was Juncken's brother-in-law and local newspaper editor John Jones – who would assist with the identification of the body – and Neild's son, Joseph, a medical student who had simply been invited along by his father for the experience.

Upon arrival at Gawler, they were met by the local medical practitioner, Dr William Popham, who had been engaged to assist Neild in the post-mortem examination. Popham was not only extremely prominent in the Gawler region for his medical prowess but he had also once sued a local newspaper for libel and been awarded the grand total of 1 shilling, without costs.

A police horse-drawn trap was waiting at the Gawler railway station to convey the officials and witnesses to Lyndoch, while a second conveyance carried a tent and the paraphernalia necessary to carry out the exhumation.

The pretty little town of Lyndoch was reached shortly before 11 a.m. and the party proceeded immediately to the cemetery. Typical of many rural resting places interspersed throughout the Australian landscape, they found the peaceful cemetery to be picturesquely situated on the slope of a steep hill, with the entrance gates just on the crown of the rise. The inhabitants of the district showed much interest in the proceedings and a large crowd had gathered to watch the events unfold. This was turning out to be a very historic occasion for Lyndoch.

Whitney had previously decided to call upon Louis' elderly mother to identify his body but even at this late stage her family members were still trying to convince him otherwise. They feared the result of the shock that was sure to occur when she viewed her deceased son's face after the body had been so long in the ground.

Mrs Juncken's regular medical practitioner, Dr Richter, spoke to Whitney on the family's behalf and offered his professional opinion that the old lady was too upset by these recent troubles to have this further tax on her strength. The untimely sorrow of losing a son had done much to age her and had left her extremely feeble.

Based on this advice, Whitney decided to spare Mrs Juncken this unpleasant duty and, immediately after his decision was made known, she was taken home again. In many respects, this grief-stricken old lady had also been a victim of the Black Widow.

The exact position of the grave was pointed out to Whitney and he immediately directed the couple of labourers on hand to start the 'sickening task' of excavation. The digging was supervised by Herbert Engel, the labourer who had dug the original grave five weeks earlier. The grave was located a few metres from the front gate; next to it was buried Louis' father, who had passed away almost four years previously.

Louis had died on 15 May and been buried four days later. As the soil had only covered the coffin for about five weeks, the gravediggers were pleased to find it comparatively loose. Their work was certainly easier than that of the original diggers, who had to deal with a sinking that was, for the greater part of its depth, in limestone.

The coffin was reached in a surprisingly short time but the task of raising it to the surface was by no means an easy one. Apart from the weight of the body itself, it had been encased in a lead casket within a wooden shell. After considerable heaving with ropes and pulleys, it was brought to the surface and placed on trestles near the mouth of the grave. The outer lid of the coffin was removed by the undertaker, King, the man who had originally screwed it on.

The glass plate that had been fitted at the front of the coffin was now covered in mould. But once cleaned by King, it clearly showed the features of Louis' face, which was still recognisable but very disfigured and black from decomposition. Louis' moustache, too, had increased considerably in length since the time of interment.

The witnesses required to identify the body were called forward in quick succession. King, Jones and Herman Juncken all gazed for some time at the decomposing face on the other side of the glass plate and all agreed they were viewing the body of Louis. Likewise, Engel was able to confirm that the coffin was the same one he had buried five weeks earlier.

King was then given the nod to cut open the leaden covering and remove the lid of the outer shell. One parochial South Australian reporter observed, 'Everybody immediately moved to windward of the coffin, although the visitors, probably becoming inured by long residence in Melbourne, appeared to be the least affected by the horrible stench which arose immediately the cover was lifted'. This journalist must have been acutely aware that the unflattering nickname of the heavily polluted Melbourne was then 'Smellbourne'.

The body of Louis was then carefully taken out of its coffin and placed on a table inside the tent. By this time, the doctors were bearing up much better than the gravediggers. As one observer noted, 'The men who had to perform this nauseous work [removing the body] were completely prostrated, and for hours afterward looked white and ill. Dr Neild and Dr Popham with professional sangfroid then began the autopsy, which seemed dreadful to the lay mind'.

At this point both Neild and Popham were confronted with a difficulty that always presents itself in connection with bodies that have been buried for some time. The corpse had become badly decomposed – and decomposition can mask very materially any appearance of injury, disease or the presence of poison. The brain was now only semi-fluid but the heart appeared to be of natural size and quite healthy, showing no telltale signs of disease. The lungs were collapsed and pulpy from decomposition and could not afford any indication of their condition at the time of death.

Neild nonetheless set about his melancholy task with considerable enthusiasm. During the grim post-mortem examination, he had two main things to look for, both of a somewhat negative character. He firstly had to determine whether Louis had died from injury, accident or a self-inflicted wound. The body was carefully examined externally for unexpected damage. Neild found nothing – there were no recognisable marks of violence and no fractures of the skull.

Then Neild had to determine whether there was any appearance of disease, which would justify the opinion that Louis had died from natural causes. Neild and his assistant examined very carefully the internal organs for evidence of disease but as far as they could judge they found none that would cause death.

The doctors then proceeded to examine minutely the organs that would be affected by irritant poison. They found clear evidence of congestion of the stomach and bowels, plus also of inflammation of the stomach and the small intestine – all telltale signs of arsenic ingestion.

The mucous membrane of the stomach was reddened throughout and a large portion of the small intestine was also reddened in patches. Neild formed an opinion that the appearance of these organs was consistent with death caused by a mineral irritant poison. He was less conclusive about the other organs, given that the liver had changed a good deal due to decomposition, as had the spleen and kidneys.

One remarkable feature of the post-mortem examination was that, in Neild's opinion, it failed absolutely to disclose any symptoms of endocarditis, which had been certified by McColl as one of the causes of death. Nor were any indications of gum disease discovered, even though McColl had presumed that Riggs' disease had also adversely affected Louis before he died. Neild did not feel the need to dissect the jaw – from his examination, he was satisfied that there was no disease of it.[80]

All up, Neild spent about two hours examining the brain and other organs for traces of disease while placing the contents of the stomach, lungs, heart, liver, kidneys, spleen and intestines into jars for transmission to Melbourne.

Although conducting an autopsy could scarcely be considered a glamour-filled activity, Neild became a central figure of fascination and willingly participated in graveside press interviews when his work was done. After explaining the purpose behind Louis' post-mortem, he finally uttered the words that the clamouring reporters were hoping to hear. 'We found nothing to lead us absolutely to determine the cause of death and we found only appearances consistent with poisoning by arsenic,' he said, before adding a cautionary note. 'The presence of arsenic or otherwise will have to be determined by Mr Blackett.'

The members of the press gallery barely heard the last sentence. They already had their story: The post-mortem *had* revealed 'appearances consistent with poisoning by arsenic'.

By 2 p.m., the now mutilated body of Louis was returned to its coffin and buried again, this time presumably in its *final* resting place. The officials present were in a self-congratulatory mood – the preliminary findings of Neild's autopsy had franked their theories and made their work all the more worthwhile.

The official party, with their jars containing various pieces of human anatomy, left Lyndoch before 4 p.m. and caught the 5 p.m. train to Gawler. They arrived in Adelaide 'about dinner time'. In light of the day's activities, it must have been a subdued meal.[81]

Presumably in between bouts of indigestion, Whitney was quick to fire off a confirmatory telegram back to Melbourne, which was received by Superintendent Brown that evening. It stated that everything connected with the exhumation of the body of Louis had been completed and, even more importantly, 'that poisoning symptoms were visible'.

The Victorian officials returned to Melbourne the very next day and were met at the station platform by Blackett, who immediately took possession of the anatomy jars. Blackett was fully aware of the seriousness of the task before him. He was now literally dealing with a case involving questions of life or death; there could be no shadow of mistake or inaccuracy. He warned that his analysis would take several days to complete – an agonising amount of time to wait for a hyperactive throng of pressmen faced with a hot story and a case 'marked by sensationalism' at every step.

By 29 June, Blackett had informally told the excited detectives that arsenic was present in the remains he had analysed in sufficient quantities to have caused Louis' death, although he needed more time to state the exact amounts. He followed up these discussions with an official telegram.

Whitney immediately handed over this information to reporters. The *Herald* was the first newspaper to break the story – on the very same day as the news arrived – quickly followed by the *Age* and the *Argus*.

The gee-whiz journalistic piece written in the *Age* provided even more shameless promotion for the self-glorifying detectives, informing the readership that 'Detective Sergeant Whitney and Detective Fryer, who have had direction of the case, and have managed it with great ability, do not apprehend that the trial will be a very protracted one, for they will not have more than 16 witnesses to call, and none of the witness's evidence will be long'. This contradicted a report that had surfaced four days prior – at a time when more challenges were anticipated – that had stated, 'There will be altogether about 30 witnesses engaged in the case, which is exciting more interest in Australia than any previous trial since that of the notorious Deeming'.

In any event, David Gaunson had different ideas.

A Change in Direction

The developments stemming from the autopsy altered the course of the investigation. Police would ultimately decide to put aside Martha's charge of attempting to poison Herman and replace it with the more devastating charge of wilfully murdering Louis. Sticking to one crime at a time remains a common prosecution technique. If the first charge fails, it is always possible to revisit the remaining cases and bring fresh charges if necessary.

All the while, Blackett's analytical testing of Louis' remains continued. In more devastating news for Martha, by 2 July Blackett was confident enough to announce that he had found arsenic in four of the five jars of human remains presented, the only exception being the jar containing Louis' heart and part of one of his lungs.

For the first time since her incarceration, Martha's health began to show signs of deterioration under the strain of imprisonment. Around the same time that Blackett's results were making headlines, she was momentarily seized with her customary fainting fits and was briefly removed to the prison hospital under the care of the prison's medical officer, Dr Andrew Shields. She recovered quickly. Although Martha was still confined to the infirmary the next day, Shields reported that her health had improved and he did not anticipate any serious results.

Martha wasn't the only person beginning to feel the strain. The autopsy results proudly announced by the publicity-friendly Neild had coincidentally made his fellow medical man, proud lodge doctor Donald McColl, look like an incompetent idiot. In an attempt to protect his professional reputation, McColl fired off a letter to the editor of the *Age* newspaper, to not only justify his actions but also to criticise Neild. Martha's case was now so big that this letter made headlines and was prominently published in full:

> SIR, - It has repeatedly appeared in the press that endocarditis was the cause certified by me of Louis Juncken's death. I now write to say this wasn't the case. My certificate was 'gastritis and endocarditis', which is a very different thing. Dr Neild has not been slow to state what he did not find in accordance with my certificate. Ordinary courtesy should have restrained

him to state what he did find in accordance with it. The reason for which post mortem evidence of endocarditis was not found by him will be clear when my evidence is given. Forbearing further comment on this case while sub judice.

– Yours

D.S.McCOLL, M.B., Ch.M

Richmond, 1st July[82]

Back in the Limelight

Shortly after this furore, the now infamous Martha was due back in court. Her next appearance occurred on the morning of 5 July and it caused a near riot. Although Martha would only be required for a very brief time, a large audience had congregated at the courthouse. All eyes were riveted on the door leading to the court from an anteroom in which Martha was kept prior to the calling of her name.

When she was brought forward, Martha calmly walked in front of the dock and leaned against it. She then locked her gloved hands together and let them fall in front of her as she passively watched proceedings. Again, the gaggle of reporters who were present provided varying accounts to their vast readerships about Martha's demeanour.

The Melbourne *Herald* recorded that she appeared 'with a blanched face calmly and quietly, though evidently nervous', while the journalist representing the *Sydney Morning Herald* took more poetic licence, indicating that 'The accused appeared more haggard and worn than previously, but preserved a calm demeanour throughout the proceedings'. In an effort to bolster the folklore further, South Australia's *Advertiser* went right over the top by publishing 'The accused appeared very nervous … and her eyes were tearful'.

Such was the brevity of these particular proceedings that Gaunson did not need to attend. Instead, Whitney provided a brief summary of the matter to update Magistrate Keogh and asked for a further remand of seven days to allow detectives to fully prepare the case.

When Keogh asked Martha if she had anything to say, she simply answered in a low but firm voice, 'No, sir'.

Once Keogh had granted Whitney's request, Martha turned around quickly towards the door leading to the cells and walked rapidly back to the lockup, as if anxious to shut out the stares from the crowd. The whole court appearance had taken about ten minutes, which for Martha at this stage was about eleven minutes too long.

Her next court date would be much more significant – the commencement of her preliminary hearing in the Police Court. And already the prosecution was assembling an impressive number of witnesses to give evidence.

CHAPTER 15

More Gruesome Business

Amid a maelstrom of public interest, Whitney and Fryer commenced the necessary arrangements to have Martha's deceased husband and children exhumed. They also continued to extend their investigations more exhaustively. Some of the facts they were uncovering not only added weight to the calls for further exhumations but also cast suspicions on Martha in general.

They found sufficient information to conclude that there had been 'domestic dissentions of a pronounced character' between Martha and her husband long before his untimely death. Although this proved nothing in itself, when considered with other information – such as Henry's life insurance, which was worth a colossal £200 – it was sufficient to justify considerable scepticism about his cause of death.

The detectives further found that the death had been 'attended by some remarkable circumstances'. Not the least of these had been Henry's obstinate refusal to take food offered by his wife, even though Hodgson's death certificate had indicated that 'exhaustion' due to malnutrition was present. The other maladies listed on Hodgson's certificate also made for interesting reading – 'persistent vomiting', 'sub-acute hepatitis' and 'enteric fever' – all of which were similar to symptoms of arsenical poisoning.

There were fewer suspicious signs about the passing of Martha's children. After all, she had *appeared* to be a particularly dutiful mother. Everyone who had seen her with her children was readily attesting to her love and devotion to them. Nothing stronger could be drawn by the detectives to support their request for disinterment than the monetary advantage that Martha had derived on the death of the two youngest, Elsie and May.

Under the circumstances, the detectives decided not to request permission to disturb the remains of Mabel, the three-year-old who had died at the end of 1885 and pre-deceased her father. Not only had she perished before the other members of her family but her remains rested in a different grave.

But the detectives concluded that the bodies of Henry, Elsie and May needed to be exhumed and tested for poison. This was the only way to put the story right. If their suspicions proved unfounded, all allegations could be refuted. But if their suspicions were confirmed, such evidence might be used circumstantially as part of the Crown case in the Louis Juncken murder trial that was still pending.

The relevant exhumation order was granted on 4 July 1894. As Henry, Elsie and May Needle were all buried in the same grave at Boroondara, they could all be exhumed on the same day.

Whitney and Fryer visited Melbourne Gaol the following afternoon to personally serve Martha with the notice of the intended exhumation. After hearing the contents of the notice, Martha turned to the female attendant in charge of her and said, 'There is nothing about my oldest child in that'. Martha then calmly walked away and later consumed her dinner with an unimpaired appetite.

Always under constant watch, Martha found herself the subject of even more personal scrutiny at this time – but she showed little emotion. She acted like a defeated woman. The Melbourne *Herald* interpreted this in a different way, updating its readers with the report: 'Mrs Needle still remains in the same condition in the Melbourne

Gaol. She appears well, and does not realise her serious position, judging from her outward demeanour'.

It was determined that the grisly task of exhuming the three bodies of the ill-fated Needle family would occur on the morning of Tuesday, 10 July 1894, and the necessary arrangements began to fall into place.[83]

A similar team to that which had handled the exhumation of Louis was assembled. This time, it was decided that Neild and analyst Blackett would be present. If the bodily conditions rendered post-mortem examinations impossible, the entire coffins and their contents would be taken intact to Blackett's laboratory and the anatomical matter would be subjected to analysis there. Again, handling the undertaking duties was the trusty and now overworked Herbert King. He had originally carried out the burials of Henry and the two children, so he would presumably be able to also identify the graves and coffins.

Although the unearthing of Louis' body had been gruesome enough, this time the challenges were even greater. Henry's body had been buried for four years and nine months. Elsie had passed away three years and seven months ago; the youngest child, May, had met her death about two years and eleven months prior. Considering the long period that had elapsed since the burial of the three bodies, it could not be dismissed that the 'destroying influences of the grave' may have disintegrated them beyond the limits of post-mortem medical science; in that case, the services of Blackett alone would be required.

When interviewed by the press about the matter, Blackett expressed supreme confidence in the task before him. He declared that if arsenic had been present in the systems of any of the three bodies at the time of death, his analysis would find it. He believed that arsenic was 'indestructible' and could quote a case where arsenic had been found in the remains of a person who had been buried 20 years before. Nor did Blackett believe that 20 years was the limit – in his view, the evidence of arsenic would remain for 500 years.

There was one main factor that could literally dampen Blackett's enthusiasm. Arsenic is soluble and therefore could be carried away by water. If the site of the grave had been the subject of poor drainage and rainwater, the arsenic (if it was originally present) could have disappeared. It was not anticipated that this had occurred in this case. By good fortune, Boroondara General Cemetery occupied a site on the crown of some rising ground and even the allocated gravesite – the soon to be world-famous plot B2477 – was halfway up a slight incline.[84]

A Historic and Gloomy Day

It had always been said that, under favourable atmospheric conditions, Boroondara General Cemetery was apt to fulfil one's ideal of a peaceful resting place for departed friends. But on the infamous day of the exhumations, a more dismal and foreboding morning could not have been imagined. A dense fog enveloped the earth around the entire cemetery and objects were not distinguishable from more than a few metres away.

As the sun rose in the east, it remained obscured and its rays only served to spread a dim grey light through the mist. The fog was not only thick – it was also penetrating. Members of the large crowd of spectators assembling to watch the proceedings felt their bones chill and their clothing was soon covered with a misty film.

Despite the testing weather, there remained a buzzing expectation among the very sizeable and ghoulish horde of onlookers. As the *Age* newspaper summed up, 'the resurrection of corpses that have been in the earth for many years induces a sensation at once creepy and uncanny'. In the same article, the *Age* also jumped the gun somewhat by telling its readers that the two children, Elsie and May, were 'supposed to have been poisoned', before such a statement could be verified analytically.[85]

As it turned out, the clinical nature of the exhumation may have left some of the spectators feeling short-changed. Unlike the unearthing of Louis, this time it had been decided to take up the coffins and then remove them to the morgue for opening. Any post-mortem examinations would take place there, not under the public gaze at the gravesite.

To the relief of the shivering onlookers, by 8.15 a.m. all those in the exhumation party had arrived. Prominent among them were Neild and Blackett but also representing the scientific community was none other than Dr William Boyd, whose interest in the proceedings could be well understood. In discussing Boyd, one newspaper went as far as describing him by saying 'to whose professional acumen is to be attributed the discoveries that have been made in this sensational case'.

As expected, the police were represented by Whitney and Fryer; arriving with them was Richmond's now-famous undertaker, Herbert King. Also on the guest list was Mr W. Mason – one of the studio photographers from Bridge Road who had captured the images of Martha and the Needle family in happier times. He was kept company by another gentleman who was said to 'use his camera as an amateur'.

Also scoring an invite to be graveside was the caretaker of the cemetery, Thomas Whitelaw, a couple of gravediggers, a well-known vocalist and representatives of all the daily newspapers. Whitelaw was considered to be a significant witness because he had also been present when each member of the Needle family had been originally buried. He would later be able to testify that no-one had been buried in this particular gravesite prior to Henry and that only the bodies of Henry and his two children were buried there.[86]

Those present immediately noted that the grave of the Needle family occupied a serene position in the Church of England section of the cemetery, near the eastern end, and that all the surrounding ground in the immediate vicinity had now been taken up and was lined with other graves. The elaborate metal shield usually adorning the Needle gravesite had been removed by the gravediggers and was left lying nearby. In light of what was now being alleged, the contents of the memorial now presented a surreal image.

Reporters raced over to record its inscription, which was then duly distributed on a widespread scale through their various publications. It was immediately presumed that Martha had written the poetic composition on the shield, given that the treasure trove of correspondence she had forwarded to Otto had also contained several attempts at original prose 'of the love-sick order'. Reporters also quickly observed that there was no mention of Henry anywhere on the memorial or at the well-kept gravesite.

By the time the official exhumation party had reached the cemetery that frosty morning, the gravediggers had already been at work removing the earth covering the Needle grave to more than half its depth. The grave was covered by a gravedigger's fly awning. Once a fresh start was made to the digging, it took very little time to expose the first coffin. It was that of the youngest child, May. It took only a few minutes more to remove the painted black coffin from its resting place and hand it up to the surface.

All eyes anxiously looked at the coffin and the soil surrounding it, checking for any telltale signs of moisture and decay. But even though the coffin had been in the ground almost three years, its wooden exterior looked as sound as the day it had first been put down. The soil thrown up from the grave was of a clay composition and so dry that it appeared no dampness could have touched the coffin.

Once the coffin had been handed up, undertaker King moved in to identify it. On the foot of each coffin buried by King was a leaden plate with the name of the occupant engraved upon it. It was so well preserved that, after the dirt had been scraped away, the inscription could be easily deciphered. King was able to confirm by the likeness of the photograph appearing on the grave's shield that May was the child he had buried in this coffin.

King had also provided three plain, black, wooden shells. Once he had identified this first coffin and it had been marked by Neild and Blackett, it was placed into one of these shells and the lid was screwed down, ready for removal. Then, as a precautionary measure, Blackett and Neild asked for a small sample of the soil that had rested under the coffin to also be collected and stored, for the purpose of analysis if found necessary. This process was also followed for the other two coffins.

Very little extra excavation was required to uncover the coffin containing the remains of the other child, Elsie. This coffin was also in excellent condition and the nameplate was intact and legible. The last coffin to come up was that containing the remains of Henry. Given that it had been longer in the ground, it had begun to show definite indications of wear and tear. It had parted a little at the side seams and bottom, even though the wood was still sound. The coffins of Elsie and Henry were both marked and placed in the provided shells. All three shells were then loaded onto the undertaker's horse-drawn conveyance, before being taken to the morgue.

With the exhumation now at an end, members of the official party posed proudly for photographs at the gravesite. There was an overwhelming and self-congratulatory feeling that the entire operation had been a logistical success. As one newspaper extolled: 'Most people would have expected very repugnant scenes to have met the gaze of the bystanders when remains which had been buried so long were handed up, but there was nothing of the sort. There was absolutely no unusual odour, and nothing was seen save the coffins, which were simply discoloured'.[87]

Autopsies

Once the three coffins arrived at the morgue, Neild set to work performing the belated autopsies. One by one, the coffins were opened and each nameplate adorning them was removed and kept as evidence.

As predicted, performing an accurate post-mortem examination on bodies that had been buried so long was not an easy task. In the case of Henry, Neild found that decomposition was so advanced that he could not speak at all about the cause of death. Some of the bones were loose in the coffin and the head had also become detached from the body.

The internal organs were so collapsed that Neild was unable to successfully separate them. Nonetheless, he found the chest and abdomen to be perfectly dry. He removed both as carefully as he could and wrapped them in paper. He then sealed and labelled the package before handing it to Blackett for further analysis. He also gave to Blackett the brain of Henry, which was so fluid in composition that he actually had to pour it out of the skull.

With reference to Elsie, decomposition had advanced much further and differently to the body of her father – it represented three stages of decomposition, namely the ordinary putrefactive condition, mummification and saponification. Once again, Neild could not find any indications of the cause of death. He removed the whole of the trunk, wrapped it up and sealed it, and handed it to Blackett.

In the case of May, Neild found that the body had formed adipocere (known commonly as grave wax) and undergone saponification. Several of the internal organs could not be separated. Only in one organ, namely the last portion of the large intestine, could Neild find any indication that suggested arsenical poisoning. He noted that this organ looked very red. Once again, Neild removed the trunk; he wrapped, sealed and labelled it before passing it over to Blackett.[88]

During the post-mortem process, Neild noted that at the bottom of each coffin the undertaker King had originally placed a layer of sawdust. Each body had also been wrapped in linen as part of the burial process. Neild took samples of the sawdust and cloth from each coffin, bundled them up in the same way he had done with the anatomical samples and then given them to Blackett. He also bundled up and labelled the soil samples that had been collected at the cemetery.

Determining the cause of death of these three people – if it was possible – was now a job for the analyst. Blackett made it quite clear to impatient members of the press that his results would not be publicly available for at least eight days.

In the meantime, Martha had another court date to attend.

CHAPTER 16

The Police Court

The justice system at the time of Martha Needle bore a close similarity to that which currently operates, even though the terminology differed. In serious matters, a 'prima facie' case first had to be established in front of a magistrate at the Police Court before a matter would be sent to trial.

Therefore, if it were found at this hearing that sufficient evidence existed against Martha for the ruthless murder of Louis, she would face a full murder trial in the Supreme Court. The result of that trial could see her leave the prison in a pine box.

Martha's legal counsel, Gaunson, would attempt to have the charges against her thrown out at this preliminary stage. Likewise, the prosecution would not be leaving anything to chance. Experienced barrister Charles Finlayson was appointed as the chief prosecutor for the Crown. A prominent citizen originally hailing from the town of Ballarat, Finlayson had previously acted for the prosecution as Junior Counsel in the Deeming case a few years earlier.

Like Gaunson, Finlayson had also once harboured political ambitions, unsuccessfully standing for the state seat of Ballarat West in 1880, the same year Gaunson had won the vote for the seat at Ararat. Known for his measured preparation and smooth presentation,

Finlayson would be the ideal match for his more belligerent opponent.

Police Court hearings tended to be very extensive and would often go for longer than the Supreme Court trial itself, if it eventuated. The preliminary hearing of Martha would be no exception, with a sensational five days of evidence being heard, punctuated by a number of strategically driven adjournments. And lurking in the background of this hearing was the anticipation that Blackett's results about the deaths of Martha's three family members would soon be delivered.

There was an exceptionally large attendance at the Police Court on the morning of Thursday, 12 July 1894, the opening day of Martha's proceedings. Not only were the galleries of the largest courtroom, Number Three, fully occupied but all the seats in the body of the court were also taken. A crowd of disappointed people who were unable to gain admission assembled outside. A noticeable feature was the very large number of female spectators in attendance, with the *Herald*'s reporters noting that there had not been so many members of 'the weaker sex' present in a courtroom for years.

Seated at the overcrowded bench was Magistrate Keogh (the same judicial officer who had presided over Martha's previous appearances) and five Justices of the Peace, namely Cherry, Lancashire, Andrews, Learmonth and Bird.

When the star of the show, Martha, entered the court, she was said to look 'quite composed', although showing 'traces of anxiety'. She certainly looked the part as a Black Widow, as she was again wearing mourning clothes – a neat black dress and an open veil. As she looked around the court, she slightly bowed to a female friend she recognised in one of the front rows. Many of those in the courtroom spent their entire time staring intently at Martha, which only exacerbated the already unsettling nature of her ordeal. Before long, such pressure would become almost unbearable.

Just before matters got underway, Martha was accommodated with a chair in front of the dock. She sat passively as the charge was solemnly read out: 'Feloniously and wilfully murdering Louis Juncken'.

A reporter from the *Australasian* pictorial magazine did Martha no justice by offering the following unflattering description: 'She is neatly dressed in black with a veil covering her face, which she only lifts to wipe her tears. The trouble of the trial has told on her very much, and she has lost a stone and a half in weight. Her face is drawn and thin. She must at one time have been a neat-figured, good-looking little woman.'[89]

In his opening address, Finlayson briefly summarised the case he proposed to put before the bench. He related how the accused had taken control of the residential section of the premises in Bridge Road, where Louis Juncken had carried on a business as a saddler. Louis and his brother, Otto, had boarded with her and Otto had become engaged to her. When Louis had objected to the marriage, a 'coolness' had arisen between him and Martha. On 25 April 1893, Louis fell ill and began vomiting. He also complained of pain in his gums. He consulted Dr McColl, but his condition worsened so badly that he died on 10 May.

Although McColl provided a death certificate that nominated the causes of death as 'gastritis and endocarditis', it would be shown that arsenic was found in Louis' remains. This was the same poison found in the vomit of Herman Juncken after he drank a cup of tea prepared by Martha. The poison 'Rough on Rats' was found on the premises and it would be shown that the accused had bought it on the day before Louis was taken seriously ill. It would also be demonstrated that she had threatened other members of the Juncken family.

The first witness called was Otto Juncken, a man in a particularly compromising position. After all, he was now attending a hearing about the alleged cold-blooded murder of one of his brothers and the attempted murder of another – and the accused was none other than his romantic interest, Martha. Was he completely besotted by the Black Widow, simply naïve or even part of her apparently evil plots?

Although considered a prime witness, it was still unclear as to whether Otto's testimony would benefit the prosecution or the defence. Ultimately, he would occupy the witness box for the entire first day and some of the second day.

Through questioning, Otto was able to outline details about his family's history, Martha's rental of the residential section at Bridge Road, his engagement to her and her complaints about the way his brother, Louis, had treated her. He also spoke about Louis' final illness and how well Martha had tended to him at this time.

When Finlayson produced the letters that Martha had written to Otto, her fiancé was forced to admit that they were scribed in her handwriting. Most notable of all was the rage-filled letter Martha had sent him as his 'cast off landlady'. At this point, the media-hating Gaunson objected loudly, 'This is the abominable letter these newspapers have published, crying the woman down'.

Gaunson then started his cross-examination. Before the courtroom of captivated spectators, he asked Otto to explain his first meeting with Martha at the Nicholson's boarding house and how he had become reacquainted with her during a chance encounter in Swanston Street after the death of her husband.

He also had Otto speak about his casual visits to Cubitt Street. According to Otto, he had 'no lovemaking' with Martha but he had observed how well she cared for her children, Elsie and May. 'I don't think anyone could have been a more affectionate and sympathetic person towards a sick person than she,' Otto explained. 'I don't think anyone could have been more tender. That was why I visited her, because I pitied her.'

When Otto began to speak specifically about Elsie's illness, all eyes in the court were suddenly drawn to Martha as she wept copiously into her black-bordered handkerchief.

Just as the audience members were becoming enraptured by the juicy details unfolding before them, an 1890s version of a technical glitch intervened. The clerk of courts taking down the evidence in shorthand, Mr J. Pennefather, took issue with Gaunson for proceeding so fast with the cross-examination that he was struggling to keep up. When the meticulous Pennefather asked Gaunson whether it was totally necessary to take down every piece of evidence, Gaunson gave the stinging reply, 'Yes, every line of it. I must not trust it to those sensational newspapers.'

His cynicism, while abrasive, was also well founded. A number of the major daily newspapers had begun printing word-for-word dialogues from the hearing but none of them completely matched. On some occasions, journalists would be tempted to add an extra phrase of imaginary 'dialogue' just to spice up the story a bit.

Having firmly established Martha's splendid credentials as a caring mother of dying children, Gaunson moved on to other areas of inquiry. He learned from Otto that Martha had only been in 'fairly good health' after the death of her children. When unexpectedly asked by Gaunson whether he personally stood to gain at all from the death of his brother, Louis, a stupefied Otto could only reply, 'No, I did not'. In fact, his late brother had owed him a debt and Otto held no security.

In the witness box, Otto needed to fend off further questions about a number of topics – Martha's occasional trips back to South Australia, her appearance before an Adelaide court when sued by her mother, her belief that Mrs Foran was not her real mother, the apparent 'suicide letter' he received from Martha, his discovery soon after of 'Rough on Rats' in the house, Martha's habit of taking chlorodyne for internal pains and her consultations with a horde of doctors. He believed that she had been personally consulting Drs McColl, Elsner, Burton, Lalor and Singleton.

The answers to all of these questions may have painted a somewhat bizarre picture of Martha's personality – but most interest still centred on Louis' relationship with Martha, his unexpected illnesses and ultimate demise. After all, Martha had not been charged with being an erratic and volatile person who couldn't spell very well – she had been charged with callously murdering Louis.

Otto explained how Louis had formed an opinion that Martha was a woman 'too violent-tempered' to be an acceptable wife. From the answers that he provided, Otto appeared to suspect the same thing. He told Gaunson, 'We couldn't understand the cause of these violent outbreaks. The occasions did not seem to warrant them. She manifested temper towards anyone.'

With respect to Louis' illnesses, Otto confirmed that the symptoms had been 'exactly the same' in both August 1893 and during the final onset in April 1894. His brother was also complaining that all the foods being given to him had a horrible taste.

And what of Martha's care and attention to Louis during these illnesses? 'She was very kind and attentive,' Otto answered unhesitatingly, 'and it seemed to soften him'. He went on to explain further that while Martha's conduct towards Louis had been 'at first rather impatient on account I thought of my brother and of his irritability, giving her unnecessary work', when his condition worsened 'she became very kindly towards him, so much so that I was affected by it – Louis was also very affected by it. I cannot recall any mark of unkindness on the part of the accused to my brother.'[90]

The other main topic on the first day of the hearing was Martha's health and propensity to have 'fits'. Under cross-examination, Otto began to expand on his observations, all of which enthralled the spectators in the packed courtroom. He explained how she would sometimes appear unconscious for hours and needed to be lifted from the floor and carried to her bed, all the time with her limbs rigid. Then there were the times she addressed him as if he were Henry and re-enacted a quarrel, holding up her hands to ward off an imaginary blow. Otto further described to the court how – when Martha was in this state – she would look through all the rooms of the house for her dead children and affectionately pick up an object and imagine it was one of them.

In another telling blow to Martha's self-esteem, Otto conceded to the court that he believed it was 'a mere imagination' of Martha that Mary Foran was not her mother, likewise the fantasy that she was entitled to a £700 property inheritance. But his most significant statement of all was his opinion that, if the evidence showed that Martha poisoned one of his brothers and tried to poison another, she didn't know what she was doing at the time.[91]

At several points during Otto's testimony, Martha became much affected, sobbing and crying into her handkerchief to hide her emotion. But when he suggested that if the evidence ultimately proved her guilty of murder then he would believe she was not responsible because of an unsound mind, she was impacted the most.

In the short amount of court time left on the first day, Otto was re-examined by Finlayson. He conceded that he had paid many of Martha's personal bills, even though he had since learned that she had secretly stashed away her own insurance monies. Otto largely tried to talk this away by saying, 'It all depended upon the state of her mind and whether she was in trouble. She troubled over her children.' Finlayson could not resist a retort: 'She had the memory of the deaths of her husband and children, and I think that would trouble her'. Upon hearing Finlayson's comment, Gaunson bounced to his feet, imploring to the bench, 'That is a very improper remark and should not have been made'. Keogh remained unmoved.

Shortly after, the court was adjourned for the afternoon. It had been an enlightening first day of evidence for Martha. She had now heard the love of her life publicly declare that he had really only played along with her notions about her parentage and inheritance. While he had tried to be favourable to her during his evidence, he had also articulated for the first time his opinion that she may have committed the frightful deeds of which she was accused. The only qualification he had placed on this was that she might not have been aware of what she was doing at the time.[92]

Day Two

As the hearing was ready to recommence the following morning, the court chambers were again filled to capacity, with much of the crowd consisting of 'ladies'. When Martha came into court at 10.30 a.m., it was immediately noted that she was dressed in black as on the previous day. She was allowed to sit on a chair on the floor of the court and, whereas during the previous afternoon she had tended to sit with her head bowed and her handkerchief to her face, this time she appeared 'less moved' and she looked calmly around the courtroom.

Otto found himself back in the witness box. This time, he was facing the re-examination by Finlayson – a legal eagle with much less sympathy for him and his version of events than was displayed by Gaunson. Finlayson focused heavily on one of the weakest points of Martha's case, namely the contents of the mournful 'suicide' letter she had sent to Otto and the circumstances in which it was sent.

Finlayson then moved on to address issues about Martha's mental wellbeing, asking Otto, 'I suppose you know the difference between a faint and a fit?' Otto conceded that he didn't know the difference but he described the 'fits' in a very similar way to his evidence of the previous day. In response to Finlayson's question 'Were there any signs when these fits were coming?', Otto could only utter 'None whatever. They were quite unexpected.' Finlayson then asked a few questions about Martha's hate-filled letter as the 'cast off landlady' and Otto's memory of Louis' death, before excusing him from the witness box.

Upon Otto's evidence being completed, Pennefather spent more than half an hour reading out the depositions that had been taken. At several points during the reading of this testimony, Martha again became emotional and sobbed into her handkerchief.

Martha had sat shivering all the morning up near the bench but, upon a request by Gaunson, she was now given permission to be accommodated with a seat near the fireplace in a corner of the Court. This not only allowed her to feel more physically comfortable but also kept her comparatively out of the observational range of the curious crowds in the galleries.

It was now time to move on to other witnesses. The remainder of Day Two of the hearing was to provide an entertaining mix for the assembled audience. Even though there was only enough time remaining to call on three people to give evidence, one would ultimately collapse in the witness box, one would be a bitter doctor defiantly trying to save his tattered reputation and the final witness would inadvertently leave those in attendance howling with laughter.

Clara Stevens, the trained nurse who had briefly tended to the dying Louis, was the first to be called. Even though she had never seen a case of direct poisoning of any kind, she had seen people suffering blood poisoning. As Gaunson began to cross-examine her on this point, Finlayson objected. He believed that such evidence should be sought from 'an expert medical man' and not 'a simple nurse'. Gaunson retaliated by saying that he had a great wariness of so-called 'experts' and, in his opinion, this witness was just as capable of describing symptoms as any medical man.

As the tension in the air rose, Keogh finally ruled that Gaunson could continue his questioning. But by then Stevens had inadvertently solved the problem by fainting in the witness box. Even as Gaunson and Finlayson had been arguing, she had been gradually sinking – but she was now fully stricken and needed to be carried out of court. Both Gaunson and Finlayson agreed that there was no need to immediately recall her.

The Good Doctor

Fireworks were expected when the next person, Donald McColl, was called. As the Richmond medical practitioner who had unsuccessfully attended the deceased Louis, he was now clearly facing some heat of his own. But the pompous McColl had already been demonstrating a feisty resolve to stand up for his own professional reputation, invariably putting him at odds with some of the propositions that the prosecution would present.

As an educated doctor practising in a lowly working-class suburb such as Richmond, McColl had also developed an unhealthy dose of personal ego. He was unaccustomed to having his opinions questioned and would be unlikely to concede any miscalculations. He was also still bristling at some of the comments that the effusive Dr Neild had made publicly after performing the autopsy on Louis' body.

With respect to Louis' first bout of illness in August 1893, McColl remained convinced that he had been suffering from Riggs' disease of the jaw and that the pus discharging from his gums had somehow poisoned his stomach. Despite all the information that had unfolded since, McColl still appeared to be quite satisfied – in public at least – that it had been the quality of his careful treatment that had led to Louis' first successful recovery. He remained arrogantly in denial that Martha's probable actions in withdrawing the arsenic had been secretly dictating the whole process.

Louis' second bout of illness throughout April and May 1894 had been the one that had ultimately claimed his life and therefore would be much harder to explain away. Yet, to a large extent, McColl still stood firm. He explained how Louis had come to see him on 26 April and was displaying matching symptoms to those from the previous August. McColl embarked on a similar course of 'treatment' and was pleased to see Louis recover sufficiently to be up and about again by 10 May.

Then there was the sudden and final relapse. By the morning of 11 May, Louis was vomiting again and his mouth was in a worse condition than ever. From there it was all downhill. On 15 May, McColl had first detected the problem with Louis' heart, which he described as a 'blowing murmur over the Mitral valve'. He called on Dr Grant for assistance but by later that evening Louis was dead.

The wily Gaunson realised from the outset that McColl could

prove to be a scientifically trained witness friendly to his cause, even though the doctor's primary motivation was to preserve his own reputation. Gaunson's optimism was immediately reflected in parts of his questioning:

Gaunson: The certificate of death which you gave states that in your opinion he had died from organic poisoning?

McColl: Yes.

Gaunson: There was undoubtedly gastritis?

McColl: Yes.

Gaunson: Are the symptoms of gastritis similar to those of poisoning?

McColl: To arsenical poisoning.

Gaunson: Did you discuss the subject of inorganic as well as organic poisoning with Dr Grant?

McColl: Yes. We discussed it for about 20 minutes or so very carefully, owing to the uniqueness of the symptoms.

Gaunson: The conviction impressed upon your mind was that all the symptoms which you had closely observed were consistent with organic poisoning?

McColl: Yes.

Gaunson: And consequently you gave the certificate of death?

McColl: Yes, without any hesitation.

Gaunson then began to raise the topic of the autopsy performed by Neild, a gripe for the witness. Some of McColl's self-serving responses in this area were destined to attract the biggest newspaper headlines of all.

Gaunson: You ascribed death to the condition of the heart caused by organic poisoning. Therefore, you asked for a post-mortem for the purpose of examining the heart only?

McColl: That is so.

Gaunson: Do you think in fairness you ought to have been invited to be present at the post-mortem?

McColl: I think so.

Gaunson: Would the congestion of the intestines and stomach be consistent with your theory?

McColl: Yes. The inflammation of the stomach and other organs would be quite consistent with organic poisoning.

Gaunson: Were the portions of the body taken away sufficient for an examination on the result of which life and death is to hang?

McColl: It would be sufficient to determine the presence of poison but not to determine the cause of death.

There was nothing to suggest that anyone in an influential position had taken McColl's potentially explosive testimony seriously. Most people saw it for what it was – a doctor, conscious of the need to keep his practising certificate, giving favourably worded evidence that defended his own position. Nor was McColl's credibility about arsenic consumption strong. Even during cross-examination, he had been asked 'In the course of your practice, how many cases of arsenical poisoning have you come across?' to which he replied, 'I am glad to say this is the first'.

It was during prosecutor Finlayson's stint of questioning that McColl made some brief but telling concessions to reality. When asked 'If you had seen anything suspicious in the manner of Mrs Needle, would you have given the death certificate?' he simply answered 'No'. Likewise, when Finlayson added 'Or if you had known that there was arsenic in the body, would you have given it?' he again answered 'No'.

Most intriguing of all was McColl's continued staunch defence of Martha's character during Gaunson's questioning, at least the side of it she had cared to show him:

Gaunson: Did you ever see anything in the manner of the accused that was not affectionate and kind?

McColl: No.

Gaunson: Did she, so far as you can judge, give him every attention in his illness?

McColl: She did. Her manner was very kindly and attentive.

Gaunson: Did you at any time observe any flightiness or looseness in her conduct?

McColl: I have been going to the house for two years and always thought her conduct most exemplary.

McColl had thought so highly of Martha, he even proudly conceded that he had played the role of matchmaker between her and Otto.

His words may have been intended as a good citation but, in light of what Martha was being accused of, they reflected even worse upon her. She had clearly never let her guard down around McColl and, to some degree, she still had him wrapped her around her little finger.

Some Light Relief

As the day was drawing to a close, Finlayson indicated that he would call one more witness – namely Benjamin Baker, the chemist from 100 Bridge Road, Richmond. Although Baker had not sold the 'Rough on Rats' to Martha, his pharmacy had made up five prescriptions written by McColl while he was treating Louis during his last illness. Baker was simply there to confirm that arsenic had not been added to any of them. It was anticipated that his evidence would only occupy a few minutes.

As it turned out, Baker would end up being labelled by the *Herald* newspaper as 'an interesting witness'. His peculiar performance in the witness box showed that even in a case this serious – where a woman's life was potentially at stake – the spectators could still be treated to some inadvertent lighter moments.

Baker was an elderly man and drastically short of hearing. Long before the invention of the hearing loop, he was left to battle on the best he could … and, as it transpired, so was everyone else.

After some confusing moments, Finlayson was able to ascertain from Baker that the prescriptions produced before the court had not been actually made up by him but by his assistant, Herbert Streeton. Baker then awkwardly contradicted himself by saying that while he had probably made up some of the prescriptions, his assistant had made up the others – but he could not say which. The only point he was adamant about was that if he made up any of these prescriptions, he had not included arsenic in them.

When Finlayson asked Baker the name of his assistant, he could only reply that it was 'Sefton' or 'Seften' but he couldn't say which. He then helpfully added that 'either was good enough'. Upon hearing this remark, Gaunson rose to his feet and quipped that if the witness was no more particular in making up prescriptions than in giving evidence, he would not care to have his prescriptions made up by him.

Baker would ultimately exact some revenge for this remark, although as the *Herald* noted on its front page the next day it came to him with 'most refreshing unconsciousness'. When Gaunson asked him a question about the sale of 'Rough on Rats', Baker began to give a lengthy explanation of the entire *Poisons Act* and the raft of conditions under which poisons could then be sold. Then with 'unconscious drollery that was irresistible', he tried to give an illustration: 'You see, Mr Gaunson, if you came to me I'd know you and I'd give you "Rough on Rats"'.

The *Herald* reported: 'The witness seemed to be the only person in court who was unaware of the double meaning he conveyed. The spectators simply burst out into loud and unseemly laughter and Mr Keogh, as soon as he could make himself heard, sternly declared that if the police would bring before him any person whom helped in the disturbance he would send him to gaol'. A constable on courtroom duty hardly improved matters by looking up at the galleries and yelling indignantly, 'Do you hear that now?'.

When the laughter had simmered down, the bewildered Gaunson

tried again. Having ascertained that the prescriptions contained bismuth, he remarked to Baker, 'They are sedatives, are they not?' to which Baker responded eagerly, 'Yes, they're for acidity'. It took some time for Baker to finally come to understand that he had mistaken the word 'sedatives' for 'acidity' and he finally agreed they were 'to settle the stomach'.

The worst difficulty of all was experienced when Baker was asked to differentiate between *patent* and *proprietary* medicines. What his confused answer lacked in quality, it certainly made up for in quantity. As the *Herald* stated the next day, 'The audience is probably to this moment in doubt as to what he considers a patent medicine is'. But at last Baker did commit himself to the statement that 'a proprietary medicine is a medicine to kill rats'.

'A medicine to kill rats!' exclaimed the amazed Magistrate Keogh from the bench. 'Yes' replied Baker confidently, before adding 'or cats'. At this point, even the court officials were having trouble following Baker's logic and his deposition ended up providing the extraordinary testimony, 'a patent medicine is a medicine to kill rats'.

Upon hearing this, Finlayson could take no more. 'Where did you get your licence?' he asked Baker with resignation. 'In the old country, forty years ago,' was the best answer Baker could give. With a final sigh of relief, Finlayson simply slid back in his chair and said, 'Then I'm sorry for the old country, that's all I can say'.[93]

At this point the court was finally adjourned for the end of the day. Being Friday afternoon, Martha would now be spared from hearing any further evidence until the following Monday – but she was not destined to have a peaceful start to her weekend.

The Marauding Mob

While the Baker testimony may have provided some merriment to the otherwise solemn occasion, the *Herald* newspaper would later describe the scene enacted outside the court afterwards as 'a disgrace to the community'.

The moment that the court was adjourned, the gapers seated in the galleries hurried outside and joined a number of other idlers, forming a crowd of a couple of hundred or so. Those in the swarm waited for a few minutes before having the supreme pleasure of seeing Martha emerge from the court between Whitney and Fryer and then being marched out of the courtyard, up Russell Street and down Victoria Street to the main entrance of Melbourne Gaol. The crowd followed Martha the whole way, 'metaphorically yapping at her heels'.

'It was a pitiful sight,' surmised the *Herald*. 'An unhappy woman who, whether she be guilty or not guilty, is manifestly at present suffering great mental anguish, exposed in this manner to the stare of an idle crowd happily composed mostly of police court loafers. What makes the affair more disgraceful is that there is absolutely no need for it. There is at the rear of the court a door leading from the lock-up cells into the gaol. That door was formerly used by prisoners on trial when the criminal sittings of the Supreme Court were held in the present City Court building … Why so much indulgence cannot be extended to Mrs Needle it is impossible to see. At any rate, it is simply brutal to walk her through the crowd outside, and allow them to follow in her footsteps to the gaol gates.'[94]

CHAPTER 17

Back by Popular Demand

The members of the mob who had been stalking Martha's court appearances were not likely to change their coarse behaviours due to a sudden jolt of collective conscience. This was fully evident when Martha was again brought before the bench on the morning of Day Three – Monday, 16 July 1894. In fact, some of the female members of the assemblage had even brought along more of their friends. A reporter noted that 'The Court was again crowded and there were among the audience even more women than on previous days'.

Evidence from a succession of varied witnesses would be heard on this day. While some would only be required to give brief details on a few factual points, others such as Stanley Setford and Thomas Brittain would utter comments that made headlines. And the most significant of all would be Herman Juncken.

Herbert Streeton, the chemist's assistant to Benjamin Baker at Bridge Road, was able to provide a great deal more clarity about the confused evidence his half-dotty boss had ended up delivering the previous Friday. He simply stated that he had made up four of McColl's prescriptions and Baker had made up one. To his knowledge, none of them contained arsenic.

Stanley Setford, Martha's former lodger who was now boarding at

7 Eliza Street in Burnley, gave more substantial evidence but delivered it in a very peculiar way. Throughout his entire ordeal in the witness box, he acted evasively – looking very much like a man who had a few personal secrets lurking in his background.

During this attack of performance anxiety, he opted to speak very softly and mumbled brief, incoherent answers. This was so noticeable that South Australia's *Advertiser* told its readers, 'The witness hesitated a great deal in his evidence, and was sometimes almost inaudible'.[95]

Setford also appeared to be suffering from some form of convenient amnesia, continually informing his questioner – particularly the prosecutor, Finlayson – that he could 'not remember' even the simplest of facts. As is commonly the case with those who try to play against the system in court, Setford only succeeded in attracting headlines for all the wrong reasons.

It was not clear whether Setford was simply trying to save his own personal reputation or was attempting to assist Martha's case – but either way, it soon became obvious that he was not telling everything he knew. During his cross-examination, Gaunson was so taken by this approach that he ultimately ceased his questioning altogether and informed Setford by way of additional cryptic comment, 'Do not be afraid of giving your evidence or think you may do this woman an injury. Tell the truth whether you shame a certain individual or not.'

But by this stage, such advice had come too late. Despite all of the elusive strategies he had employed, Setford had probably already done his former housemate, Martha, more harm than good.

When first questioned by Finlayson, Setford was able to guardedly confirm that he had boarded with Martha from August 1892 right up to the day of her arrest. He could clearly remember Louis' illness and then let slip that Martha and the deceased Louis were 'not on very good terms'. Finlayson quickly seized on this last comment and prodded further. Setford could only offer, 'She spoke to me after his death – a few days after. She only said that he was very selfish.' Finlayson was anxious to keep this line of questioning going:

Finlayson: She would not come to you and say, 'Louis is very selfish' and then go away. When did it take place?

Setford: At mealtime.

Finlayson: How did it originate?

Setford: I can't remember.

Finlayson: Did Mrs Needle say anything about anyone else?

Setford: I can't say.

Finlayson: Did she say anything about Louis' mother?

Setford: Yes, she said his mother did not treat her properly when she came to the house from Adelaide.

By this time, Setford had resorted to muttering so softly that Keogh felt compelled to intervene, imploring him to speak up clearly.

Finlayson: Anything else? Now come on, tell me what she said. It's no use trying to fool the court. You know you made a statement to Detective Whitney a few days ago and you cannot have forgotten it.

Setford: I have not forgotten it. I do not know whether it was at the same time as she spoke of Louis being selfish.

Finlayson: Well what did she say?

Setford: She threatened Mrs Juncken.

Finlayson: Come on, what did she say?

Gaunson, sensing danger, intervened by stating, 'I have no objection to what Mrs Needle said but I object to having it in the witness's language'. Keogh remained unmoved and Finlayson moved on.

Finlayson: Well, what did Mrs Needle say?

Setford: She said Mrs Juncken did not treat her well while she was in the house, and that she did not care if the train broke down.

Finlayson: Anything else?

Setford: Yes, she said she would like to give her a dose of poison.

The newspapers now had their long-awaited headline. Setford's last comment would be relayed around the world. That evening's *Herald* newspaper even turned it into a major heading in capital letters: SHE WOULD LIKE TO GIVE HER A DOSE OF POISON.

It was now Gaunson's time to cross-examine this curious witness and at first even the canny lawyer remained disconcerted. He simply uttered, 'See, Mr Setford, I have no question to ask you but I wish to impress upon you that you can do this woman no harm by telling the truth. I want to impress upon you that when you give your evidence in another place [clearly meaning the Supreme Court], there will be nothing to gain by appearing to hold back anything. I have no question to ask you.'

Although he was moving away from the bar table, the persistent Gaunson then had a change of heart. Setford had quickly scurried from the witness box, so Gaunson decided to take a risk and recall him. He would desperately try to mitigate any damage the witness had done.

Gaunson: You have said that the deceased and Mrs Needle were not on very good terms. That may do the woman injury and I want to know whether you refer to the time of Louis' illness or not?

Setford: No. It was before that.

Gaunson: What terms were they on at the time of his illness?

Setford: They appeared to be very friendly.

Gaunson: What was her manner to him then?

Setford: At first she appeared somewhat impatient, and she told me Louis gave her a good deal of unnecessary work, but afterwards she seemed to me to be all that was good and kind to him.

From Setford's evidence, it was clear that Martha had been smart enough to initially offer some complaints to those around her about the extra workload that Louis' condition had imposed upon her. She knew it would be very hard to suspect that someone was causing a condition when they were actually bold enough to be complaining about it.

Although Gaunson then managed to form a bit of a diversion by raising the topic of chlorodyne and the size of the local rat population, he could gain no more by continuing to question Setford. He wisely sensed it was time to stop. The witness was excused, at least for now.[96]

The next person to enter the heavily scrutinised witness box was the more precise George Miller, assistant to the chemist Mr Roberts in Swan Street, Richmond. Miller could not only confirm that he knew Martha but he could clearly recall her buying some 'Rough on Rats' between 7 p.m. and 7.30 p.m. on 10 May. He was then able to produce the store's 'Poison Sales Book', which showed the signatures of Martha and her witness, Thomas Brittain.

In response to questions raised by Gaunson, Miller was able to confirm that 'Rough on Rats' was a very popular form of rodent poison, it was a slate colour and was generally spread on bread and butter. After Gaunson asked 'When spread upon bread with butter, would the colour attract attention?' Miller quickly responded 'It would be noticeable spread upon any kind of butter'. He also confirmed that 'no element of secrecy' had been associated with the purchase in any way.

Miller was followed by Martha's 'witness', Thomas Brittain, the eminent Richmond boot salesman who must have now wished he had never encountered Martha on that fateful night. Anxious to please, Brittain had unhesitatingly closed his shop and accompanied Martha to the chemist to witness her purchase of 'Rough on Rats'. His 'Good Samaritan' act was now coming back to haunt him.

The only potential controversy that Gaunson could detect with Brittain's evidence was how the pair came to make the purchase of 'Rough on Rats' at the chemist shop owned by Mr Richards, instead of the closer chemist shop owned by Mr Stiles. Was this a twist of fate or brought about by some veiled attempt by Martha to conceal her behaviour? Was this course of action initiated by Martha or Brittain?

Gaunson: Did you not refuse to go to Mr Stiles because you were not friendly with him? Be truthful, you know.

Brittain: I think I did.

Gaunson: Was it not you who took her to Mr Richards?

Brittain: I mentioned to her that I usually make my purchases from Mr Richards and we went there.

Gaunson then asked the question that everyone had secretly wanted answered. Although it was couched in implied terms, there was no doubting its intention. He needed to find out more about the relationship between Brittain and Martha ... a mysterious friendship between a boot salesman and housewife, so close that she could call on him after an absence of 18 months and effortlessly have him close his business to witness a purchase of rat poison. Gaunson simply asked, 'When you were accustomed to see her, I presume it was in the ordinary way of business?'

Brittain played a straight bat to the hushed court, replying, 'Yes. She was living near my place then in Cubitt Street. I knew the whole family.'

The other potential point of interest for Gaunson was the very upfront way Martha had purchased the 'Rough on Rats'. It appeared that she had even ended up finalising the transaction in a busier street than she originally intended. Did this look like a woman worried about something to hide? Who better to ask than Richmond's most prominent and popular purveyor of footwear?

Brittain agreed that Swan Street was a livelier thoroughfare than Bridge Road.

Gaunson: A dull person would be more recreated by the life and brilliancy of lights there than in dull Bridge Road? If a person wanted to hide what Shakespeare called 'a potent poison', I suppose he or she would not come to you?

Brittain: I don't suppose so.

Gaunson left it there and Brittain was excused. In any event, Martha's lack of concern about concealing her 'Rough on Rats' purchase remained a largely inconsequential point and the case was unlikely to turn on it. It even presented a potential weak point for Gaunson, as it could be equally suggested that Martha had acted so brazenly because she didn't anticipate being caught.

Next came some witnesses who could talk about the exhumations. First was the busiest undertaker in Melbourne – Herbert King – who now needed to add court appearances to his hectic schedule. The court then heard from Louis Juncken's former brother-in-law, newspaper proprietor John Jones of Port Adelaide, who testified that he had been present on 19 May when Louis' coffin had arrived in Adelaide and had seen it being interred at Lyndoch. He had then been personally present on 23 June when the grave was reopened and had identified the remains of Louis.

Jones had also spent three days staying with Martha at Bridge Road during the previous November. In response to some prompting from Gaunson, he told the court, 'She was very kind and attentive to me … nothing occurred to suggest to my mind that there were strained relations at that time between her and any of her household'.

The final witness for the day was none other than Herman Juncken, the man Martha had at one time stood accused of attempting to murder and who had only been a gulp or two away from certain death. Given the massive press coverage already circulating about the case, most of Herman's story was already very well known. But now he had to relate it out loud in a courtroom and then allow himself to be exposed to cross-examination.

Like his brother Otto, Herman presented as a plausible witness, providing his answers in a clear-headed way while being led by prosecutor Finlayson. The only controversy that arose occurred when he discussed the 'trap' set by detectives for Martha at Bridge Road. Unlike accounts given by others, his recollection was that Martha had told the detectives that there was chlorodyne *and* 'Rough on Rats' in the house but he was not certain whether the detectives found the poison or whether Martha had given it to them.

Gaunson's cross-examination of Herman was potentially a crucial moment in the Police Court proceedings. Rather than try to destabilise the clear facts that Herman had outlined, he saw more advantage in exploring what possible *motive* Martha could have had to attempt to murder him. This approach was typified by Gaunson's very first question, 'Can you conceive any reason why she should try to harm you?' to which Herman could only answer, 'None whatever'.

Gaunson then turned to the 'treacherous' events of 13 June, seeking to highlight the atmosphere of entrapment while also trying to gain mileage from any slightly different recollections of events between Herman and the detectives.

Gaunson: Knowing that a warrant had been issued and the errand you were bent on ... there was a sort of feeling that it felt like treachery?

Herman: Yes.

Gaunson: How did she seem when she heard the accusation?

Herman: She seemed dazed.

Gaunson: The finding of the 'Rough on Rats' was only confirming what the woman said?

Herman: Yes.

Gaunson: Did you see her try to possess herself of chlorodyne?

Herman: Yes ... When she snatched at the bottle, I thought that she intended to take it.

Gaunson: Did they turn over mementos of her little ones?

Herman: Yes.

Gaunson: What was the accused's demeanour then?

Herman: She burst into tears and asked them not to touch them as they belonged to her dead children.

Returning to his trump card – Martha's possible *motive* for finishing off Herman – Gaunson tried to step up his questioning. He sensed that Herman's 'treacherous' role in her arrest was still playing on his mind. And, of course, the deceased Louis was no longer in a position to defend himself by giving evidence.

Gaunson: It has been put that the unfortunate woman could have no ill will against you and Louis except that you were obstacles to her marrying Otto. To your knowledge and to the knowledge of the accused, have you at any time put obstacles in the way?

Herman: I never did.

Gaunson: Then can you see any possible reason or motive for the alleged crime?

Herman: Well, I have an opinion of course.

Gaunson: Then what motive could she have for putting you out of the way?

Herman: I thought it was to spite my mother.

Gaunson: Then that's madder than ever. You still think that the motive in her mind was to revenge herself upon the mother by murdering the children?

Herman: Yes.

Gaunson: Wouldn't you think that a mad thing?

Herman: It seems most unreasonable.

Gaunson: Would it not be the very maddest thing you ever heard of?

Herman: Yes.

At this point, the usually subdued Finlayson could take no more. He sprang to his feet and interjected, flatly interrupting Gaunson's cross-examination at a crucial point. He asked Herman in a loud voice, 'Do you see any madness in poisoning your tea and not her own?' It was an extremely insightful question.

Although Herman did not answer, it immediately took the sting out of Gaunson's offensive and the courtroom became hushed. All Gaunson could eventually say to no-one in particular was, 'The old wild beast theory of right or wrong'. Rather than Gaunson, it was Finlayson who had taken the advantage.

As if to confirm the ultimate ineffectiveness of Gaunson's cross-examination, Keogh chimed in with one last question of his own that bore no relationship to the line of questioning that Gaunson had pursued. Keogh simply asked Herman, 'Did you notice anything peculiar in the taste of the tea?' to which Herman replied, 'Yes, it had a very peculiar taste'. The witness was then excused.

This concluded the hearing of evidence on Day Three, at which point Keogh promptly announced that the case would be adjourned for eight days. Although this break would interrupt the flow of the case, it had become increasingly obvious that there was good reason for such an adjournment.

To this point the entire proceedings had taken place under a cloud of uncertainty. To use a more modern expression, it was becoming increasingly difficult to ignore the elephant in the room. After all, while all this evidence was being heard, Blackett was still diligently completing his analysis of the remains of the accused's husband and two of her children.

This had become far more than a mere distraction. Although in theory the court was only hearing evidence on its own merits in relation to the murder of Louis, this was not how matters were working out in reality. Clearly the outcome of Blackett's analysis would be pivotal to interpreting the strength of the current evidence. And, as it played out, things were about to become a whole lot worse for Martha.

Jaw-Dropping Results

On 19 July 1894, Martha's case was to officially take on its new twist. It was on this date that Blackett was in a position to announce the news that an anxious public had already been suspecting – he had found arsenic in the remains of Martha's late husband, Henry. Within a day or so he could also confirm the presence of arsenic in the remains of Martha's late children, Elsie and May.

Blackett was now another person becoming famous on the back of the Needle case. He soon found himself having press interviews in his house at bayside St Kilda. It could be said that the public had never found the field of chemical analysis to be so fascinating.

Blackett had commenced with Henry's body parts. He had dissolved them in chlorine and treated the liquid by various processes before he was able to declare that arsenic was present – and, what's more, it was in sufficient quantities to have 'undoubtedly' caused Henry's death.

In the meantime, Blackett had also been treating the remains of the children in similar fashion. When he first tested the very badly decomposed portions of Elsie's body, he could initially not find any arsenic – but the body parts of May quickly revealed arsenic aplenty. Blackett then persevered with portions of Elsie's remains without immediate success. At last, he tested the bones of the trunk and found unmistakable traces of arsenic.

In the mode of an objective scientist, Blackett was to provide an official report on his findings to the Criminal Investigation Department. It was a damning report for Martha. The main text read in a matter-of-fact way:

No. 1 – HENRY NEEDLE'S REMAINS

Brain – Careful analysis of this organ, which was very soft and converted into adipocere, revealed nothing in the shape of poison.

The thorax and parts corresponding to the abdominal region

– As so little was remaining, I removed as much as possible for analysis, washing and macerating the bones with distilled water in a perfectly clean, glass dish. This was added to the soft matter, and on analysis found to contain a considerable quantity of arsenic. The flannel shirt found on the skeleton was in a good state of preservation.

The sawdust taken from under the body contained no arsenic. The earth taken from beneath the coffin was found to be free of arsenic.

No. 2 – ELSIE NEEDLE'S REMAINS

Found to be far advanced in decomposition: adipocere abundant and very alkaline. I followed the same method of analysis as in No. 1 and, after much care and perseverance, detected the presence of arsenic in small quantities.

Earth from underneath Elsie Needle's coffin was found to be free of arsenic.

Sawdust taken from coffin immediately underneath the body gave no indication of containing arsenic.

No. 3 – MAY NEEDLE'S REMAINS

I cut out the parts pointed out to me by Dr Neild as containing the rectum. I then removed as much as possible of the internal organs. The lungs and the intestines were still recognisable, but very soft. The liver still contained what appeared to be biliary matter. The decomposed organs were very alkaline. On analysis, I found a considerable quantity of arsenic. The earth from beneath the coffin did not contain arsenic.

In each case I have preserved specimens in tubes, etc. etc. to be produced if required.

All the chemicals and apparatus used in these investigations were previously proved to be free from arsenic. Each analysis was conducted separately with its own set of materials.

C.R. BLACKETT

All of Blackett's results and reports were leaked to the press and they were excitedly reported in each of the daily newspapers.

As the next court date of 24 July began to draw closer, Whitney and Fryer decided to ask for another seven-day adjournment to more formally compile evidence about Blackett's analysis and the deaths of Martha's family members.

Blackett's results had provided a new development and a different *type* of evidence was now required. The detectives had already begun to investigate certain statements that Henry made just before his death, in which he had raised his suspicion that he was receiving foul play at the hands of some person in his house. They also let the press know that Henry had been 'allegedly' very jealous of his wife and had frequently accused her of being too fond of male admiration. It had also been said that he occasionally beat her.

Based on the information flowing in an unfettered fashion from the Criminal Investigation Department, the *Herald* was able to dramatically inform its large readership, 'The detectives have already collected a quantity of evidence of a startling and sensational character'. Likewise, the *Argus* newspaper was able to announce even more specifically, 'It was known that Henry and Martha frequently quarrelled ... Witnesses have now been found who will give testimony to this effect, and it will be shown that Mrs Needle several times subsequent to her husband's death complained of his cruelty to her, and said she was glad that he was gone'.

Very early on the morning of the next hearing day, 24 July, Whitney and Fryer visited Martha at Melbourne Gaol, where Whitney informed her that an adjournment would be sought and evidence would now be given about the discovery of poison in the bodies of her husband and children. Martha remained perfectly calm upon hearing this news.

It was also at this point that she uttered infamous words to the effect that more of her friends had died in recent times. She willingly offered to give their names and burial details, suggesting that such information would be useful if the detectives wanted to dig them up. But, rather unwisely, Whitney had said, 'No, I have quite enough at present'.[97]

Shortly after, Martha was brought before the court in an early example of a brief 'out of sessions' hearing, even though members of the press were notified and granted entry in large numbers. One journalist took some expressive licence, noting that Martha looked 'very greatly depressed and thin' – which, in the circumstances, was probably quite understandable.

Whitney applied for a remand of seven days, adding that arrangements had been made between Messrs Finlayson and Gaunson for hostilities to resume on 31 July. The adjournment was granted. While before Keogh, Martha said nothing. She was marched back to prison long before the court opened for normal business that morning, leaving a disappointed crowd of onlookers in her wake.

Initially, very few of the pathetic scrum looking for free entertainment were even aware that Martha had already come and gone. They had gathered at an early hour in the hope of seeing her. The moment that the court doors opened, a multitude of men rushed into the galleries, pushing against each other in an endeavour to reach the most convenient seats. But it was the scores of women and accompanying children who also scrambled and pattered up the stairs as rapidly as they could that drew the most attention.

As one newspaper reported that evening:

> The curiosity of some women is simply astounding at times. Some had infants with them, and one child made its presence felt most annoyingly. Its mother caught it by the frock, and let it play its infantile feet most noisily against the parapet of

the gallery. The mother was heedless of the interruption of the Court by her child, and looked mortally offended when a constable told her in so many words that such applause from one so young in such a place went very near contempt of Court.

The females were sorely disappointed when they heard that Martha had already been before the Court and remanded. About a dozen of them rushed around the courthouse and even pelted away towards the lockup corridor in a belated attempt to gratify their curiosity. [98]

Martha now had to cool her heels for another week before her case would recommence. She needed to do so in the knowledge that her case was now looking even grimmer and that her courtroom experiences were likely to become more harrowing with each and every appearance.

CHAPTER 18

The Heavily
Anticipated Resumption

Martha's bizarre popularity had certainly not diminished by the time her case resumed on 31 July. Her capacity to attract a courtroom crowd had even forced court officials to think up some strategies to minimise the inevitable disruptions. This time, by arrangement, her case was not called until 11 a.m. – but even before the courtroom doors opened just before 10 a.m. there was a considerable crowd waiting outside, again including a great many females.

A large number gained admission the moment the doors were opened. The women rushed to occupy all the seats in the south gallery of the court, while their male counterparts quickly filled up the north gallery. The body of the court was reserved for witnesses but this didn't deter a number of women spectators, who simply secured seats there. They were disappointed when one of the police officers on duty later ordered them to move on.

At 10.40 a.m., it was announced that the ordinary business of the court was finished and the court was adjourned. Clearly the object of this manoeuvre was to mislead the idle spectators into believing that the Needle case would not be going ahead. But the attempt was a failure. Only two or three people were convinced enough by the ruse to shuffle out of court. The rest stubbornly kept their seats and were ultimately rewarded.

It was reported that Martha looked 'composed but anxious' when she was brought into court shortly after 11 a.m. One scribe even made the rather deflating observation, 'Otherwise she looked much as she had done on previous days'.[99]

Although Martha was still only charged with the murder of Louis, the publicly known arsenic results relating to her deceased husband and two children would now overshadow the entire proceedings. Witnesses would be seen in a different light and, inevitably, so would Martha. The laws of coincidence and unintended consequence no longer appeared to apply and it was easy to join the dots. The battle facing Gaunson was now more uphill than ever.

Also, Magistrate Keogh did not hesitate to allow all the 'similar fact evidence' to be fully admitted, even though Martha only stood accused of murdering Louis. While these details could point to striking similarities and Martha's trademark calling cards, in normal circumstances such information is thought to be highly prejudicial and would not likely be permitted today.

As an emerging hero in the story, the first important witness of the day was Dr William Boyd. Having blown the whistle on Martha in the Herman Juncken situation, he could clearly provide some insightful comment about that case. But as a more diligent doctor than some of his more relaxed peers, he was also valued for any medical and scientific information he could provide.

According to his own accounts, Boyd began to strongly suspect that Herman was suffering from the effects of irritant poison after he had visited him a number of times and unsuccessfully prescribed a bismuth mixture. It was then he issued his fateful instructions about collecting Herman's vomit.

Gaunson wasn't totally accepting Boyd's gallant story. When he commenced his cross- examination, he was anxious to confirm *who* had actually first mentioned the possibility of poisoning. Was it Boyd who had first raised it with Smith, or was it in fact the other way around? Had Smith – clearly a man with a low opinion of Martha – planted the idea in Boyd's head?

Gaunson asserted, 'As a matter of fact, at first you had not the faintest idea of anything of the kind when you prescribed that bismuth,' before he asked, 'When were your suspicions first aroused?' Boyd gave the guarded answer, 'Mr Smith had not spoken to me of his suspicions at that time'. The last three words of Boyd's curiously worded reply – 'at that time' - implied that he had been aware Smith harboured some suspicions about Martha.

Rather than completing his questioning of Boyd at that point, Gaunson sensed an advantage in continuing to delve further. After all, Boyd was now a respected medical man (in the words of the newspapers at least) and apparently not afraid to offer a diverging, forthright opinion. Gaunson hoped that Boyd might actually say something that could add some credence to Martha's case. He might be used to confirm the inexperience most general practitioners of the day had in relation to poisons, leaving them prone to making inaccurate accusations. Perhaps he could even be led into saying something that might support the besieged McColl and his 'auto-intoxication' theories and 'Riggs' disease' diagnosis.

But, to a large extent, Gaunson's hunch backfired and soon Boyd was making statements in the witness box that provided little comfort to Gaunson's client.

Gaunson: Have your experience or reading brought you into contact with the subject of auto-intoxication?

Boyd: Yes. It is a difficult subject and it is hardly fair to call it auto-intoxication.

Gaunson: What do you understand by it?

Boyd: The absorption of the products of putrefaction …

Gaunson: Is not auto-intoxication a new discovery to the profession?

Boyd: Yes.

Gaunson: Are you acquainted with a disease known as Riggs' disease?

Boyd: Not by that name ... before Dr McColl gave his evidence, I had known Riggs disease as pyorrhoea alveolaris. I had a case of Riggs' disease about 12 months ago. I diagnosed it at the time.

Gaunson: Ulcerative endocarditis is a very rare disease?

Boyd: It is. Ulcerative endocarditis is a very rare disease. It does arise from aseptic processes going on in other parts of the body. It causes certain forms of pneumonia.

Gaunson: Does it not arise from auto-intoxication?

Boyd: It may.

Gaunson: Have you had any cases of arsenical poisoning in your practice?

Boyd: I think I can remember two in my hospital experience. I have attended autopsies for poisoning cases as a student. At two autopsies, I had cases of arsenical poisoning.

Gaunson: You have heard Dr McColl's evidence as to the pus from the jaw in cases of pyorrhoea alveolaris or Riggs' disease. Do you still adhere to your definition of the infection by germs from without?

Boyd: In that case I think the germs came from without – originally from without.

Gaunson wisely stopped his questioning there.[100] With the witness starting to make statements such as 'Ulcerative endocarditis is a very rare disease' and 'I think the germs came from without', he couldn't have Boyd leave the witness box quickly enough.

The next three witnesses called gave those in the courtroom a slight break from hearing 'medical' evidence. The caretaker of the Pharmacy College, Joseph Lowry, was able to confirm that Boyd had indeed handed him the jar containing Herman's vomit – he was even able to identify the specific jar when it was produced as an exhibit. He stated that he did not interfere with it any way and handed it to Blackett's assistant, William Wilkinson, on 9 June. Likewise, Wilkinson was able to confirm that he passed the jar to Blackett undisturbed on 11 June. Gaunson chose not to seek controversy with this 'chain of custody' evidence and both witnesses were quickly excused.

The next witness provided evidence of an entirely different nature. It was Edward Croker, the overworked Registrar of Births and Deaths at Richmond, who among other duties was required to retain records of death. Presumably Croker was being called by the prosecution to suggest that Martha had given him extra work to do in recent years. Croker was immediately asked if he could produce as exhibits the death certificates of Henry, Elsie and May Needle.

In keeping with the administrative custom of the day, whenever Croker received an original certificate of death he would transcribe all of its particulars into a central Register. Although he was unable to produce the original certificate of death of Henry, he was able to hand up his Register entry, which was entered as an exhibit. Croker explained that while he had searched extensively for the original certificate, he could not find it. He could not recall giving it to anyone, adding that these original certificates were generally not retained after a certain time.

Croker's scrawly handwritten Register entry confirmed that Henry had died on 4 October 1889 from 'sub-acute hepatitis and persistent vomiting, enteric fever and exhaustion due to obstinacy in taking nourishment' and that the physician supplying the original death certificate was George Hodgson.

Helpfully, Croker was able to produce both the original death certificate and Register entry for Elsie, the original also being signed by Hodgson on 9 December 1890 and indicating the cause of death to be 'exhaustion and gangrenous stomatitis'. But in the case of May, it was a similar story to that of her father – Croker had searched for the original death certificate but could not find it. The court was nonetheless satisfied to receive his Register entry as an exhibit, which indicated that May had died on 27 August 1891 and Dr Charles Payne had certified that the cause of death was 'tuberculous meningitis'.[101]

After hearing briefly from a series of relatively uncontroversial witnesses, it was then time to return to the medical theme – the next witnesses in line being the besieged lodge practitioners Charles Payne and George Hodgson. These men were likely to enliven Gaunson's interest to a much higher degree than the previous witnesses and, in a similar vein to his cross-examination of Dr Boyd, he would use this opportunity to question them about the world of science and medicine in general.

Payne must have drawn the short straw. He went first. In response to leading questioning by Finlayson, he explained that to the best of his recollection he first saw May Needle on 20 August that year and visited her daily until the date of her death on 27 August. He had been puzzled about the symptoms at the time, which had included obstinate vomiting, but diagnosed brain irritation. Still unsure, he took the added precaution of seeking more advice from another medical practitioner – Dr Burton from Richmond.

Payne could not directly recall what he had prescribed for May but he could definitely swear that it was not arsenic. He explained that prescriptions for lodge patients were always written in a lodge book that was kept by the patient, or in this case, by the mother of the patient. He confirmed that he wrote the certificate of death, citing the causes listed in Croker's grisly Register.

When Finlayson asked, 'Has anything come to your knowledge that you did not know then that has caused you to change your opinion?' Payne emphatically answered, 'Yes – I have since been told that arsenic was found in the body'. He agreed that he would 'certainly not' have issued a certificate of death if he knew this at the time.

While Finlayson's questioning of Payne had been relatively gentle, Gaunson's cross-examination would be less so. He quickly established that Payne had already seen a case of arsenical poisoning about ten years previously in which six or seven people had been poisoned at once, even though it had been accidentally administered on that occasion. In response to his question, 'Arsenic is a poison easy to absorb through a sore and in other ways?' Payne had rapidly confirmed, 'It is one of the most easily absorbed poisons'.

Gaunson then decided to concentrate on the agreement between Payne and Martha to allow another medical practitioner, the agreeable Dr Burton, to give a second opinion about May's condition. Martha had also made suggestions to Gaunson that she had willingly put forward to Payne other names from her stable of doctors to examine her ailing child. Had Payne first made these suggestions to Martha, or was it in fact the other way around? Either way, Gaunson was trying to raise a suspicion – was this truly the action that a guilty woman would take?

Gaunson: It is not usual, is it, for lodge patients to get outside advice? I suppose it is the poor people who go in for this lodge business?

Payne: Not always, I am sorry to say. [Laughter]

Gaunson: Well, the additional advice in this case would be a charge upon the accused?

Payne: It would.

Gaunson: Do you recall the accused suggesting any second doctor?

Payne: No.

Gaunson: Do you recollect whether she suggested Dr Snowball?

Payne: No, I do not recollect.

Gaunson: You would not say she did or did not? At all events, you had confidence in Dr Burton and she agreed?

Payne: Yes. So far as my recollection goes she suggested Dr Burton herself.

Gaunson: You see, Doctor, she is charged with being a dreadful person, who murdered this little child for the sake of a few pounds. If she did so, it would be very likely when you suggested Dr Burton for her to say you were quite good enough and that Dr Burton would be an extra expense, which she could not afford. Did she say so?

Payne: No. So far as I can recollect she suggested Dr Burton herself.

Gaunson: Do you recollect her saying she would like to have Dr Elsner and you saying that you did not know where to find him?

Payne: No, I don't recollect that.

Gaunson then stated, 'I suppose Dr Burton was paid a fee,' before asking Payne, 'Do you know how he was paid?' Payne's answer largely shot down Gaunson's advancing argument in flames: 'I cannot say, I do not take note of such things. I know there is an account of £1 and 1 shilling still owing to me by the accused for insurance certificates for May Needle'.

Under normal circumstances, Gaunson's theory about a 'poor widow' doing the best she financially could for the welfare of her only surviving child may have tugged at a few heartstrings. But two factors were now heavily playing against it. The rumour had now been firmly established that Martha had been collecting insurance bounties upon the multiple departures of her loved ones and should have been well and truly cashed up. And now those in the court learned that she hadn't even fully paid Payne for his work.

Gaunson abandoned this line of questioning and turned his attention to the slightly more promising 'contaminated bismuth' theories – even though this was a long shot in itself. While he wasn't in a position to raise bismuth as a direct defence, he could use it to air a few doubts and cause a useful distraction.

Gaunson: Is there anything about bismuth which renders it liable to be adulterated by arsenic?

Payne: Undoubtedly it is liable to be adulterated by arsenic – impure specimens, that is.

Gaunson: Well, Dr Boyd prescribed bismuth for Herman Juncken. And Dr McColl prescribed it for Louis Juncken. Doctors have to rely on the chemists making up the prescriptions as directed and of course they have always the best drugs on hand. You have heard of adulterated bismuth?

Payne: Yes.

And what about Martha's behaviour in general?

Gaunson: Was there anything in the attention of the prisoner to the child which attracted your attention – anything that you could object to?

Payne: I have already said I had no suspicion, and that, I think, answers every question of that sort. I had no suspicion.

Payne left the witness box. Now it was the turn of George Hodgson, a medico who had forged the unfortunate record of losing two members of the Needle family while they were under his medical care.

Unlike the slightly more progressive Drs Boyd and Payne, Hodgson was more typical of the all-knowing suburban practitioner who was fixed in his ways and opinions, however out of date they may actually be. He was also more argumentative and would probably be a much tougher medical stickler to disturb.

Although he had moved from the poor, ramshackle area of Richmond in the middle of 1891, Hodgson still had some memories of the deaths of Henry and Elsie Needle. What he was not able to readily recall, he could piece together from the surviving documentation he previously provided. The danger of this referral method was that such documentation had been somewhat sloppily attended to in the first place.

Hodgson recalled that Henry was a strong man but could only rely on his paperwork to recollect that vomiting was present in the case.

With respect to Elsie, Hodgson needed to refer to her death certificate to see when she had died. He could no longer definitely say how long he had treated her before her death but thought that it was probably about a week. From her death certificate, he could presume that she must have been in a very low state and that there would have been a discharge from her gums and vomiting. When Finlayson asked him, 'Were the symptoms consistent with arsenical poisoning?', Hodgson only gave the general reply, 'They are not usual but they have occurred in arsenical poisoning'.

Although Hodgson may have been a reasonably effective suburban medical practitioner, Gaunson clearly suspected that Hodgson's actual medical knowledge might not be totally up to speed – at least in comparison with that of his more inquisitive colleagues, Boyd and Payne. Gaunson was astute enough to realise that this observation could be used to his advantage. He saw shades of Dr McColl in Hodgson, a professional man with plenty of pride, not averse to contradicting other medical witnesses. In general questioning, Hodgson could be coerced into saying something very useful that could be seized upon by the defence.

To add to the dynamic, Hodgson could be outspoken and was not likely to take a backward step. This made for a lively exchange with Gaunson:

Gaunson: Is it not rather a big jump for a medical man to say that arsenical poisoning was the cause of death because arsenic was found in the body?
Hodgson: It depends upon the quantity.
Gaunson: Are the symptoms always the same?
Hodgson: No, they are not.
Gaunson: They vary in every case?

Hodgson: No, they do not. They are similar in nearly every case and vary rarely.

Gaunson: What are the symptoms of arsenical poisoning?

Hodgson: Pains over the abdomen and persistent vomiting are symptoms.

Gaunson: Say that for a whole month a quarter of a grain of arsenic was taken daily, would that be a fatal dose?

Hodgson: The fatal dose is put down at from two grains to two grains and a half, but it varies with the person.

Gaunson: But taking a dose such as ladies take to beautify their complexion – say a quarter of a grain a day for a month, or seven and a half grains in all – would you expect that to cause death? Would the system absorb it, or would death occur? You know horses are given as much as ten grains at a dose?

Hodgson: I should be very sorry to give a horse ten grains. I gave a horse four grains quite recently myself daily.

Gaunson then took the time to read to the court a lengthy extract from a work that discussed the doses of arsenic to be given to various animals, before he turned immediately to the touchy subject of bismuth.

Gaunson: Did you order the inevitable bismuth?

Hodgson: I cannot say, but it is highly probable … I have ordered it extensively but I do not always order it in vomiting.

Gaunson: And you ordered the common bismuth for Henry. Perhaps that accounts for the milk in the coconut.

Gaunson began to rattle Hodgson's chain further.

Gaunson: Did you see anything of him [Henry Needle] on the day of his death?

Hodgson: Yes – I saw him three times and there was a great change in
him.

Gaunson: What religion was he?

Hodgson: A carpenter, I believe. [Laughter]

Gaunson: If he were a carpenter, he would be a Christian I presume;
but what church did he belong to?

Hodgson: I cannot say.

Gaunson: Did you suggest to him that it might be advisable for him to
make up his accounts? It is usual, I think, for medical men
to suggest such things?

Hodgson: I did not suggest anything of the sort.

Gaunson's most telling exchange with Hodgson hit upon the inevitable
questioning about Martha's care for her ailing loved ones, with a
predictable result. When he asked, 'Was there anything in the prisoner's
demeanour that caused you to think that she was acting neglectfully or
unkindly to her husband and child?', Hodgson immediately fired back,
'Certainly not'.

It was surprising that while Hodgson could not directly recall all
the medical details about his dying patients and was even a bit touchy
about whether or not he asked the dying Henry to settle his accounts,
one crystal-clear thought remained in his memory. He could remember
Martha's kindness.

A Change of Pace

On a day that had been somewhat dominated by medical men, next
came one of the more intriguing witnesses in the case – a man who
would provide the type of gossipy 'evidence' on which the newspapers
were thriving. It was none other than the highly questionable Owen
Evans, the self-reported former close confidant of the Needles who
was now forging a living as a penal warder at faraway Maryborough.

Of all the people who claimed to know the Needles while they resided in Richmond, it was never made perfectly clear how Evans – a former boarding companion of Henry – had found himself embroiled in the case. Nor how he had been considered so significant that he was now giving evidence before a court of law. But there was a strong implication that he had either approached the police or they had approached him and that he was willing to provide a healthy version of events favourable to the prosecution's case for financial reward. He had certainly not been called by Gaunson, who took an instant disliking to him.

In the witness box, Evans formally explained to Finlayson how he had first met Henry in 1885 and knew him well right up to his death. He also knew Martha and considered himself to be on 'intimate terms' with both of the Needles. According to Evans, Martha had seen fit to confide in him about three years before her husband's death that she had made a mistake in marrying him and should have become hitched to someone else.

At this point, Gaunson interjected with the wisecrack, 'You, I suppose'. Evans retained his composure and simply answered, 'She said someone else who was on the other side'. Those in the courtroom became intrigued by this comment about 'the other side'. 'Did it refer to a deceased person?' asked Finlayson. 'No, it's a term used, meaning Adelaide,' answered Evans. Gaunson wasn't buying the theories about geographical borders, articulating out loud, 'What this person [Evans] may have thought she meant is quite another thing. She might have meant on the other side of the room and he was there'.

In reality, Martha had probably meant the other side of the ocean, referring to her former boarder, Archibald Martin, who had moved to New Zealand.

Undaunted, Evans continued his story:

> I told her as near as I can remember that Henry was a very decent fellow. About a fortnight after Henry's funeral, she called at the house of Mrs Tutt, where I was residing, and I

went with her to the house of a person where she visited. I don't know the name. I waited outside until she came out and went back with her but can't remember clearly where I parted company with her. During the conversation, I expressed my sympathy with her in having lost her husband. She told me she was not sorry he was dead and that he had left marks of violence on her when he died.

Even to this stage, the version of events Evans was reciting was exposing its limitations. While he could remember some things favourable to his story, he couldn't recall other facts. Some parts of the conversations that Evans was suggesting had occurred also didn't seem to fit into the normal context of what would be discussed between suburban acquaintances.

It appeared that Evans was well versed in knowing what to say. Even though he was merely confirming some of the stories that had already been in circulation about Martha, he was also attempting to add some spice and credibility to them by quoting in Martha's own alleged words.

While there was little doubt that Evans had engaged in conversations with Martha after Henry's death, in all likelihood he was now embellishing the content of these private conversations. But there was no real way of knowing for sure. Only two people knew what had really been said – and Martha was no longer talking.

Gaunson relished the thought of cross-examining Evans. He paid little regard to the need to avoid leading questions:

Gaunson: Well, I suppose you saw a good deal of Henry Needle?

Evans: Yes.

Gaunson: Did he use to knock her about in the presence of people, or did he do it secretly, like a coward?

Evans: I never saw him knock her about.

Gaunson: Now, have you invented all this cock-and-bull story you have told us, or did the detectives ferret you out?

Evans: They ferreted me out.

Gaunson: Oh, come now. Did you not say that you could give valuable evidence that she was going to marry again if she got an offer? In these times of retrenchment, you come down for a holiday from the penal establishment in Maryborough?

Evans: The detectives ferreted me out.

Gaunson: Was Henry a kind husband?

Evans: He was as far as I know.

Gaunson: You were intimate, you know, and you would know if he knocked her about with his hobnail boots? Did he do so?

Evans: Not that I know.

Gaunson: Did you ever notice anything unkind on her part or anything to show that she was wanting in her duty as a wife?

Evans: Well, on one occasion about the middle of 1886, returning home from work with Henry Needle I found her at my house and I thought she ought to have been at her own house getting her husband's tea.

Gaunson: Do you mean to say you come here to tell the Court that this is the only instance of unkindness on her part that you remember?

Evans: Well, not exactly unkindness.

Gaunson had now had enough of Evans. In more modern times, Evans may have even attracted the label of 'male chauvinist'.

Gaunson: You can get out of the box so far as I am concerned. I don't want to ask you any more questions … Was she ever in love with you?

Evans: Not that I know.

The stylish but deadly Martha Needle.

Martha Needle's stark mugshots – taken on the day of her dramatic arrest.

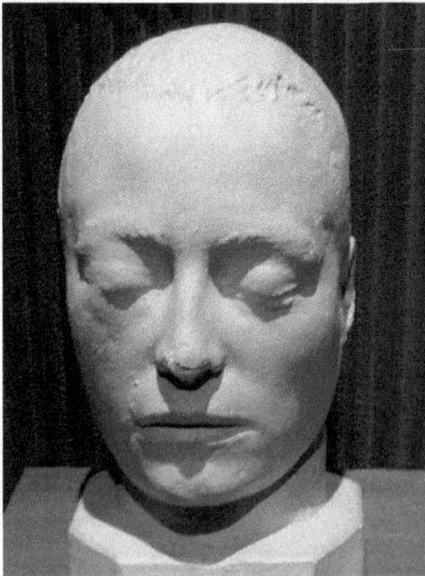

The haunting death mask of Martha Needle – still on public display today.

The soon-to-be unhappy couple – a posed photograph of Martha and Henry Needle taken shortly after they were hurriedly hitched.

A rare photograph of the infant Mabel Needle, taken at the Hammer and Co Studios in Rundle Street Adelaide, whilst Henry and Martha Needle were still residing in South Australia.

The power of the camera – a classy snapshot of Martha Needle taken at one of her favourite local studios.

A sketch of Henry Needle, circulated after his untimely death.

The Needle family's rented residence at 110 Cubitt Street – it proved to be the unluckiest house in Richmond.

A studio print of the youngest and ill-fated Needle children – May (left) and Elsie (on the right, holding the hoop). This eagerly-sought image was ultimately distributed throughout the world.

Otto Juncken, the man destined to become the last target of Martha Needle's affections.

Detective Robert Fryer, who rose to prominence on the back of the Martha Needle case.

1.—Dr. M'Coll.　2.—The Late Louis Juncken, Whose Death is the Subject of the Inquiry.　3.—Mrs. Needle, Sketched in Court.　4.—Mr. Otto Juncken.
5.—Mrs. Needle (From a Photograph by Thompson and Co., Royal Arcade).

An artist's impression of a chilling scene - the exhumation of the Needle family at Boroondara General Cemetery.

The plush environs of Melbourne Gaol – Martha Needle's final accommodation.

A portrait of Martha Needle, highly circulated at the peak of her infamy .

A woman under intense scrutiny - the uncomfortable Martha Needle in court.

Defence lawyer David Gaunson, who fought valiantly to save Martha Needle's life.

The celebrated Dr William Boyd – his vigilance finally shed light on Martha Needle's devious activities.

The imposing Supreme Court building in Melbourne, as it stood in the days of Martha Needle.

The solemn and business-like entry for Martha Needle in the 'Particulars of Executions' book.

The gaol mugshot of Martha Needle's assistant executioner Robert Gibbon, aka William Smith... proof that sometimes you can judge a book by its cover.

The Needle family's infamous gravesite at Boroondara General Cemetery, as it looks today.

The marker stone for Martha Needle's final resting place − it was later transported from Melbourne Gaol and is now at Brighton beach.

Those in court burst into laughter at Evans' final cringing response. He left the witness box and returned to well-earned obscurity, forever damning Martha for not getting her husband's tea in a timely manner. Evans had aimed low and missed, all the while catapulting his credibility to new levels of weightlessness. It was never explained why Martha had been at Evans' house in the first place.[102]

In an unusual move, a witness from a previous day was then recalled. It was Herbert Streeton, the assistant to the entertaining chemist Benjamin Baker. By now Gaunson was beginning to focus on the bismuth that had been prescribed, more specifically on the possibility that this substance itself had been contaminated.

Streeton began to methodically recite the supplied prescriptions again in strictly clinical terms, prompting the impatient Gaunson to cut straight to the chase and say, 'Mr Streeton, give them in English'. Streeton simply answered 'Bismuth'. Not wanting the moment to pass unnoticed, Gaunson then said with considerable irony, 'I thought we would get to the bismuth' before immediately asking the loaded question, 'Is that the leading contaminant?'

But Streeton refused to be bluffed any further. He referred to a respected English reference, the *British Pharmacopoeia*, which cited that commercially available bismuth was 'practically pure'. When Gaunson asked, 'You never tested it?' Streeton logically replied, 'No. If we tested everything in the shop, we would be at it all day long.'

But it was Streeton's last word on the matter that resonated most powerfully around the court. When asked by Finlayson during re-examination, 'So far as you know, there is no arsenic in bismuth?' he replied emphatically, 'No'.

With his definitive words, Streeton had effectively squashed Gaunson's arguments about bismuth and the potential for contamination.[103] The shrewd lawyer would need to find different angles to explore.

CHAPTER 19

It Pays To Be Insured

Questions relating to the world of insurance are rarely the most uplifting topics that can appear before a court of law. But this all changed when Martha was involved.

A series of commercial-based witnesses would now appear, all providing exhibits and carefully catalogued items of correspondence – each one inevitably adding a piece to the puzzle about how Martha had insured those closest to her and then managed to procure the resulting financial proceeds after tragedy struck. Although these were witnesses who would normally light up a room by leaving it, this time those in court were captivated by every word they uttered and every damning document they tabled.

First was John Donaldson, the Secretary of the Australian Widows' Fund Life Assurance Society. He indicated that Henry's life had been insured for £200 and that the initial application had come from the town of Warragul. He naïvely explained that he didn't know whether Henry had taken out the policy entirely 'on his own notion', or whether his loving wife had suggested he insure his life. The answer to this question was becoming more self-evident.

Donaldson confirmed that the first premium payment had been punctually made on 16 June 1889, at which time Donaldson believed

Henry was residing again at Cubitt Street.

Upon Henry's untimely death, the amount of the claim had been paid over to the Trustees Executors and Agency Company, under Administration. The accountant from this company, John Ariell, was next to step into the spotlight of fleeting fame.

From the witness box, he crunched the numbers. Although two-thirds of Henry's estate had been kept in trust for his surviving two children, Martha had managed to get hold of the remaining one-third by way of an uncrossed cheque, the ease of such a transaction even seeming to surprise Gaunson. He said to Ariell, 'I see it is marked "pay cash"' to which Ariell explained, 'Yes, we open all our cheques in that way and she would get the cash'.

Of course, that wasn't the end of Martha's windfall, with Ariell meticulously tabling details of all the other cheques being made out to her upon the deaths of her children, Elsie and May. All up, with expenses taken out, Martha had pocketed a sum amounting to £194 from the Trustee. Exclusive of the value of Henry's work tools and clothes that had to be sold, her cash 'profit' had been no less than £188.

Gaunson tried to use these figures to his advantage:

Gaunson: As a matter of fact, supposing the woman were engaged in a nefarious plot to take away the man's life, she might be doing a foolish thing, for if there were a will she might not get a penny?

Ariell: Yes.

Gaunson: And as there were children, she would get only a few pounds?

Ariell: Some £61 odd.

Gaunson: So the woman would be engaged in taking away a man's life for £61?

Ariell: Yes.

Gaunson: The total payments, exclusive of the value of tools or

clothes, and leaving out your expenses, I make out to be
£188, 10 shillings and 8 pennies, so that would be murder
at the rate of about £62 per head?

Gaunson's attempt to massage the figures fell flat. It had already
been clearly established that Henry had not left a will, so making the
suggestion that Martha was too simplistic to know about this looked
disingenuous. And although his catchcry of 'murder at the rate of
about £62 per head' had been designed to downplay the financial
implications, the opposite effect emerged.

This amount of money was still considered substantial and such a
quote could not dispel the theory of an evil person acting for reasons
other than money. Much to Gaunson's chagrin, 'Murder at £62 per
head' was now destined to become a catchy newspaper headline *against*
the case of his renowned client.[104]

Those in court next heard some brief evidence from three
representatives of the banking sector – all helping to outline Martha's
rather diversified approach to her finances. Most significant of all was
Robert Summers, the manager at the Savings Bank at Richmond. He
testified knowing Martha, who had opened an account at his bank. For
a number of years, she had been in the habit of cashing large cheques
at this institution and departing immediately with her bounty onto the
local streets.[105]

On that lucrative note, the court adjourned until the next day, at
which time those lucky enough to gain a seat would hear more about
Martha's escapades into the world of insurance.

Premium Discussions

When the court resumed on Wednesday, 1 August, the first witness
called was John Holt, the suburban insurance agent who had peddled
a multitude of insurance policies to Martha on behalf of the grandly
titled Temperance and General Mutual Life Assurance Society Limited.

A quarrelsome type, Holt was prepared to clash heads with the equally forthright Gaunson, so fiery scenes would soon erupt.

Holt immediately recognised the photographs of the children, Elsie and May, going on to explain that he had insured each of their lives for £5 in separate policies. The diligent Martha paid the premium right up until the death of Elsie, with her last payment being made only two days before the death occurred. Her presence of mind while tending to a dying child and another toddler had indeed been admirable. Upon Elsie's passing, Martha not only received the £5 but she also received an additional 11 shillings in endowment.

After Elsie's death, Martha followed Holt's advice and kept up the one penny a week premium payment that she had been making when both children were alive. This allowed her to load up with an additional life insurance policy on May. After being notified of the death of May, Holt paid the claim. All up, this time Martha pocketed an additional sum of £7 and 10 shillings. And no warning bells rang.

As a man who was effectively visiting Martha and her children every week to collect his penny premium, Holt was in a good position to comment on her evident treatment of them. When Gaunson asked him, 'Did you ever see anything wrong in the prisoner's treatment of her children?' Holt readily replied, 'No, they were always clean and nice when I saw them'.

But under the weight of the case's publicity, it soon became apparent that Holt's opinion of Martha had now changed. As the questioning became more targeted and aggressive, he began to glare towards her in the witness box and answer the questions in a defiant tone, as if justifying his own position.

Much to the discomfort of Holt, Gaunson was quick to allude that this purely profit-driven approach to insurance could lead to haphazard results. All the hallmarks were there – desperate door-to-door salesmen willing to hawk their products to anyone, very little regard given to the suitability of the products sold or their associated risks and, worst of all, little or no investigations made before settling claims.

Gaunson: You go around pointing out the advantages, I suppose. In fact, you are prepared to insure their lives on the shortest notice.

Holt: We are very glad to do business whenever we can but I am very glad I did not take one that I wanted – and that was Henry Needle.

Gaunson: Did you insure his life?

Holt: No – but I wanted him to insure his life for the sake of his children and I believe it was in consequence of what I said to him that he did insure himself.

While giving this particular answer, Holt took it upon himself to glare accusingly at Martha, prompting Keogh to make a rare interjection and warn, 'That will do, Mr Holt'.

But Gaunson was never going to let the matter rest there.

Gaunson: You would make a nice juryman in this case, would you not? It shows your Worships that this witness has made up his mind that Henry Needle died from some illegal causes. It shows how the newspapers have already tried this woman. [To Holt] Yours is a nice little thriving institution, I suppose, but it requires some little care to make ends meet? You are the Adam who tempted Eve, it seems. It was you who wanted them all to insure?

Holt: I believe I asked them.

By this time, any hope of a useful rapport existing between the increasingly desperate Gaunson and the unyielding Holt had disappeared completely. There was only arguing and one-upmanship left, which ultimately even embroiled the presiding Magistrate – who

Gaunson would then also turn upon mercilessly.

Gaunson: Did you see them [the Needle children] in bed while they were sick?

Holt: I do not think I did. I have no recollection of it.

Gaunson: If she swears you saw the children ill in bed, will you contradict her?

Holt: I say I have no recollection of it.

Keogh: Mr Gaunson, this appears to be a waste of time.

Gaunson: Your Worship has no right to address me that way. I say it is not a waste of time. This woman's life is not in your hands and the responsibility rests with me. I am prepared to go on for two hours if necessary …

Holt: I say I have no recollection of seeing them.

Keogh: There, you have the same answer again, Mr Gaunson. He has answered you several times.

Gaunson: If your Worship interrupts me in this manner, I will throw up the case. It is most improper.

Keogh: I cannot help that, Mr Gaunson.

Gaunson: I am trying to refresh his memory and you interrupt me.

Keogh: Then suggest some facts to refresh his memory.

Gaunson: [To Holt, very energetically] If this woman swears you did see the children while they were ill, will you contradict her?

Holt: Are you addressing me, Mr Gaunson?

Gaunson: Yes, I am.

Holt: Then address me respectfully.

Gaunson: I am addressing you energetically and I want an answer. If this woman swears you did see the children while they were ill, will you contradict her?

Holt: If she says I saw them more than once while they were ill, I will contradict her – but I have no recollection of seeing them even once.

And so, it went on ...

By this time, the increasingly hostile demeanour of Gaunson was becoming a story in itself. And, not surprisingly, he wasn't receiving favourable reviews from the very arms of the media he had seen fit to attack. That evening, a reporter from the *Herald* newspaper took delight in reporting: 'Mr Gaunson and Mr Keogh P.M. had a slight "breeze" in the court this morning. Mr Gaunson also fell foul of one of the witnesses. Likewise, he continually abused the newspapers; but as that has now become monotonous, no one heeds it.'[106]

As Holt's cross-examination was coming to a close, Gaunson chimed in with a different line of questioning:

Gaunson: At one time in your examination, you said you were very glad that you did not insure Henry Needle's life. What did you mean by that?

Holt: Well, that I was very sorry that I have to be in this at all. It is very unpleasant having to come here and if I had insured Needle's life I should have been worse in it than I am.

Gaunson: Then you have a singularly infelicitous way of expressing yourself.

Holt: I beg your pardon.

Gaunson: Don't.

Holt vacated the witness box.[107]

Friendly Fire

The next witnesses – Martha's acquaintances from the Richmond area – were able to provide considerable background information about her. While, as expected, most of this evidence was favourable, there were still some very worrying implications raised.

First was the motherly Hannah Tutt, now a restaurant keeper in

North Melbourne. Tutt had continued to have contact with Martha and her 'fine, healthy, pretty children'. She retold the story of how she had seen Martha only a fortnight after Henry's death and, after expressing her sympathy, was surprised when Martha told her she was not sorry he was dead because he had not treated her well.

Martha had then told Tutt that on one occasion when Henry was supposed to be working in the country, he had backtracked and stayed at his brother's house nearby. He had waited there until evening and then at 7 p.m. had burst back into the house at Cubitt Street, presumably expecting to find Martha in a compromising situation. But Henry's plan was foiled, because Martha was simply getting ready to go out with some friends. According to Martha, this still didn't prevent Henry from later 'ill using' her after she had returned home.

Martha also complained to Tutt that her husband was very wilful and would not take nourishment when he was ill. When Tutt suggested to Martha that it was a pity that Henry had not made a will, Martha explained that she had asked him to do so but he was too stubborn to comply with her requests. Tutt would go on to tell Gaunson that her only visit to the Needles' house had been when May was born, so Martha's revelations about her unhappy marriage had taken her aback a great deal.

It was now time for Gaunson to get to the nitty-gritty – he even asked a few questions that bordered on being scandalous:

Gaunson: Do you remember whether the accused told you in whose favour she wanted him to make a will?

Tutt: I don't remember.

Gaunson: Did you hear it from her or that redoubtable gentleman and caretaker of convicts, Owen Evans?

Tutt: I heard it from her. I know Evans. He boarded with me at the time Henry did.

Gaunson: Do you know whether there was anything between him and the accused?

Tutt: I do not and don't think there was.

Gaunson: I should hope not – but I thought it right to ask you. Did you understand that there was no impropriety in her arranging to go out with friends, when she believed her husband was away?

Tutt: I did not understand that there was any impropriety.

Gaunson: You saw the children frequently. Were they kindly and tenderly kept?

Tutt: Very – I never saw children more nicely kept.[108]

As a person who had known Martha for most of her life, the next witness, Mrs Eliza Martin, was one of the best placed to provide an insight into Martha's personality. She would prove to be an enlightening witness, providing the human background story of Martha, in contrast to the many blunt and unfavourable facts that had been aired in court to that time.

Although due to the nature of her deeds, Martha was bound to be a private person, she had developed enough trust in Martin to confide in her every now and again about what she was thinking – whether that be good or bad. While Martin could scarcely have qualified as a tell-all bestie, in the shrouded world of Martha she was the closest thing to it.

On a few occasions, Martha had confided in her that Henry had been 'very unkind' to her and had 'knocked her about' while they were living in Cubitt Street. Martin also knew the Junckens, although she had not known Louis very well. Her main memory of Louis was listening to Martha complain about him, telling her he was unsociable and how he would move about his place without taking any notice of her. For good reason, Martin also recalled having a conversation with Martha about Louis' mother. One day, Martha had arrived at her place in a very excited and angry state, declaring that she would kill Mrs Juncken.

At this stage, the ordeal of giving such evidence began to take its toll on Martin. She started to cry and almost broke down completely. She was accommodated with a glass of water, before composing herself sufficiently to continue. Finlayson initially asked her only one question – 'What else did she say about Mrs Juncken?' – to which Martin responded, 'She said she would kill Mrs Juncken if she walked all the way to Lyndoch to do it'.

It was now Gaunson's turn to re-examine the witness and he was determined not to let slip such an opportunity. He knew that this witness could not only provide valuable information about Martha's childhood and dysfunctional upbringing but could also shed light on her unusual behaviour as an adult.

Gaunson: You have known this woman all her life and I think you can give us some information which can do her a great deal of good. Did you know her mother?

Martin: A woman who was supposed to be her mother.

Gaunson: What was the name of this supposed mother?

Martin: Mrs Mary Foran.

Gaunson: Do you know in what way did her supposed mother treat her?

Martin: Very unkindly.

Gaunson: Did she beat her?

Martin: Yes.

Gaunson: Did you ever see her tie her up and thrash her?

Martin: No – but she has told me she did and I have seen the mother running after her with a stick.

Gaunson: And you have reason to believe that this home was particularly wretched?

Martin: Yes … Mrs Needle told me she was not her mother. She said her mother died when she was born and Mrs Foran was only taking care of her.

Gaunson: Had you any other reason for believing Mrs Foran was not her mother?

Martin: Well, Mrs Foran was kinder to the two boys [Martha's stepbrothers] than she was to Mrs Needle.

Gaunson: Did you ever see Needle ill-treat his wife?

Martin: I saw him strike her a blow which was sufficient to bring water to her eyes and also strike her on the side with a piece of wood. That was just before the birth of Elsie. She told me that once in Cubitt Street he knocked her about and caused a premature birth of a child. She was always kind to her children. She was very proud of them. After the death of the children, she went to the Junckens' place. After that, I remember her coming to my place at night-time, with Otto following her. She came twice in that way at night. On one of these occasions, I was in bed and it was pretty late – about midnight. On the other occasion, it was about seven or eight. On these occasions she talked very wildly and on the time when she came so late at night I had great difficulty in persuading her to come inside. She said she was going to Kew cemetery to the childrens' grave …

At this point, Martin again became very much affected before soldiering on. She took a big breath before further explaining Martha's frightening behaviours when struck down by her fainting fits. But, significantly, she also declared: 'She has been subject to these fits all her life almost – for a good many years at least. She has had these since she has been married but I do not recollect them occurring when we were children together.'

These comments reinforced the theory that Martha had displayed no evidence of epilepsy in childhood. The 'fainting fits' had evidently intensified as she increased her chlorodyne usage to deaden the pain of her marriage.

A Good Little Woman

Sensing Martin's sympathy for her old childhood chum, Gaunson saw this as a prime opening to pull a good reference for his besieged client.

Gaunson: Now, Mrs Martin, I am sorry to say that some efforts have been made by the newspapers to blacken this woman's character. So far as you know, was she a sober woman?

Martin: Yes, she was sober.

Gaunson: And a good little woman?

Martin: Yes, as good a little woman as I ever knew.

Gaunson: As to her treatment of her children, was she kind to them?

Martin: She was very kind and brought them up a credit to herself or a credit to any woman.

Gaunson: Can you account for Henry Needle's ill treatment of her?

Martin: Only that she told me he was jealous of her.

Gaunson: Did she ever give him cause to be jealous?

Martin: No. I have asked her what he had to be jealous about and she said nothing.

Gaunson: Have you ever heard her talk about her claim to some property?

Martin: Yes – but I took no notice of it.

Gaunson: You have very properly regarded it as moonshine but it is now important to know about it. I regarded it simply as lunacy. Was the conversation generally to the effect that her father had died, leaving her some property?

Martin: Yes – but that was only lately.

Gaunson: Was her statement not that her father was a man of property and that he died in England, leaving her money?

Martin: Yes, she said he died in England and left her, his only child, some property.

Gaunson: Was any amount mentioned?

Martin: Yes, £700.

Gaunson: What did you think of it?

Martin: I thought it was strange and hoped it might be true but I did not trouble much about it.

Gaunson: Did you notice anything else besides the fits about her?

Martin: She sometimes gets strangely excitable.

Gaunson: What is the reason for that?

Martin: She said it was caused by pains in the head. Two or three times she said, 'Oh, these pains in my head. They will either kill me or drive me mad …' When talking in her fits, Mrs Needle rambled and appeared to be talking to her children, telling Elsie to take May's hand and take her to school and take care she was not run over. Among other things, she said, 'You will hit me once too often, Henry Needle'.[109]

It was significant that during the questioning of Martin, Gaunson had uttered the word 'lunacy' for the first time. And while Martin had hardly been a completely unbiased witness, she had been an important one. She was at least providing some corroborative evidence of Henry's perpetration of domestic violence. Martha had no reason to speak to her about this at the time she did and Martin was now saying she had directly witnessed some of the actions.

But Martin's lauding of her friend as a good little woman with superlative mothering skills nonetheless looked shallow – particularly as Martha was now heavily suspected of putting her own children in the ground.

Robert Robinson - The Nosy Neighbour

The next person called to the witness box was the enthusiastic former neighbour of Martha, Robert Robinson. He was destined to delight many of those attending court, although presumably not Martha or Gaunson, by spouting all sorts of information about Martha's personal life. He was also willing to 'name names' in the process, much to the agony of those on the receiving end of his so-called 'evidence'.

Robinson had known Martha for a little over nine years and, for some unstated reason, he considered himself the closest of confidants. He recalled that when he was first acquainted with them, the Needles had two children, Mabel and Elsie, and he saw the family frequently. He considered Mabel to be much healthier and stronger than Elsie but thought this was 'perhaps because she was older'. He recalled that when Mabel had died, Dr Elsner had 'certified to tumour on the brains'. Robinson then gave evidence about the marital state of the Needles, suggesting, 'At that time the husband and the wife lived on very good terms, so far as I know'.

But then Robinson began to notice a change. He keenly took up the story, again inadvertently confirming Martha's propensity for confiding in men other than her husband about her personal life:

> I remember the husband going to Adelaide on a visit and I had a conversation with Mrs Needle about him after his return. It was in my house. She was referring to Needle's treatment of her at the time. She was greatly annoyed at the manner in which he had treated her. She said he was suspicious of some impropriety between her and some man who was lodging with them at that time.

Other than Dr Hodgson, Robinson had been Henry's most frequent visitor during his final illness. Almost daily he would trek from Wellington Street to Cubitt Street to be by his former neighbour's bedside for extended periods of time. At that time, Robinson noted that Martha was nursing her sick husband. 'I thought Mrs Needle was most kind and attentive to her husband during his illness,' he added.

The seriousness of the matter suddenly struck Robinson the night before Henry died, when he went into his old neighbour's room and found him in a delirious state of mind. As Robinson explained:

> I was in the habit of visiting Henry Needle during the illness
> which preceded his death. My wife was alive then and the two
> wives were very intimate. I frequently spoke to Mrs Needle
> about her husband's illness but on the night before his death
> she told me his illness was likely to be fatal, as Dr Singleton
> had visited him a day or two previously and said to him that
> he could not live.

Even though he departed for Morwell with his wife and family on the
next calendar day after Henry's demise, this was certainly not the last
time he would see Martha. He explained how Martha would regularly
endure considerable inconvenience and expense to visit his family
and stay for a few weeks at their new country abode whenever the
chance arose.[110]

Hired Help

With Robinson's words still ringing in the ears of spectators, the
next witness was called – Georgina Lillis, the woman who had been
employed by the Junckens as an additional housekeeper when Martha
had apparently been too ill to complete her duties. Lillis recalled that
she had initially stayed about two months at the house and helped to
look after the boarders. Lillis had also become quite close to Martha
throughout this time, close enough to also be regularly told by Martha
about the mistreatment her former husband and Louis had dished out
to her.

But Lillis' most memorable observation of Martha related to her
poor health and the fainting fits she used to take. 'She would very often
go into these fits in bed,' she told the court. 'The first time I saw her in
one I ran down and told Louis as I was afraid. He told me I need not
be afraid as she was often in them and to put her to bed.'

And what was the nature of these 'fainting fits'? Lillis explained: 'Sometimes she would have two faints a day and some days she would be free of them. I would not have any warning when these attacks came on … I have heard her speak of her children during these fits. You could barely understand what she would be saying but you would hear the names Elsie and May … They would last sometimes 10 minutes, sometimes 20 minutes and at times an hour.'

In terms of Martha herself, Lillis remained a friendly witness, remarking, 'There was nothing in the conduct of that household that was in the slightest degree objectionable. The accused seemed to me to be a person of character.' Turning directly towards Martha, Lillis then continued, 'She frequently complained of headaches and I have noticed her put her hand to her head as though suffering from headaches when she complained. I have noticed her do the same thing in court. She used to say, "My head is dreadful".'[111]

The Police Contribution

As Lillis left the witness box, Martha's headache was about to get a lot worse. The next witness was one of the most prominent in the case and would ensure that she was no longer in friendly territory. It was Detective-Sergeant Alfred Whitney. Well versed in the strategies of the courtroom, Whitney was more than capable of matching legal wits with the wily Gaunson.

Although there was little court time left for that day, Finlayson was anxious to have as much of Whitney's testimony heard as possible. And hopefully to have it delivered without being constantly interrupted by Gaunson.

After being sworn in, Whitney settled in for the fight and began to methodically tell his version of Martha's arrest, a well-known tale that had already done the rounds of all the newspapers. Although most of the ghouls present in court could probably recite this story word for word, the retelling would now be subjected to Gaunson's cross examination.

The first controversy emerged when Whitney discussed the official 'warning' he had provided to Martha. According to his prodigious recollection, he had said, 'This is a very serious matter. Be careful what you say, as what you do say may be used for or against you in this case.' Gaunson sprung to his feet to interject during Whitney's detailed run-through. He protested in a formal way that Whitney had not warned his client in a 'fair and square' manner. Whitney should also have told Martha that she did not have to answer any questions. While theoretically correct, Gaunson appeared to be clutching at a minor technicality and his argument did not gain a great deal of traction.

Still perfectly composed, Whitney continued to present his evidence. He explained how Martha had agreed that she had given Herman the relevant cup of tea. She had then pointed out the kettle from which she had taken the water, as well as the tea and sugar she had used.

Blessed with a superb memory, he also confidently remembered asking Martha, 'Have you got any poison in the house?' to which she said, 'Yes, I have got chlorodyne.' While he was looking through a cupboard, Martha had allegedly said to him, 'You can search away – you will find nothing'.

All the while she had remained seated on a chair and, in Whitney's eyes at least, looked perfectly calm. He did not detect the slightest appearance of fainting. Whitney found the box iron and inside this iron he found a wooden box of 'Rough on Rats'. This box was now exhibited in court. He reassured the court that the box was in the same condition as when he had seized it.

With little court time remaining for the day, Whitney was able to answer some questions from Finlayson about the exhumations he witnessed at Lyndoch and Kew. The court was then adjourned. Gaunson's much-anticipated cross-examination would need to wait until the following morning.

CHAPTER 20

The Final Day

Friday, 3 August 1894, was now shaping up to be one of the most dramatic days in the history of Australian criminal proceedings. Not only would Whitney face a full-barrelled cross-examination from Gaunson that morning but the only other remaining witnesses to be heard by the Police Court were also highly significant – Robert Fryer, James Neild and Cuthbert Blackett.

And if all the evidence could be put forward by the end of the day, there was a high likelihood that the Magistrate would reach a decision that very afternoon – either dismissing the initial case against Martha and allowing for her release, or sending her on to the Supreme Court for a full murder trial.

The large group of onlookers fortunate enough to gain admission were dismayed when Martha occupied a seat where she was partially obscured by the Court's clerk, meaning that very few of the 'spectators' could actually see her.

From his very first question to Whitney, Gaunson was subtly on the attack. 'You have not omitted anything of importance?' Unclear about Gaunson's intentions, Whitney answered guardedly.

Whitney: I may have omitted something.

Gaunson: Did anything happen in the house or in the yard that you have not mentioned?

Whitney: Not to my knowledge. If you mention anything, I may remember.

Gaunson: You remember taking a bucket out to the yard for her to vomit in?

Whitney: Yes, she was about to be sick and if she did retch I wished to take possession of the vomit.

Gaunson: Oh, that was very thoughtful of you. Was it dry retching or vomiting?

Whitney: There was no vomit. It appeared to me to be dry retching.

Gaunson: You asked her if she had taken anything. Perhaps you thought she would be likely to frustrate the end of justice? Did you say, 'Have you taken potent poison'?

Whitney: I asked her what she had taken.

Gaunson: When in the yard, did she say, 'I would be more likely to poison myself than anyone else'?

Whitney: No, not in the yard. She said that upstairs and I mentioned it in my evidence ... I recollect what took place. One thing I left out is I took her away in a [horse-drawn] cab.

Gaunson: You wouldn't take her away in your arms and walk her around the streets like you have recently when bringing her from the jail. You were in a terrible state when you asked if she had taken anything?

Whitney: I was anxious that she would not commit suicide while in my custody.

By raising a series of technicalities and personal asides against Whitney, Gaunson was clearly hoping to ruffle the detective – perhaps even intimidate him. If he could get Whitney angry enough, the experienced walloper might even say something in retaliation that could later be used against him. But Whitney was far too controlled to fall for these types of sucker punches.

Gaunson: If she says that she told you there was poison in an iron on the cupboard and pointed to it, will you contradict her?

Whitney: Yes. She did not say anything of the sort.

Gaunson: Weren't you standing on a chair?

Whitney: Yes. I had been standing on a chair for some time.

Gaunson: Of course, you were like a preacher at a revivalist meeting. [Laughter] She told you without the slightest trouble that she had purchased the 'Rough on Rats' at Richards, the chemist?

Whitney: Yes.

Gaunson: As a matter of fact, she answered your questions straightforwardly?

Whitney: Yes.

Gaunson: You knew this was a case of life and death for this poor creature?

Whitney: I did – and for that reason I was particularly careful.

Gaunson: No doubt you were, Whitney. Far be it from me to say anything else. When I do want to say anything about you, I will say it straight out. You have read in the newspapers what a splendid witness Herman Juncken was and how cool and collected he was?

Whitney: I have not read anything of his evidence in the newspapers. I have been too busy.

Gaunson: Yes, I suppose so since you gave them your portrait to publish. Do you know any reason why the accused was refused food from outside?

Whitney: I know nothing of what goes on inside the jail. It is a matter for the Governor of the jail.

Gaunson: Do you not know that people on remand are allowed to be supplied with food from the outside?

Whitney: I have heard they are supplied from the outside.

Gaunson: Why, every little boy in the street knows it. There must have been some reason for refusing it in her case. What was it?

Whitney: I only know that application was made to me by certain persons to supply her with food and I referred them to the Governor of the jail.

Gaunson: Come now, who was the person who made the application? We have no objection to it being known who it was. It is all to his credit. Was it the man she was engaged to be married to?

Whitney: It was Mr Otto Juncken. I have no feeling in the matter. I have supplied her with dinner myself every day she has been at the Court, at Mr Juncken's expense.

Gaunson decided to drop his attack over the catering arrangements.

Gaunson: Do you remember what took place and what you said when I applied for bail?

Whitney: I have a very clear recollection of every word I said. I gave evidence that I believed if she were admitted to bail she would commit suicide – and I believe so still.

Gaunson: She might, you believe, escape your clutches before you could give your portrait to the newspapers to publish in connection with the Supreme Court trial. Do you think sane people commit suicide? Have you had any experience of mental disease?

Whitney: I have seen a good many cases.

Gaunson: Cases of persons who have committed suicide?

Whitney: Yes. I believe more sane than insane people commit suicide.

Gaunson: The doctors are the only people who know anything about mental disease, you know, as they tell us. Have you heard them say after post-mortem that persons who committed suicide were insane?

Whitney: Yes but I regarded that as a bit of polish in most cases.

Gaunson: Then the medical men swore to what was untrue, just as a bit of polish?

Whitney: I don't say that.

Gaunson: How did the accused seem after you had searched the house?

Whitney: She seemed to feel her position very much at the end of the investigation.

Gaunson: Did she weep?

Whitney: No.

Gaunson: Herman Juncken says she did. Will you contradict him?

Whitney: If she did cry, I did not see it, I confess.

At this point, Gaunson could sense that he was unlikely to find a chink in Whitney's armour about all the minute details pertaining to Martha's arrest. He decided to alter the topic immediately to the arrangements put in place for the exhumation of bodies at Lyndoch and Kew. Gaunson began to point out the contradictions between the two sets of procedures. Why was no analytical chemist present at Lyndoch? Why were two doctors present at Lyndoch but only one at Kew?

Whitney had obviously anticipated this line of questioning and rehearsed a series of answers. He was able to take on board Gaunson's questions in one hit, providing a masterful response. 'There was no analytical chemist at the exhumation at the Lyndoch Cemetery but two medical men. The only reason why there were two medical men at Lyndoch and only one at Kew was that at Lyndoch the death was a recent one and at Kew the deaths occurred a long time before.'

Whitney further commented that this was his fourth poisoning case and recalled that one of the other three was an arsenic case. But Martha's matter was the 'largest' poisoning case that had occurred.

Gaunson decided to leave this topic alone. His other questioning continued:

Gaunson: You went to the jail to give the accused notice that it was the intention of the Crown to produce the evidence as to the exhumation and analyses in the Needle cases?

Whitney: Yes.

Gaunson: What was the reason for serving the notice on the accused and not on her solicitor?

Whitney: I served a notice on you as well and I served it on her.

Gaunson: What was the reason for serving this notice on the accused and not serving her solicitor with notice of the intention to do so, so that her attorney or someone representing him could also be present at the interview?

Whitney: I had no interview with her. I served the notice on her and she asked me to read the notice to her. I served the notice on you and also notices at the exhumation at the Lyndoch and Kew cemeteries, so that the accused could be represented by medical men if she chose. You knew of the exhumation and it was your duty to be present if you thought fit.

Gaunson: Now you think fit to put it forth that I have neglected my duty but I can afford that … And you know that medical men want fees to attend exhumations at 8 o'clock in the morning – you know what I mean?

Whitney: Yes.

Gaunson: Why did you not leave notice at my office that you intended to serve the notice on her?

Whitney: I did leave a notice at your office.

Keogh sensed that this stand-off between the two adversaries could end up going around in circles. He intervened and spoke to Whitney personally. 'Mr Gaunson wants to know why you did not give him notice of your intention to serve the accused personally. Did you do so?' Whitney replied simply, 'No, I did not'. But Gaunson was in no mood to let the matter rest:

Gaunson: [To Whitney] You have insinuated that I neglected my duty.

Keogh: I don't think so, Mr Gaunson. I don't think it would convey that impression.

Whitney: I would be very sorry to suggest anything of the kind about you, Mr Gaunson. I do not suggest it.

Gaunson: Very well, I apologise to myself and I apologise to anyone else when I think I am wrong. What I want to do is to protest against this iniquitous system of interviewing witnesses under cover of serving them with notices. What did she say when you served her?

Whitney: She said, 'Would you like the names of a few more of my friends with a view of taking them up?' I said no, I had quite enough at present.

Gaunson: Was that said jocularly?

Whitney: Neither she nor I took it jocularly in any way.[112]

Gaunson had now exhausted his line of questioning of Whitney. The experienced detective was excused from the witness box, knowing full well there was a high likelihood that the case would proceed to the Supreme Court and he would be required to cross swords with Gaunson again.

The next witness called was Whitney's colleague, Robert Fryer. As the more junior detective on the case, he may have been a prominent player during the sensational investigations but he would spend a surprisingly brief amount of time giving evidence.

Although Fryer wasn't in the witness box very long, he remained staunchly loyal to his superior. At one point, he simply said, 'I have heard Whitney's evidence about her arrest. It is quite correct.' About the only new observation he added was that he recalled seeing children's clothing both upstairs and downstairs in the house.[113]

The last two witnesses to be called were the men of science – James Neild and Cuthbert Blackett. They may have had differing personalities – Neild the eccentric showman and Blackett the studious analyst – but both would provide enough grisly details to enthral the court observers in attendance.

More importantly, both of these experienced witnesses would be crucial for completing the precise technical details of the case. They were both sure and definite in their testimony, moving away from subjective opinions, and they advanced the level of evidence to scientific facts.

The entertaining Neild went first. He immediately launched into a rapid and unsanitised description of exhuming the remains of Louis. This was the type of information that the gruesome audience was hoping to hear. He explained that the body was that of a solidly built, well-nourished man, but was much decomposed. Externally, Neild could not detect any recognisable indications of violence.

He further clarified:

> I examined the mouth … and found there no appearance of disease whatever. The brain was much decomposed – in fact, semi-fluid. The heart was perfectly healthy and showed no indications of disease … The mucous membrane of the stomach was reddened throughout and the larger portion of the smaller intestines was reddened in patches. The first portion of the large intestines was intensely reddened – of a vermilion colour.

Neild then outlined the actions he performed:

> I took one lung, the stomach, the small intestines, the last portion of the large intestine, the liver and the kidneys and I

placed these separately in jars supplied to me. Having placed the portions of the body in the jars, I saw the jars placed in a box and the lid of the box screwed down ... I delivered that box to Detective Whitney.

It took a while for those in court to realise that rapid-fire talker Neild had finished his speech. After a pause, it was left to the lawyers to move through the pertinent points, the prosecutor going first. None of Neild's matter-of-fact answers fell in Martha's favour, nor provided any relief to the original certifying Dr McColl.

Finlayson: From your examination, can you say what was the cause of death?

Neild: The opinion I then entertained was that the appearances found were consistent with death from an irritant mineral poison.

Finlayson: Did the appearances disclose that the deceased had died from endocarditis?

Neild: Not at all.

Finlayson: With references to the mouth, doctor. Did you particularly examine the gums?

Neild: I did.

Finlayson: Were there any appearances of disease there?

Neild: Not that I could discover.

Finlayson: Presuming that the result of the analysis of the parts you removed disclosed arsenic, and taking that in connection with what you observed, what, in your opinion, was the cause of death?

Neild: I feel certain death was caused by arsenic.

Scarcely taking the time to draw breath, Neild then moved on to describing the exhumation of the remains of Henry, Elsie and May

Needle in similar morbid detail.

As Gaunson stood and prepared to cross-examine Neild, he decided to focus heavily on each step of the autopsy process. Given that McColl had certified Louis died from endocarditis of the heart, the biggest concern for Gaunson was that Neild was now saying he had detected no disease of the heart at all.

Gaunson had obviously done his preparation, swatting up all he could about the anatomy of a human heart and how it worked. He began by asking Neild whether he had weighed the heart, measured its apex or taken the diameter of the valves. Neild replied quickly, 'No. I did not take any of these measures,' before adding rather bombastically, 'I have examined so many hearts that I know exactly what the normal conditions of a heart should be'.

Gaunson refused to be shaken off, asking Neild if he had examined the auricles of the heart. This time Neild agreed that he had – but he provided no joy for Gaunson when he made comments such as, 'It was perfectly healthy', 'There was no irritation whatever' and 'There was no perforation of any part of the heart'. When Gaunson probed further by asking, 'Did you look for it?', Neild shot him down with the snappy reply, 'What is the use of looking for a negative?'

The increasingly frustrated Gaunson moved on to the gums:

Gaunson: Did you examine the jawbone?
Neild: I cut down to it.
Gaunson: Did you lay it bare?
Neild: I did not dissect the jaw. There was no need for it.
Gaunson: That may be a matter of opinion with other men.

Gaunson began to read out a list of body parts that Neild had taken away from the autopsy, diligently writing each one down as Neild agreed he had removed it from the body. He stopped when he reached the brain, asking what became of it. 'The brain I left,' Neild stated, 'as there was no indication of any disease in it. I did not require the brain.'

Neild refuted McColl's rare 'diagnosis' of Riggs' disease, commenting that 'A good many things are called by names which they are not entitled to now'. And what about McColl's unwavering theory about the absorption of poisonous pus? Was it an irritant poison, as McColl initially stated? 'No, it is not' said Neild blankly. 'I have taught the subject for 29 years at the University and it is not an irritant poison.'

As part of his pre-trial research, Gaunson had procured a copy of Alexander Wynter Blyth's *Poisons: Their Effects and Detection*, a commonly used reference in its day. He now waved it in the courtroom, sparking an exchange with Neild.

Gaunson: Do you know anything about Blyth's book on poison?

Neild: Yes, I have heard of it.

Gaunson handed up the book, which was in turn passed to Neild.

Gaunson: See whether you can find any mention about putrid animal substances being irritant poison.

Neild: He puts it down here but I don't accept his dictum.

Gaunson: But this man prints it in a book.

Neild: All those big men print big books, which are absolutely worthless.

Gaunson: I hope when your books are printed they will not be useless!

Neild: Oh! I'm wise enough not to print a book. [Laughter] What are those words, 'Oh, that mine enemy would write a book. Where are they to be found again?' Some respected authority. It's something that they won't say about me, as I know better. [More laughter]

Gaunson: Well, we'll leave it to the medical profession as to who is an authority?

Neild: Oh, I don't set myself up as an authority – but I have consulted Dr Taylor.

Gaunson: Is Dr Taylor still alive?

Neild: No, he is dead. They say 'the good is oft interred with their bones' – Shakespeare says so.

Gaunson: Then Shakespeare is always right?

Neild: Not about poisons. [Laughter]

Gaunson: I am sorry Shakespeare's dead.

Neild: So am I. [Laughter]

While Neild's delivery amused all in court, Gaunson knew it was now time to return to the seriousness of the matter. Neild was there because of his extensive expertise, not as a stand-up comedian.

Gaunson: How many cases of poisoning have come under your notice – arsenical poisoning?

Neild: About 30, I should think. Some I have seen before and some after death. About two-thirds I saw after death.

Gaunson: I understand you form your decided opinion both as a result of your examination and what you have heard since as to the analysis?

Neild: Well, if I had no corroboration in the way of analysis, I should have felt – if you will pardon me the word – morally certain that death was caused by an irritant poison but being supplemented by the analysis makes me feel quite certain.

Gaunson moved away from the analytical and anatomical discussions, which weren't proving helpful to his client. Instead, he began to question Neild about the graveside press interviews he had seen fit to give. Neild acknowledged that he read all the newspapers and felt a compelling duty to participate in these exchanges. The first interview had been published in Adelaide and he recalled there had been some inaccuracies. As for those published in Victoria, they were largely correct, except for a few verbal errors that were not vital.

That completed Neild's evidence. After hearing macabre details about every body part imaginable (and at one stage even hearing detailed evidence from Neild about Louis' reddened rectum), those in court were instructed to adjourn for lunch.[114]

Paralysis By Analysis

The court resumed with the analytical chemist, Cuthbert Blackett, sitting sharply in the witness box. He provided a great deal of thorough technical information about the methods he had used to establish his findings. Under Finlayson's guidance, he was then able to go straight to the core issues.

Blackett explained that he had submitted the stomach and intestines of the late Louis to both an initial analysis and then a check analysis. The results were the same in both instances. To be precise, he had found 2.936 grains of arsenic in the stomach and intestines, 0.363 grains in the liver and 0.06 grains in the spleen and kidney. The heart and lung had given negative results but the quantity of arsenic obtained from the rectum was 0.04 grains.

With regard to the matter that Herman was said to have vomited, the results were even more dramatic. Blackett had discovered a considerable quantity of arsenic in it. More alarming still, the liquid in the cup of tea that Martha had poured out and handed to Herman had been analysed and found to contain 10.56 grains of arsenic. Although the newspapers had beaten him to it, Blackett noted that the type of arsenic found in this concoction was the same as that contained in 'Rough on Rats'.

In Henry's long-buried remains, Blackett had found 1.4 grains of arsenic. The quantity of arsenic found in Elsie's remains was too small to be determined – but it was there. May's body yielded 2.81 grains; spots containing yellow sulphide of arsenic were also present in the body's tissues.

In order to provide some perspective to the quantities of arsenic that Blackett was quoting, Finlayson asked a pivotal question: 'Can you say from your knowledge and experience what is a fatal dose of arsenic in an adult?'

Blackett replied: 'The minimum fatal dose is from $1\frac{1}{4}$ to $1\frac{1}{2}$ grains – but one grain is considered dangerous. 2 to $2\frac{1}{2}$ grains are considered fatal. In the case of children, a smaller quantity, of course, according to age and constitution.' And what did this translate to in this case? 'The quantity found in the portions of Louis would be fatal,' Blackett explained, 'but according to the opinions of toxicologists, the arsenic found is the surplus after the poison has done its work'.

Blackett's evidence had been distinct, unmistakable and objective. Upon his last words, Finlayson indicated that the case for the Crown had been concluded. All that was left now was Gaunson's cross-examination of the last witness.[115]

Under the weight of constantly working against compelling evidence, even the normally indefatigable Gaunson appeared as though he was beginning to tire. He spent less than half an hour cross-examining Blackett and his questioning darted from one topic to another.

Blackett agreed with Gaunson that his opinions were not based on medical training but he also asserted that he was 'relying on general analytical knowledge acquired by experience and reading'. He explained further that the first effort of any living organism would be to expel arsenic as rapidly as possible and that the levels of arsenic he had found in the victims' remains would not be all that was taken.

As one of the most rapidly absorbed poisons, arsenic might be diffused in the muscles, brain, bone or spinal marrow. It was also possible to absorb arsenic through environmental exposure, with Blackett agreeing that people could be poisoned by sitting in a room lined with arsenic wallpaper or 'by quacks putting ointment on a wound'. These were all interesting examples but none appeared to apply in the case of Martha.

Gaunson then moved on to the topic of equines, asking Blackett, 'Now, you know sometimes 10 grains of arsenic are given to a horse?' After a pause, Blackett answered, 'Yes, by foolish grooms and others, who do not know what they are doing'. Gaunson retorted, 'The woman who puts paint on her face or who dyes her hair is a fool?' 'So she is', answered Blackett.

Gaunson was still anxious to use the example of a horse being slowly poisoned. He asked, 'Supposing five grains of arsenic a day were given to a horse and at the end of the week that horse happened to die, and there was found in him sufficient arsenic to cause death if given one dose, would anyone say that horse died of arsenic?'

Blackett wasn't budging, simply answering, 'A toxicologist would, if he found arsenic there'.[116]

Gaunson then raised a bizarre story that had emanated from the Styrian peasantry (cited in the New South Wales arsenic case of Louisa Collins) – namely that arsenic needed to be taken during the full moon to be effective. 'That is all nonsense' sharply summarised a bemused Blackett.

This led to Gaunson's most precise question: 'What I want to get at is whether because of what is estimated to be a fatal dose was found in a body therefore it was administered in a fatal dose?' Blackett offered Gaunson no joy, answering, 'It is my opinion it would … the analyst would be right in concluding that death was caused by poison'.

That was the end of the evidence before the Police Court. Blackett – the 38th and last witness – was allowed to leave.

It was now time for the Magistrate to make his big decision – would Martha be committed for a full murder trial? Was the evidence sufficient at this stage to justify this action? There was ultimately no time wasted and a remarkably quick ruling would be delivered.

Firstly, the Magistrate was required by a mixture of law and custom to ask the accused if she wished to make a statement. Before this occurred, he also needed to read her a formal caution, namely that

241

she was not obliged to say anything but anything she did say could be used as evidence. Gaunson confirmed, 'She has nothing to say', just as Martha muttered 'No' in a firm voice.

Keogh then delivered his finding. He rejected Martha's preliminary case and she was then immediately committed for a full trial in the Supreme Court, where her life would well and truly be on the line. What's more, her trial was scheduled to commence on 15 August, less than two weeks away. Gaunson reserved her defence. Rather impetuously, Gaunson also reapplied for Martha to be granted bail but his brave application was immediately rejected.

It soon came to be understood that Gaunson — who had appeared for Martha in this 'court below' — would also undertake the onerous task of defending her in the Supreme Court. It was noted in the newspapers that Gaunson already had 'such a grasp of the case' that it would take another learned gentleman 'many hours of study and labour' to reach the same level of knowledge. Once again, the methodical Finlayson would appear as prosecutor for the Crown.

Gaunson in particular now had a lot of work to do. In the limited time available, he would need to analyse all the statements made in court, desperately looking for any contradictions that he may be able to exploit in the full trial. Finlayson also had his challenges, albeit in a different direction to Gaunson. With all the Police Court witnesses also bound to appear at the Supreme Court if required, he would need to ensure that no major cracks emerged in the Crown's case.[117]

This was a time when the prosecution reviewed its strategy for the upcoming battle. The lawyers and detectives involved were aware of the vagaries that juries could display when the accused was a woman. A decision was reached not to persist too obsessively with the *motive* behind Martha's alleged actions. With this in mind, it was determined not to revisit her financial inducements, meaning that none of the 'insurance' witnesses would be required to give evidence in the Supreme Court. This probably also suited Gaunson, who had little desire to reacquaint himself with the impossibly argumentative insurance agent John Holt.

As it turned out, Martha's Supreme Court trial would ultimately be delayed by mutual consent until the September sittings of the court. On 15 August, Gaunson appeared briefly before the Chief Justice and applied to have the matter adjourned until the last week of September; Finlayson offered no objection. Both men were obviously relieved that the adjournment was granted, given the amount of legal homework they needed to do. Inadvertently, Gaunson had also bought Martha another month of life.[118]

Meanwhile, Martha had stayed in the news – but for all the wrong reasons. Life-sized effigies of her suddenly began to appear around Melbourne, the most notable being in two separate shopfronts along the frenetic inner-city thoroughfare of Bourke Street.

As the legal advisers to the accused, the law firm Gaunson and Wallace immediately dispatched a letter to the Victorian Attorney General, stating, 'As by virtue of your office you protect as well as prosecute, we beg to ask your immediate intervention to stop this scandal'. To add to its impact, this letter was also handed over to the press, presumably by Gaunson himself.

A Crown Law Department officer was immediately dispatched to Bourke Street to make inquiries. While the power available to the Attorney General in such circumstances was regarded as doubtful, he indicated a willingness to legally interfere in the displays by making an application to the Supreme Court.[119] In the end, the effigies of Martha were taken down voluntarily.

Martha's Supreme Court trial was now ready to begin.

CHAPTER 21

The Supreme Court

Martha's final trial for the murder of Louis Juncken commenced on Monday, 24 September 1894. Proceedings took place at the gothic-looking Supreme Court building in William Street, Melbourne, which had first opened ten years earlier.

Already, the *Herald* newspaper was predicting that Martha's trial was 'likely to be remembered long as one of the most extraordinary on record'. The newspaper's editorial explained further, 'The case presents many interesting features, both from a medical and legal point of view, and will probably figure in the text books of each profession'. This prediction proved to be accurate.

The judge assigned to preside over the historic case was the grandiose and humourless 50-year-old Justice Henry Edward Agincourt Hodges. To dispel any doubt of the perils that Martha was potentially facing, only two years earlier Hodges had sentenced the notorious murderer Frederick Deeming to death, a punishment that was mercilessly carried out a few weeks later. It was said of Deeming at the time he dropped through the gallows that this had been the first time he went straight in his life.

Hodges came from a privileged background and a very different stratum of society than that occupied by Martha and many of the spectators who would soon invade his court. The son of a ship's captain, he had been born in Liverpool and arrived in Victoria with his parents at the age of ten. After attending a private school, he enrolled at the fledgling University of Melbourne and studied both arts and law, before establishing a substantial legal practice as a strong advocate. At the age of 45, he had moved to the other side of the bench to become a judge.

Although at the time he presided over Martha's case he had only been a judge for five years and was considered the judiciary's most junior member, Hodges was also one of the strongest, brightest and most opinionated. His flaws were his demeanour and his resentment over anything he perceived as impertinence. Hodges had developed a sharp and sneering manner in court and was criticised for his biting sarcasm towards barristers and any witnesses he thought had departed from the truth. He had already shown in the Deeming case that he was also cynical about prisoners who sought refuge and tried to plead 'insanity' to explain their crimes.

And, like Magistrate Keogh before him, Hodges would not hesitate to allow 'similar fact evidence' to be admitted during the trial.

The Usual Flurry

Once again, the cultish popularity of the Needle case prompted special arrangements to be put into place. The trial preliminaries were planned to commence at 10.30 a.m. on the opening day, with Hodges first taking his seat on the bench at 10 a.m. to sentence a couple of prisoners who had pleaded guilty in other cases. But it was 10.20 a.m. before the court even opened and the sentencing went right through to 11 a.m.

It had already been a testing day for Hodges. Not only did he need to adjust to the uncustomary crowd-control problems but one of the prisoners he had been required to sentence for robbery took advantage of performing before the unusually large crowd, impetuously yelling out his refreshing self-appraisal 'You might as well hang me' before the judge sentenced the habitual criminal to 12 years' hard labour, 30 days of solitary confinement and one flogging.[120]

In Martha's case, time then needed to be set aside to empanel a jury. This process began shortly after 11.15 a.m. In keeping with the requirements of the day, the jury would consist solely of men – at that time, women were not able to act as jurors. It literally had to be 12 'good *men* and true'.

From a very early hour that morning, a large crowd of 'certain classes of laymen' had eagerly waited outside the courtroom, hoping to gain admission. As soon as the doors were opened, every seat in the gallery was quickly filled, while court ushers tried desperately to ensure there was no jostling. In any event, potential jurors had already filled most of the seats on the floor of the court. Forty-three such men had already answered their names and been sworn in.

It was then time for the famous defendant to arrive. Martha entered the court from a side door, accompanied by a beefy female warder. As had been the case in the Police Court, Martha was dressed solely in black. She also wore a fashionable black hat.

A great deal of newspaper attention was again paid to her appearance and fashion sense. Many of the reports were contrasting and did not particularly comply with journalistic rigour.

The *Herald* noted: 'Towards the close of the long inquiry before the magistrates, the unhappy woman had become much thinner and looked more careworn. Today, if anything, she looked thinner than ever, and her incarceration and the mental strain had made her look more haggard ... She came with faltering step and appeared to have some difficulty in restraining sobs.' In keeping with this theme, the *Sydney Morning Herald* stated that 'The prisoner, who is very small in stature and of slight build, looked very ill and careworn as she was placed in the dock'. The word 'careworn' had obviously done the rounds among the reporters that morning.

In contrast, South Australia's *Advertiser* informed its readers that Martha 'was firm and composed and appeared improved in health' and the *Age* wrote that she 'appeared to be perfectly calm and collected'.

Irrespective of how she looked, Martha moved intently into the dock and sat down in the ordinary seat. She would afterwards be given a cushioned chair on which to sit, in lieu of the hard, box-like seat usually allowed. This was not only more comfortable but also enabled her to sit more forward and look over the ornate wooden bar of the dock. When the Court Associate read the presentment and asked Martha whether she wished to plead guilty or not guilty, she rose to her feet and said in an unfaltering voice, 'I am not guilty'.

She remained standing and leaned on the dock rails for support while the jurymen were being selected. Under the advice of a solicitor's clerk, she challenged sparingly, rejecting just five potential jurors in clear tones. The Crown ordered another six to stand aside before the final jury was speedily empanelled.

Even the melodramatic *Herald* was by now adjusting its initial observations of Martha, conceding that 'She had quite recovered her composure ... in fact, during the remainder of the morning, she was perfectly calm ... though when the first reference was made to her children, she took out her handkerchief and shed a few tears'.

Rightly or wrongly, some newspaper reporters were already trying to guess the likely notions the jurymen may hold according to their age and background. But this wasn't very helpful with this jury – they could best be described as middle aged, middle class and all residing in the middle Melbourne suburbs. The youngest man selected was at least thirty years of age and the oldest not more than fifty.

In keeping with the custom of the day during large and important trials, the 12 men set to decide Martha's fate were fully named and identified in the newspapers. These new-found luminaries were:

Albert W.H. Major, South Melbourne, foreman

James Mitchell, Balaclava, tram employee

Henry Harding, Prahran, tobacconist

Charles T. Mason, Windsor, ironmonger

Cecil Forrester, South Melbourne, actor

John Gordon, Carlton, driver

Patrick W. Ryan, Fitzroy, draper

Joseph Hutchinson, Brunswick, blacksmith

Edward Batty, Toorak, baker

William J. Wheeler, North Melbourne, carpenter

Samson Grattige, Balaclava, greengrocer

Thomas Douglas, Moonee Ponds, cashier

These men would not be allowed to go home until their function in the trial had been completed. Overnight they would occupy the jurors' quarters in the quadrangle of the courts. While this was hardly an exotic holiday destination, a newspaper report assured readers that the jurymen would be allowed all the indulgences that could be permitted in the circumstances.

Even at this stage, it was being predicted that their stay might not necessarily be a marathon one. Given the completeness of the evidence presented in the lower court, Finlayson was expressing a belief that a replay of such evidence could possibly see the trial finished within three days. Defender Gaunson saw it differently.

Once the jury had settled, it was time for the trial to begin. The first presentation would be the Crown Prosecutor's opening address and it was approaching noon before Finlayson rose to his feet and commenced his practised spiel. He would speak for nearly three quarters of an hour, methodically outlining Martha's personal history and all of the key points related to the case. It was largely a repeated summary of all the evidence that had been given in the Police Court, which was already very well known by the public.

More significantly, by this time Finlayson's courtroom style was standing in favourable contrast to the permanently abrasive Gaunson. The admiring *Herald* noted:

> Mr Finlayson's style is quiet and unassuming, but incisive – perhaps the more effective because of its very quietness … From all that appeared from his tone, Mr Finlayson might have been relating to the jury some of the most ordinary events of everyday life, instead of unfolding to them the story of what, if the contention of the Crown be correct, is one of the most extraordinary and sensational poisoning cases of modern times.

Otto Juncken, the man still seemingly supportive of Martha, was the first witness called. Despite his harrowing position, his clearness and modest manner in the witness box again impressed all courtroom observers, as had also been the case before Magistrate Keogh.

From the outset, the moralistic Otto was again determined to emphatically declare that there had never been 'anything improper' or 'wrong' between Martha and himself, either before or after their engagement. By 'improper' or 'wrong' he meant sexual.

Otto's evidence before the Supreme Court was spread over a number of hours but it was fundamentally the same as he had given before the lower court. But before he could be cross-examined by Gaunson, a noticeable problem had emerged with the uncouth crowd in the courtroom.

A number of women who had managed to secure seats in the front row were spending their whole time turning around and staring at Martha in the dock. Hodges would no longer stand for it. He announced, 'I must ask those persons not to turn around and stare at the prisoner. She is placed in a position of great peril and her mind ought not to be disturbed by persons staring at her … If anything of the kind occurs again, I shall have such persons removed from the Court.'

For the rest of the unfolding drama, these 'ladies' needed to be content with back seats. At least one newspaper was willing to offer a stereotypical explanation. 'A woman (in trouble or otherwise) does not object to the critical glares of men but she sometimes shrinks from the too keen and searching glares of members of her own sex.'[121]

While Otto was giving his evidence, Martha sat with her hat off and her head leaning on her arm, which in turn rested on the front rail of the dock. Although Gaunson's cross-examination of Otto largely went over the same ground as previously, the anxious fiancé was able to further emphasise that Martha had always seemed to have 'motherly love and affection' for her children. In response to Gaunson's questioning about whether Martha had been 'a proper living woman', Otto was only able to remark, 'I never had any doubt in my mind regarding that at any time'.

The only other witness to be heard on the first day – Dr Donald McColl – was then called. Given the tensions and professional rivalry between the medical men giving evidence at the Police Court, McColl would offer Gaunson an opportunity to introduce some new eye-openers to this trial.

Still smarting over comments made by Neild, McColl remained unshakable about his treatment of Louis for Riggs' disease. He was particularly insulted about not being invited to view portions of Louis' body brought over from Lyndoch. Even though Neild had previously sworn that no symptoms of jaw disease had been revealed during the post-mortem, McColl now sought to flatly contradict him.

McColl believed that the head of the deceased should also have been brought back to Victoria. This would have allowed the jaw to be fully dissected. Although conceding that the arsenic had killed Louis, McColl remained convinced that he had also suffered from Riggs' disease and that this would have been easily discernible if Neild had properly looked for it. On that gory note, the court adjourned until the next day.

The second day of Martha's fight for life began with the jurymen taking their seats punctually. They were said to be 'looking quite blooming' after their night in official custody. The press also noted that Martha seemed calmer this time around and sat up, taking a deep interest in the proceedings.

The day actually began with a request from the jury, although it was not related to a point of law – they simply wanted access to the daily newspapers. Hodges had no objections to the request but he warned them that they were not to read any reports about the Needle case.[122] Given the widespread reporting about Martha that had already occurred, this comment probably came a bit late. There would not have been much left to read.

Once the trial continued, a series of minor witnesses appeared in quick succession – nurse Clara Stevens, boarder Stanley Setford, chemist assistant George Miller and boot salesman Thomas Brittain. They were dispensed with efficiently – even the *Herald* newspaper indicated that their evidence had all been previously given before Magistrate Keogh. All four were examined and cross-examined within half an hour.

The only addition to the previous testimony came from the young carpenter Setford, who was still curiously trying to come up with some positive points to bolster Martha's case. He told the court he had once detected a foul smell at 137 Bridge Road and took up some floorboards to remove four or five dead rats – the implication being that this mini rat plague explained Martha's need for an urgent purchase of 'Rough on Rats'. But it didn't make much sense. Setford thought that this had occurred just prior to Christmas, whereas Martha's controversial purchase of the poison had occurred on 10 May.

The next three witnesses – Herman Juncken, James Neild and Cuthbert Blackett – were never likely to be disposed of so rapidly, with Gaunson seeking to target their previous evidence as exposing potential weak points in the prosecution case.

Herman went first and was led through his now familiar and

dramatic story. While his brother, Otto, had remained convinced that Martha's 'fits' were genuine, Herman told the court that he believed she was shamming. He had only seen her faint once and this was after he had spoken to her about leaving the house and seeking alternative employment.

In replicating his Police Court tactics, Gaunson's cross-examination opened on the question of motive. What reason would Martha have for wishing to do harm to Herman, a man with whom she had been seemingly friendly? Herman repeated his theory that Martha may have thought that by killing him and other members of his family she would be inflicting pain upon his mother. He could offer no other reason.

In response to Gaunson's questioning about the final cup of tea seized by the detectives, Herman told the court that he had taken a sip and the brew had a peculiar taste – 'sort of metallic, coppery' – and there 'was stuff like tea dust floating about the top'. Gaunson then delighted in telling the jury that arsenic 'has no taste whatever'.

Towards the end of his cross-examination, Gaunson also stumbled upon another contentious point. Through some means or other he had heard that Otto had found some pieces of bread and butter, liberally sprinkled with 'Rough on Rats', at the house at Bridge Road sometime after the detectives had left. He was now hopeful that Herman would corroborate this story.

When Gaunson queried Herman about this, he answered straightforwardly, 'I did not know that'. Gaunson intimated that he might have to recall Otto to the witness box to find out.

During the final stages of Herman's evidence, the jury intervened to collectively ask a question of its own, a relatively common occurrence during major trials at that time. They had a note passed to the bench, wanting to know if Herman had suffered any pain in his stomach before he vomited. He replied that he had not, 'only an empty feeling in the stomach, and a sort of nausea'.

Apart from the minor hiccup about the alleged bread and butter laced with 'Rough on Rats', the intelligent Herman had again provided consistent evidence. Like Otto, it was said that he came through the ordeal in a manner that impressed all who heard his testimony.

But Gaunson now wanted to keep the 'bread and butter' theme going. After Herman left the witness box, Gaunson proved true to his word and took the unusual step of recalling Otto to also quiz him about this point. Otto explained to him: 'After the prisoner was taken away from Bridge Road … I found pieces of bread and butter with some dark substance spread over them, lying in the dresser … The colour I saw on those was of a similar colour to "Rough on Rats". I left the pieces of bread and butter where they were.'

This potential revelation even aroused prosecutor Finlayson. After he sought more information, Otto explained to him: 'I found these pieces of bread and butter the Sunday evening after Mrs Needle was arrested. On the Wednesday – the day she was arrested – I did not make a thorough search of that dresser.'[123]

Otto's fresh evidence had raised a curiosity. Surely the detectives had closely searched the house both immediately after Martha's arrest and on subsequent occasions before sending her down for murder? In all of the copious documents and evidence being presented to the court, no mention had ever been made of finding pieces of bread and butter in the house, apparently sprinkled with 'Rough on Rats'. Such 'evidence', although flimsy and only relying on Otto's account, might at least provide some credence to Martha's story about why she needed to urgently buy the poison.

Was it possible that the detectives were selectively ignoring evidence? Was Otto now manufacturing a snippet of a story to shed a more favourable light on Martha's case? Or did Martha simply still have a sympathetic supporter, such as Setford, with access to the house, who was willing to plant some evidence to assist her cause?

Irrespective of the answer to the 'bread and butter' issue, as Otto left the witness box for the last time he knew he could no longer be of assistance to Martha in these proceedings. Her fate now rested elsewhere.

With the Juncken brothers now fully done, the next witness was called – James Neild. The medico's previous evidence was also likely to be targeted by Gaunson. In turn, the brilliant but idiosyncratic Neild was not the type to back down from an argument. This part of the trial promised to be lively, perhaps even somewhat ugly. Neild got right down to business, again scoffing at McColl's previous suggestions. He asserted that no signs of either Riggs' disease of the jaw or endocarditis of the heart were present in the body of Louis.

Shortly after Neild began to give his evidence, Martha appeared to give way to emotion for the first time that morning. The female warder standing nearby moved across and had a conversation with her through the bars of the dock before passing up a message to the bench. Hodges then called an adjournment to allow Martha to be removed from the court. Those nearby saw her trembling as she held her handkerchief to her face while being led out the court's side door. When Martha was returned to the court about a quarter of an hour later, she appeared to have regained her composure.

An explanation about what had upset Martha was given soon after. The seats at the back of the press box commanded a full view of the dock and had been invaded by inquisitive 'ladies'. While Hodges had rebuked some spectators the day before for staring at a woman 'placed in a position of great peril', this time he directly requested the sheriff to move the offenders to seats at the rear of the court. Some complied with the request. Upon being deprived of their spectator status, others decided to leave the court altogether.

Neild continued to give his evidence. But for such a credentialed witness, he also proved to be poorly prepared. He had arrogantly preferred to rely on his showmanship, rather than going to the trouble of reacquainting himself with what had already been said in the Police Court. This was an unexpected bonus for Gaunson.

Most of the controversy rested upon the parts of anatomy Neild removed from the corpse of Louis, with particular reference being made to the heart.

Gaunson: Did you hand Louis' heart to the Government Analyst?

Neild: No.

Gaunson: Are you positive?

Neild: Quite.

Gaunson: If the Government Analyst says he received the heart, would he be right?

Neild: I have no recollection of removing the heart.

Gaunson: You said you are so positive about it, just now, and it's upon the positiveness that this jury …

An increasingly agitated Neild cut Gaunson short and interrupted:

Neild: Oh yes! I know all about that. There is no need to go through all that. If I removed the heart, I have no recollection of so doing.

Gaunson took great delight in reminding Neild that in his previous evidence given before the Police Court, Blackett had referred to 'Jar Number 4' that was labelled 'Heart and Lungs'.

Gaunson: In your evidence, you say, 'I took one lung'. Which is correct?

Neild: It is correct that I took one lung.

Gaunson: And no heart?

Neild: Not to my recollection.

Gaunson: In the court below, I examined you as to whether you had weighed and measured the heart?

Neild: Yes.

Gaunson: Now, with your memory refreshed, are you able to say positively whether you took the heart?

Neild: I don't remember.

Gaunson then moved on to 'Jar Number 1', as quoted in Blackett's previous testimony, which purportedly contained Louis' 'Stomach and Intestines'. He also referred to a prominent textbook by Alfred Swaine Taylor, *On Poisons, in Relation to Medical Jurisprudence and Medicine.*

Gaunson: Taylor's *On Poisons* says the stomach should be removed and placed in a jar separate from the intestines.

Neild: So it was.

Gaunson: The analyst swears 'I examined jar Number 1, labelled Stomach and Intestines'. Which is correct?

Neild: If Mr Blackett says so, he is right. My recollection is that I put the stomach into a separate jar.

Gaunson: Then if that be so, it must have been interfered with.

Neild: I don't say that.

The argument hit a peak when Gaunson gestured towards Martha and began to inform the fractious doctor of some of his responsibilities. Gaunson had now well and truly managed to get under Neild's skin and the doctor would respond angrily.

Gaunson: You see it is upon the accuracy of your recollection, especially on the redness of the stomach, that the life of this poor creature depends.

Neild: I know that Mr Gaunson. Don't tell me that. It is only elocuting.

Gaunson: It is you who are elocuting.

Neild: I am not. I am the last man in the world to do so. I am only here to state facts and give opinions and I will do so.

After a pause, the moralistic Gaunson said, 'Don't think I intend to quarrel with you, doctor. We are only here to investigate the cause of death.' He then continued, 'I want to know if it is true that you did not place the stomach and intestines in separate jars'. The slightly rattled Neild could only reply, 'My recollection is that I placed the stomach in a separate vessel'.

The conversation then turned to the topic of Louis' head and jawbone. Although resolutely declaring there was no sign of Riggs' disease, why had Neild not dissected the jaw during the post-mortem, as Dr McColl had suggested? The increasingly agitated Neild gave an emphatic answer. 'I did not dissect the jaw, because as far as my examination went I was satisfied there was no disease of it. If you come to dissect a body, instead of taking two or three hours it might take a week.' Then Gaunson asked why the head was not removed and brought to Melbourne for examination.

Neild was no longer in the mood to tolerate Gaunson's cute little questions and unleashed a stinging speech from the witness box: 'I might as well have brought the whole body for negative diseases. My business was to examine the body to discover evidence of disease or evidence of poison … You have to remember that I was placed at a disadvantage in examining a body that had been dead six weeks and in which decomposition had been considerably advanced … In the examination I made, one of the objects was to determine with the greatest possible accuracy the cause of death. That is the object of all post-mortem examinations.'

Neild had made a good point. After all, it needed to be remembered that the analysis of Louis' body parts had also revealed enough arsenic to kill him.

As to the poison itself, Gaunson continued to delve into the possibility that it had been inadvertently introduced through adulterated prescriptions. He was particularly interested in the qualities of bismuth and calomel, both drugs being present in prescriptions given by Dr

Boyd to Herman. Although Gaunson's cross-examination of Neild on this topic was lively, it did not produce the answers that Gaunson was hoping for. Gaunson had hoped that these prescriptions may have explained Herman's symptoms and even been responsible for finishing off Louis in his weakened state. But all Neild would say was that these drugs were perfectly safe in medicinal doses.

Soon after, Neild was allowed to depart. He had turned out to be a poor Crown witness, at one time exclaiming during his evidence, 'I cannot quite remember what I deposed to in the Police Court. I have not read the depositions since.'[124]

In contrast, the next witness, Cuthbert Blackett, had certainly done his homework. He was able to provide meticulous details to Finlayson about the seven sealed jars he had received from Whitney and he knew exactly what was in each of them. He gave precise descriptions of the tests he had undertaken and clearly stated the quantities of arsenic found in each body and in the cup of tea Martha had generously prepared for Herman. None of this evidence was favourable to Martha's cause.

Gaunson had done his homework as well. With Blackett, he would try to move down the unlikely path that a massively unlucky environmental contamination might have occurred.

Gaunson: Is not arsenic extensively used in the manufacture of fabrics, colouring lollies, etc?

Blackett: It used to be but is not now, owing to the stringency of the *Health Act*.

Gaunson: Is it not a fact that there is an enormous quantity of wallpaper in which arsenic has been very largely used?

Blackett: It is used. Arsenic is sometimes mixed with the paste in paperhanging with a view to destroy vermin.

Gaunson: If Taylor's *On Poisons* says persons have been poisoned through keeping stuffed birds in rooms and inhaling the arsenic used in their stuffing, would you contradict this?

Blackett: I do not remember reading of a case in which persons have been poisoned by inhaling the arsenical dust from stuffed birds but if Taylor says so, I will not dispute it.

Gaunson: In cases where the life of a human being is concerned, do you not consider it a proper thing that all surroundings should be tested to see if there was any arsenic such as in the wallpaper, articles in the room, bottles and what not?

Blackett: I think that in all cases of this every possible precaution should be taken that can be found.

By this time, Hodges had heard enough of Gaunson's environmental theories about wallpaper and stuffed birds. In any event, it all failed to account for the multiple properties across which Martha had been potentially 'unlucky' – 137 Bridge Road *and* 110 Cubitt Street. Hodges squirmed and prepared to interrupt Gaunson's questioning.

Gaunson: Is it not a fact that an enormous number of poison cases occur to which no crime attaches?

Hodges: Are you asking the witness as an expert in criminal law?

Gaunson: I am asking if he is aware of it?

Hodges: How can he be aware of it?

Gaunson: There are statistics which make it plain.

Hodges: But as he did not prepare the statistics, I don't know upon what hypothesis those statistics are based.

Gaunson: [To Blackett] Has arsenic any taste?

Blackett: Yes, a slight sweetish taste.

This expert evidence contradicted Gaunson's previous unqualified declaration that arsenic has 'no taste whatever', so he wisely allowed Blackett's testimony to end on that note.[125]

From there, the witnesses rolled on in reasonably quick succession.

Chemist assistant George Miller informed Gaunson that upon opening a box of 'Rough on Rats', some of it would inevitably fly away. He used the example of taking it down to smear on bread and butter – in such circumstances, some of it was likely to spill.

Dr William Boyd denied that anyone else had suggested to him that poisoning was involved. But he did concede that Thomas Smith had told him 'something with respect to the case' and from that point he gave directions that Herman's vomit was to be preserved.

Right on cue, the next witness was Thomas Smith, who largely confirmed all that Boyd had said. Then came Pharmacy College caretaker Joseph Lowry, analytical chemist William Wilkinson, undertaker Herbert King and the Junckens' brother-in-law, John Jones, all of whom were quickly dispensed with before the court adjourned for the day.[126]

Gaunson and Martha had started the day from a low base – and their position had not noticeably improved.

CHAPTER 22

A Trial to Watch

Day Three of the trial commenced with Martha reportedly looking well. She was outwardly calm and she sat in the dock with her hands crossed on her lap. The *Herald* informed its readers that the 'little hysterical trouble' of the previous day had passed, although Martha still held a handkerchief in one hand 'in case her feelings should get the better of her'. At least this time there were no 'ladies' seated immediately in front of the dock glaring at her, with such people being relegated to the back of the court.

As one reporter put it, the first witnesses of the morning were 'speedily polished off' by Finlayson and Gaunson. Richmond chemist Benjamin Baker, South Australian graveyard labourer Herbert Engel and Boroondara General Cemetery caretaker Thomas Whitelaw gave similar evidence to that provided to the lower court and they were permitted to leave after merely formal cross-examination.

Gaunson detained the next two witnesses – Hannah Tutt and Robert Robinson – in the box a little longer. Given that Tutt had been on visiting terms with Martha, Gaunson sought to add a personal touch by having her repeat her previous statements that the Needle children were 'nicely, cleanly and tenderly' kept by their mother. Indeed, according to Tutt, she knew of no woman who performed her maternal duties with more kindness than Martha.

From Robinson, Gaunson was able to extract an opinion that Martha was also invariably kind to her husband, at least as far as Robinson knew, and that May had always been a sickly child. On the flipside, Robinson repeated his unfavourable story to Finlayson about the time after Henry's death that Martha had been asked by Robinson's wife if she would be glad if Henry was still alive, only to have her coldly remark that she would not speak to him if he came through the door.

It was then time to hear from the principal witness for the day – Alfred Whitney. This was the moment for which Gaunson had been waiting. Although five other witnesses were still to come, he already knew that this probably represented the last genuine opportunity he would have to seriously shake up the prosecution's all-powerful case against his client.

Whitney started by methodically outlining to Finlayson his established and renowned story about Martha's arrest. All the while it was noted that Martha 'listened with marked attention' to the narrative. Whitney scoffed at the suggestion that some pieces of bread and butter sprinkled with 'Rough on Rats' had been left unseen in the house. He asserted, 'It would be utterly impossible for them to be there … I did not leave a corner of the house unsearched'.

Gaunson's cross-examination of Whitney commenced in an antagonistic manner. He immediately fired at the detective, 'Did you or Fryer have any poison on you when you visited the house in Bridge Road?' With a smile, Whitney assured the court he had nothing of the kind with him.

'Did you submit Herman to a search for poison?' continued Gaunson. 'I did not' was the reply. 'Had Herman opportunities of placing poison in the teacup?' The measured reply was 'I should think he had'. Even at this early stage, Whitney was prepared to make some concessions along the way to the self-evident questions, confident that the jury would recognise that Gaunson was merely taking stabs in the dark by trying to belatedly imply that the poison may have been planted to set Martha up.

The cross-examination proceeded with great vigour – one scribe noting that Gaunson and Whitney were watching each other's 'moves' with the keenness of expert chess players. Gaunson again sneered at Whitney because he did not properly inform Martha (whom Gaunson described as 'this unfortunate creature') that she was not legally obliged to answer any questions at the time of her arrest. Determined not to lose his temper because of Gaunson's vehemence, Whitney calmly answered that he had administered a fair caution.

Throughout his extensive time being goaded in the witness box, there was only one occasion when Whitney momentarily forgot himself. After Gaunson insinuated that the detective had made a mistake in describing the kitchen at Bridge Road, Whitney snapped back, 'You have been in the kitchen and know as well as I can tell you'. Hodges, wishing to quell all digressions in his court, sternly intervened with, 'Better confine yourself to the answering questions, witness'.

But Hodges would also intervene in the other direction, when Gaunson asked Whitney, 'Did you refuse Otto Juncken access to the prisoner during the progress of this trial?' and Whitney replied in the affirmative. 'That is the ordinary course of events,' Hodges observed out loud to Gaunson, stopping this line of questioning in its tracks. Always one to have the last word, Gaunson retorted, 'I don't know that it is the ordinary course but it seems to mean illegal course – and I mean to mention it to the jury'.

Gaunson returned to his questioning and even tried his hand at a little flattery. 'You searched the house with a keen anxiety to preserve the woman from the consequences of an unfounded charge?' he put to the witness. 'I did' Whitney replied matter-of-factly. 'It is your duty to be cool and collected in the box and I must say you really are,' noted Gaunson. 'I am' answered Whitney, metaphorically giving himself a pat on the back.

Then the versatile Gaunson tried to engage the witness in a discussion about Martha's mental condition. 'Do you regard Mrs Needle's determination to commit suicide as evidence of her soundness of mind?' he inquired. 'There are more instances of sane people committing suicide than of insane,' postulated Whitney. 'Your theory then,' continued Gaunson, 'is that attempts at self-destruction are evidence of soundness of mind rather than otherwise?' That was enough for Whitney. Realising he was now moving into the realm of questions he wasn't qualified to offer a learned opinion on, he allowed the question to pass unanswered.

After some 60 minutes of cross-examination, Whitney was allowed to leave the witness box for the last time. A newspaper article would later describe the exchanges between Gaunson and Whitney as 'a keen encounter of wits' and noted that 'Upon the whole ... they parted excellent friends'.

Well, maybe not exactly 'friends'. And, more significantly for the prosecution, Gaunson had made no ground.

Next came lodge doctor George Hodgson, the suave medical man who had already told his tale (at least his version of it) numerous times. The *Herald* newspaper critiqued his presentation favourably, telling its readers, 'The doctor's voice ... is "low and sweet" and the reporters, who hanker after learned medical and surgical terms, are reluctantly obliged to "pass" several polysyllable names of diseases which the witness "rolls off" with comparative ease'.

In keeping with what had been said before, Hodgson explained to Finlayson that none of the prescriptions he provided for Henry or Elsie had contained arsenic. He could also recall that Martha never appeared to be unkind or inattentive to the patients whom she closely tended.

Gaunson took the opportunity to ply the witness with a number of queries about the properties and medicinal effects of calomel, bismuth and arsenic. In general, Hodgson came through the grilling unscathed. But by this time Gaunson probably knew more about these substances than the doctor himself. Indeed, one reporter remarked that he had 'forgotten more about drugs than the ordinary medical practitioner or the ordinary pharmaceutical chemist ever knew'.

Dr Charles Payne followed Hodgson into the witness box. For some reason, he felt the need to assume the high moral ground by quickly asserting that he was prepared to speak the truth – and that he would speak the truth whether Gaunson liked it or not.

Payne repeated that the case of May, who he certified died of tubercular meningitis, had particularly attracted his attention because he had not arrived at a satisfactory diagnosis himself and he had to consult another practitioner. He now firmly believed that this was a case of arsenical poisoning. He further told Gaunson, 'I don't think the prisoner objected at all … Nothing that came under my observation caused me to think that she was in any way unmotherly'.

The keynote of Payne's testimony actually came as he was excused and invited to take a seat in the body of the court. A woman's voice broke the stillness of the court. It belonged to Martha, who had advanced to the front of the dock and asked Hodges in a clear tone, 'Am I allowed to speak?'

All eyes in the court immediately darted in Martha's direction. Somewhat taken aback, Hodges replied, 'Yes, you may, but it would be better if you consult your legal adviser'. Gaunson moved over to the dock and Martha knelt down and whispered something to him, before Gaunson ventured back to the bar table. Martha wanted the witness to be recalled for one more question. Hodges agreed to this, so Payne returned to the box.

Gaunson: Was it at your suggestion or that of the prisoner that Dr Burton was called in?

Payne: I cannot say positively but I believe I suggested it.

Gaunson: If the prisoner says that it was her desire and suggestion, and that you delayed three or four days, and that she was dissatisfied, would you swear that was false?

Payne: I will swear it was false I delayed for three or four days.

Gaunson: Then you cannot say as to the rest of the question. That is very important.

Payne: I cannot say at this length of time whether it was I or the prisoner who suggested it but to the best of my belief it was I.

Gaunson: Well, doctor, if the prisoner says she desired it and that she was the first to desire extra medical attention, will you contradict her?

Payne: I won't contradict her. I cannot tell whether it was the prisoner or myself who first suggested extra medical skill.

On that note, Payne was finally allowed to leave the witness box for good.

In a display of confidence, Finlayson then indicated that all the evidence he had proposed calling for the prosecution had now been heard by the jury. While there were still two further witnesses in attendance – Georgina Lillis and Eliza Martin – he would not call them unless Gaunson desired it. He was now prepared to close the prosecution case.

Gaunson unhesitatingly indicated that these witnesses would be required. As both Lillis and Martin could be considered old female acquaintances of Martha, Gaunson knew they would provide a welcome conclusion to the evidence and stand in contrast to the proliferation of clinical and medical-based information the jury had heard.

More to the point, by this stage Gaunson sensed that Martha's case was looking bleak and he needed all the help he could muster. Although the defence of insanity had not been formally raised or entered, Lillis and Martin would help emphasise the mysterious 'fits' to which Martha had evidently been prone.

Georgina Lillis explained to the court that the Junckens had employed her for about six weeks in early 1892 as a backup housekeeper after Martha fell ill. Throughout this entire time, she witnessed Martha regularly having fits, or 'faints' as she called them. Lillis said that these 'faints' would usually last between ten minutes and half an hour, although one early morning episode lasted from 1 a.m. to 5 a.m. During these 'faints', Martha would fall to the floor and ramble in her talk – generally about her children. She would speak as though she was waiting on her children while they were ill. She would ask them to take their medicine.

'I have seen the trinkets of her children preserved by her. She used to always speak of her children in very endearing terms', Lillis added. Likewise, she observed, 'I never saw anything that would show that Mrs Needle had any ill will against Louis'.

Gaunson's last shot at the legal dartboard came in the form of Eliza Martin. As had been the case in the Police Court, she was able to explain that she had known Martha since she was a girl living in South Australia. She also recalled that Martha had lived at that time with a woman she did not believe was her mother and had been the victim of cruelty during her childhood.

Martin again outlined how Martha – in adulthood – had complained of pains in her head and been subject to fainting fits. She trotted out the heavily reported story of a dishevelled Martha arriving at her house about midnight, complaining that a strange man had followed her. The man was none other than Otto, who Martha did not appear to recognise. Once inside, Martha kept talking about her children, then went searching for them in the house and asked to go to the cemetery to see their graves.

Gaunson asked the obvious question, 'Did all this appear to be genuine?' to which Martin opined, 'It was genuine. Her eyes had a nasty expression and a glassy sort of look. On another occasion when I went to her house, she complained of her head and fell over on the sofa and lay there.'

Gaunson then rounded out his questioning:

Gaunson: You were fond of her?
Martin: [With emotion] Yes.
Gaunson: And you believed her to be a good woman?
Martin: I believe her to be a good woman now.

As the very last witness, Martin had done all she could to help her old friend – even though this type of information had already been heard before. Finlayson did not cross-examine.

With the hearing of all testimony completed, only three more stages of the trial remained – the final addresses of Finlayson and Gaunson, followed by Hodges' summing up.

Finlayson's address to the jury was relatively brief. He referred to his opening statements and contended that the evidence had borne them out. He also pointed out that no evidence had been given, notwithstanding her fits and faints, to show that Martha did not possess an equally balanced mind, fully capable of distinguishing between right and wrong.

It was then Gaunson's turn to speak. He explained that the case had finished much quicker than he had expected and he applied for an adjournment to the following morning. He estimated that his address would occupy about three hours. The adjournment was granted and Gaunson went home to work on his oration.

It would need to be the speech of his life. In fact, it would be the speech *for* Martha's life.

CHAPTER 23

The Final Roll of
the Legal Dice

At 9.40 a.m. the next day, Gaunson's crucial address to the jury began. As suggested the day before, he would prove good to his word and ultimately speak for three hours about the 'most painful and dramatic case' he had ever heard.

Although eloquent, Gaunson's address was also rambling. He did not focus on one specific defence or one particular thread of evidence. Instead, he spoke about a range of matters and provided some emotional commentary and criticisms about life and the justice system in general.

In many respects, this monumental speech was representative of the whole way he had conducted the defence. He had not honed in on one possibility – such as the established defence of insanity – preferring a scattergun approach. Gaunson's crusades were always aggressive and entertaining but they did not always directly assist Martha's cause.

Gaunson commenced by attacking the role of the newspapers – one of his permanent bugbears. He called on the courts to pay attention to the 'extraordinary, ill-advised, improper and grossly illegal printings' that had occurred throughout Martha's trial.

After this rant, Gaunson returned to the law of the case. He correctly reminded the jury that Martha had only been charged with the alleged murder of one person, Louis Juncken. Although they were not trying five cases of murder and one of attempted murder, the circumstances surrounding all of these cases had been put before them. Gaunson believed that this was a 'monstrous' process that could prejudice the case against Martha.

According to Gaunson, it should never be a case of trying to determine which side's lawyer was the cleverer of the two. The jury should only have a clear and absolute determination to arrive at the truth, as far as human nature would allow. He further told them – somewhat biasedly – that he was struck by the absence of evidence that would clearly establish the guilt or innocence of Martha. He also suggested he would show them what a 'rubbishy' case this was.

Gaunson then criticised the police and their hastily put together investigation. While avoiding the temptation to label them 'dishonest', he preferred to accuse them of possessing too much 'professional zeal' in their efforts to bring about a quick result. The detectives had ransacked the Bridge Road house looking for evidence, 'not to establish innocence, but to convict'. Once they had stalked into this property, Martha had found herself 'shut off from the world, except by the gracious permission of Detective Whitney'. The arresting officers had even prevented her from speaking to Otto. To Gaunson, this looked like oppression.

Gaunson chose not to steer away from Martha's relationship with Otto and the bizarre ravings and threats appearing in her letters. Instead, he tackled both head on, trying to reflect all the personal information in the best possible light. He reminded the jury that Otto, a man showing 'singular ability of mind', had been so impressed by the 'loving care she showed her children' that this attracted him to her.

Around the same time, Otto and Louis needed a housekeeper and Louis suggested that Martha was a fit and proper person for the position. But she initially rejected the offer because her only remaining child, May, was 'a sickly child' to whom she needed to attend.

During the course of the trial, the prosecutor Finlayson had suggested that it was extraordinary to think that Otto would allow himself to become engaged to a person of unsound mind. Turning directly to the jury, Gaunson sought to tug at their heartstrings, telling them rather soppily:

> Love was a thing they were not able to control and once it was in the heart of a man, it could not depart. The true loving heart of a tender earnest man would be more drawn to a weak, frail miserable woman under such circumstances as these. It only showed what knowledge the Crown Prosecutor had of love when he did not understand what the divine passion of love was capable of.

Upon hearing these words, Finlayson squirmed in his seat, in the knowledge that his opponent Gaunson was not a recognised authority on love and sweetness.

Gaunson went on to remind the jury that after Martha became engaged, she had written a suicide letter. Laying it on with a trowel, Gaunson told them he was afraid to read the letter aloud lest he 'should break down'. He read it anyway, emphasising her opinion that she was not in a fit state for marriage. From that point, Martha put off her proposed nuptials for 12 months. Gaunson considered that this was a startling fact and he begged the jury not to forget it.

Coming to the demise of Louis in that 'death stricken house', Gaunson reminded the jury that when Louis' mother and his brother, Herman, came over from South Australia, there was no suspicion associated with Louis' death whatsoever. In fact, Martha had done so many good deeds for Louis during the last days of his life that she filled him with a feeling of love and gratitude. Her fiancé, Otto, had told the court that on the day of his death Louis was only happy when the accused was by his side. Surely Louis would have known if any hostility existed between the two?

After Louis' body was buried, Martha sent her lengthy, bitter letter to Otto – in which, among other things, she said she would kill his mother even if she had to walk all the way to Lyndoch to do it. Gaunson urged the jury to view such behaviour as 'the pure language of a miserable, unsound, mental condition'. Even though Gaunson had not formally entered a defence of insanity, it was clear that his thoughts were now belatedly leaning in that direction.

Moving on to the analytical procedures, Gaunson told the jury that although the content of the cup of tea that Martha had provided to Herman was analysed, it had not been collected and preserved 'in the way that was laid down by the best authorities'. In such circumstances, he optimistically asked the jury to reject the evidence of the analyst.

Many of Gaunson's prime points – at least in his eyes – emerged when he began to speak about the exhumation and autopsy of Louis' body. This topic also gave him a gleeful, free opportunity to take a swipe at his old adversary, Dr Neild. The first question he asked the jury to consider was rather gruesome – 'Where was Louis Juncken's head?' There was said to have been disease in the jaw. Why had the jaw not been brought back to Victoria? Gaunson asked the jurymen aloud did they 'dare upon their solemn oaths, in the absence of such evidence as that, to convict the accused?' He then said that they 'could not with propriety or safety do anything of the kind'.

Turning to the processes employed during the autopsy, Gaunson labelled it 'extraordinary' that local medical practitioner Dr Popham had been invited by Neild to participate and yet the initial treating physician, McColl, was excluded. He also queried why Popham had not been called upon to give evidence. Was this because he might not have agreed with the version of events given by Neild?

Taking up the cause of McColl, Gaunson was insistent, if nothing else:

Dr Neild should have gone to Dr McColl and asked him to describe the symptoms of the disease, so that he might have more carefully searched for it. There is a law of fair play, which required that all reasonable care should be taken, especially in the grave issues of life and death ... If the head had been brought here, Riggs' disease would have been found and Dr McColl's reputation would have been justified. Dr McColl had been unfairly treated by the Crown in this case.

Gaunson asked the jury not to accept the evidence of Neild. He reminded them of Neild's 'hoity-toity' manner in the witness box, which had even seen the doctor dare to tell Gaunson 'don't elocute' in response to a simple question. Gaunson asked aloud, 'Was that the sort of evidence that could convince their consciences?' When asked why he had not dissected the jaw, Neild's only response had been, 'If I had dissected the whole body, it would have taken a whole week'. Instead, the head of the body had been left behind, which according to Gaunson was 'the front of Dr Neild's offending', in addition to conducting a 'careless' post-mortem.

Gaunson then briefly spoke about the exhumations of Henry, Elsie and May, taking the opportunity to criticise the decision not to exhume the body of little Mabel, who had died several years earlier. Once again, was this a situation of authorities selectively choosing the evidence to match their case?

He asked the jury to consider what possible motives Martha would have had to take the lives of her family members. 'None whatever', he confidently declared, conveniently ignoring the insurance money Martha had collected (even though this was not raised at the trial) and the secondary gain she may have received through the sympathy being offered.

Finally touching on the money side of things, Gaunson then made his most extraordinary and sexist comment of the whole trial – and there had already been a few. He asked the jury to think about whether Martha really needed the money at all. Surely, if she was the low-living woman that the prosecution was trying to portray her as, she could easily 'have obtained plenty of money with her good looks'.

Gaunson was implying that Martha could easily have turned to prostitution and made more money plying that trade than by over-utilising the application of 'Rough on Rats'. Realising that he had probably just overstepped the mark, Gaunson quickly conceded that 'It was a horrible suggestion to make, but was it worse than murder?' He asked the jury to ask themselves the same question 'as men of the world'.

If she didn't realise it already, upon hearing such dialogue the dismayed Martha must have finally understood once and for all that the justice system she was facing was a male-dominated and judgemental one.

Gaunson was anxious to raise the circumstances associated with the death of Martha's last child, May. The 'poor miserable woman in the box, who was fearful of the prospect of losing her last child' had been the person insisting that Dr Burton attend. Yet the prosecution was asking them to believe 'that this woman was a wicked murderess of the worst type, who, while her children were prattling around her knees, saw them dying away while she was administering poison to them'.

As proof that he had certainly done his 'research', Gaunson began to talk to the jury about evidence he had uncovered in reference books that would show that, in his opinion, Louis had not died of arsenical poisoning. Although Neild had said in evidence that chronic arsenical poisoning set up salivation, Gaunson had been unable to find any book in the medical library confirming that such poisoning produced the type of pus caused by Riggs' disease. So maybe McColl had got it right in the first place. Even at this late stage of the trial, Gaunson challenged the prosecution to produce a reference that contradicted this view.

He then started to quote another work on the subject, until Hodges intervened: 'Mr Gaunson, I am very unwilling to entertain your reference to books ... I have already allowed you to use more than I ought. The only books you can refer to are passages to which reference has been made in evidence.' Gaunson readily agreed with the direction and put his books away.

More relevantly, Gaunson then queried the bismuth taken by Louis. He again quoted Neild, who had informed them during his lively evidence that bismuth poisoning and arsenic poisoning would display similar symptoms. Was it possible that the bismuth given to Louis had been contaminated? Gaunson directly put to the jury, 'Had not doctors made mistakes before today while honestly trying to do their best for their patients?' He also reminded them that McColl had administered digitalis to Louis when he believed he had a dodgy heart and that digitalis could act as a cumulative poison.

These arguments may have sounded reasonable but, in raising them, Gaunson was blatantly ignoring the contrary evidence that had already rejected them during the trial.

Having now listed every possible reason he could think of to prevent the jury concluding that Martha was responsible for the death of Louis, Gaunson then navigated in a different direction. He told them that should they form the opinion that Louis had indeed died from arsenic 'wilfully and feloniously administered by the accused', they had to then ask themselves one further question – 'Was she responsible?'

They had heard all the evidence and now had to say not only whether it was evidence of her unsound mind but also whether it demonstrated that Martha was often unaware of what she did. A person needed to know that they were committing an illegal act for it to be punishable.

Given that Gaunson had ultimately sensed 'insanity' would emerge as Martha's best chance for beating the rap, he raised the recent case of the man named Setford – who just happened to be the father of Stanley Setford, one of the witnesses in this case. This man had given himself up at the City Watch House after cutting the throat of his young child. But he was then found to be of 'unsound mind' and not sane enough to plead.

With a freshly found enthusiasm, Gaunson began to speak about another recorded 'insanity' case – this one from Scotland – for the jury to consider. It was a case involving 'homicidal somnambulism', where a father had murdered his son while in a state of sleepwalking. But just as he was preparing to hand up copies of the case for the jury to consider, he again hit a stone wall in Hodges, who bluntly informed him, 'It would be better if you did not … It would not be of the slightest use to me'. It was clear that Hodges was not embracing this new insanity line. In any event, it had not been advanced in a spirited way before him as an organised defence during the trial.

'Very well,' Gaunson replied to the bench. 'They had it in evidence that this woman was constantly in those fits of unconsciousness. There were cases of somnambulism in which curious things were done.'

Gaunson admitted that some evidence related to Martha's fits had suggested that she had been 'shamming' but he scoffed at these allegations, telling the jury, 'It was not a sham for her to come downstairs at two o'clock on a cold winter's morning and stay there till six o'clock with nothing on but a sheet'.

Gaunson's implied suggestions about Martha's possible 'insanity' had all come too late. In any event, he would have needed to satisfy the jury of the very well established legal standard required for such pleas – which is still used today and referred to as the M'Naghten Rule. Named after the accused, Daniel M'Naghten, in a 1843 British murder trial, this judgement dictated that for an accused to be found insane, it needed to be proved that the perpetrator's mind had been so defective at the time of the offence that he or she was unable to understand what they were doing and they could not differentiate between right and wrong.

Moving over the insanity question, Gaunson then told the jury that he did not want them to understand that he thought that Martha had committed any of these crimes. He was simply putting it to them so that if any of them thought she had done any of these acts there was a 'humane and lawful consideration' for them to make – whether she was a responsible being or not. He reminded them that Martha was 'an unhappy creature', no matter the result of this trial alone. In all likelihood, there were other charges waiting. 'What was her future if freed from these charges?' he asked the jurymen. 'Could she survive them?'

At precisely 12.40 p.m., Gaunson thanked the jury and finished his optimistic presentation. He took his seat at the bar table and prepared to hear the summing up by Hodges.[127]

The Judge's Review

The summing up allows the presiding judge the opportunity to explain the relevant aspects of law, remind the jury of the factual evidence that has been presented and identify the relevant issues upon which the verdict will turn. The courtroom hushed as the poker-faced Hodges prepared to reveal his thoughts to all present. As it turned out, he would offer no positives to Martha.

Hodges commenced his address in a soft, low voice but with a grave tone. He started with some customary warnings. He firstly reminded the jury that their role was to exclusively determine the guilt or innocence of the accused according to the evidence that had been presented. They were to exclude anything that had sensationally appeared in the newspapers. They should also exclude any opinions that had been expressed by the advocates in court. In Hodges' words, they were opinions expressed hotly 'under the very strong excitement which naturally stirs a man who is pleading in a case of life and death' and were of no more authority than what had appeared elsewhere.

Hodges went on to correctly instruct the jury that while he was responsible for explaining the law to them, he had no role to play as to finding on the facts. That responsibility rested solely with them. They would need to be satisfied beyond reasonable doubt of two things, namely that Louis had died from arsenical poisoning and that Martha had administered the arsenic.

It was important to remember that the accused was only being tried for the murder of Louis. The facts relating to the deaths of Henry, Elsie and May Needle, and the alleged attempts to poison Herman Juncken, had only been raised to ascertain whether or not Louis had died from poisoning and whether the poison had been administered intentionally or accidentally.

Occasionally referring to some notes sitting in front of him, Hodges then began to read out the issues that the jury needed to determine. He gave a brief retelling of the whole story.

But throughout his dialogue, Hodges would sometimes stop and provide more in-depth commentary about points he believed were most relevant. He spent a fair amount of time mulling over the 'remarkable' letter that Martha had written to Otto in April 1892, in which she had alluded to a desire to take her life. He described the letter as 'pitiable with a tone of despair'. He added carefully: 'It showed she had feelings for Otto, which as an unmarried woman at the time would have indicated that he would not have been unacceptable to her as a husband … That letter might be a genuine expression of her state of mind, or it might not'.

But despite this expressed cynicism, Hodges was prepared to laud the character and impressiveness of Otto – a man faced with the trying circumstances of giving evidence against the woman he purportedly loved. Although the judge again reminded the jury that it was a matter for them to say who was telling the truth, he had absolute confidence in every word this man had said and believed it had been delivered 'in a manner worthy of the highest praise'.

Hodges remained puzzled about the question of motive for Louis' alleged murder but he suggested that Martha may have formed the view that Louis and his mother were working together to prevent her marriage to Otto. 'If she did, and if she were a person who placed little value on human life,' he told the jury, 'it might furnish her with some motive to induce her to do the act with which she is charged.' But Hodges was also quick to qualify his statement by adding, 'I only mention that as a slight suggestion of a motive which the prisoner may have had'.

He also noted that it had been said that Martha had suggested another doctor see Louis, in addition to McColl. (She had done a similar thing for her dying daughter, May.) If that was so, such action may be favourable to her. Alternatively, of course, this may simply indicate that she was satisfied as to her success.

The judge then repeated the circumstances connected with the accused's arrest at the Bridge Road house. He was at pains to mention that while no arsenic was found in the cup of tea that Martha intended for her own use, ten grains of arsenic were found in the cup intended for Herman. 'How did the arsenic get in the cup?' he asked the jury rhetorically.

The crucial part of Hodges' address came when he broached the topic of insanity. At that point, he appeared to have trouble containing his indifference. After instructing the jury, 'It had been suggested that she might have done it when she was not sound of mind', he quickly dismissed the notion from a legal perspective.

He added: 'I do not know where you will get evidence on which you would arrive at the conclusion that when she administered the poison, if she did administer it, she was in that frame of mind [insanity] but if you can see any ground on which you can arrive at such a conclusion, of course you are entitled to arrive at it. I don't know of any evidence to suggest such a conclusion.'

This was clearly a time when juries were not bamboozled by the psychological theorising that is poured out to them in almost every trial for graphic crime today.

The dispassionate Hodges then explained further, 'The mere fact that a man was what a medical man would call insane did not discharge him from liability. Philosophers, physicians and scientists might dispute and wrangle and argue but the law could not wait until they had settled their disputes and prisoners could not be kept awaiting trial until they had solved metaphysical problems. The law must act in the administration of justice soon after the commission of an act, surely and swiftly.'

At that point of Hodges' oration, the pending noose tightened a bit more figuratively around Martha's neck.

While we will never know whether any members of the all-male jury had harboured genuine thoughts about the possibility of Martha's insanity, Hodges had quickly impacted such speculation by speaking powerfully against it. Under the weight of such guidance from an influential judge, it was now highly unlikely that any jurymen would see fit to disagree.

Towards the end of his summing up, Hodges urged the jury not to waste time trying to understand Martha's potential motives, telling them it 'was not necessary' to establish them. He confirmed that the required standard of proof 'beyond reasonable doubt' did not extend to entertaining speculative possibilities – giving far-flung examples such as Blackett had not in fact found any arsenic in the bodies or had somehow taken it from the wrong body, or that all the witnesses were lying.

Adding to the pressure, Hodges asked them to remember that a human being's life was at stake, as if they needed reminding at all. Hodges left the jurymen with three possibilities: Martha Needle could be guilty, not guilty or not guilty on the ground of insanity – and they could only arrive at the last conclusion if they were convinced that she did not know what she was doing. He then left the solemn decision to them.[128]

Overall, Hodges had spoken for about an hour and a quarter. The jury then retired to consider their verdict, filing out of the courtroom a few minutes before 2 p.m. Adhering to his 'sure and swift' principles, Hodges told them he would return to the court about 3 p.m.

The Prisoner in the Dock

After the summing up by Hodges, Martha remained in the dock until the court had been cleared of all spectators before she prepared to be taken out. But the ever-present members of the press stayed behind, intently watching her every move. Before she left, Martha had a conversation with Gaunson for a few seconds and appeared to be in very good humour, smiling as she talked. One reporter later wrote, 'As she left the dock, she laughed at the police officer who opened the door for her'.[129]

This brief report would later be widely quoted throughout history as some sort of 'proof' that Martha must have been stark, raving mad after all. Given what she had just heard from Hodges, many presumed that Martha could not have possibly remained the slightest bit uplifted.

In reality, Martha was simply relieved that the trial was almost over and she was just battling on as best as she could. The intensity of the stares upon her would see her over-reported for her every conceivable move and every flickering emotion displayed.

'Surely and Swiftly' - the Verdict

As it turned out, Hodges would not have to wait around very long. The jury returned to the court just before 3.30 p.m., ready to deliver their unanimous verdict. Such a short deliberation time would go close to setting a record for a murder trial.[130] Martha was brought back to the dock and the courtroom quickly filled with eager observers, anxious to witness the finale to the unfolding drama.

When prompted by the Judge's Associate, Henry Pearson, the jury foreman quickly announced the jury's finding – the accused, Martha Needle, was guilty of wilful murder.

One of the multitude of newspaper reporters present later recorded that upon hearing these words, Martha 'gave a slight gasp, but beyond that showed no emotion whatever, her colour never even changing'.[131]

Although some people in such a position would react hysterically or commence to rattle off a bitter or compassionate speech, Martha remained staunch. When asked by Pearson if she had anything to say before Hodges passed sentence, she simply said in a faint voice, 'I am not guilty of the charge'.

Hodges then commenced his last oration in the trial. After he formally placed the infamous square of black cloth on his head, he offered no mercy. His delivery was remarkably brief:

> Martha Needle, it is not my intention to give you one moment of suspense. If conscience is not already doing its work, nothing that I can say will have any effect. It is my duty only to pronounce the sentence of the court and that is that you be taken from the place whence you now stand to the place from whence you came and that you then be hanged at such time as his Excellency the Governor may appoint, be hanged by the neck until you are dead, and that your body is buried within the precincts of the prison in which you were last confined. And may the Lord have mercy on your soul.

While her unfortunate predecessor, Frances Knorr, had wailed uncontrollably from the dock when informed that her life was as good as over, Martha accepted the news unflinchingly.

She was standing between two female warders when the abominable death sentence was pronounced. Each warder placed a hand upon Martha to steady her while the judge was pronouncing his last words. But Martha remained perfectly composed. She lifted her head towards the warders, gave a weary sort of smile and was heard to say, 'I am all right, thank you, let me alone'. Martha took a seat at the back of the dock, where she impassively waited for the court to be cleared.

There the three women remained – the prisoner apparently the least disturbed of them all – until the courtroom, the passages and the courtyard outside were vacated. Then Martha firmly stepped from the dock without assistance and walked earnestly to the horse-drawn wagonette waiting to convey her for her final and quick one-way trip to Melbourne Gaol.[132]

Even though they had delighted in writing about Martha's emotional demeanour throughout the trial, different reporters would now comment about her 'great courage' and the 'extraordinary' and 'marvellous' calmness with which Martha had accepted her fate. But the reality of her ordeal would hit her powerfully while she was in the wagonette rattling towards the prison. Now largely out of public view, she buried her face in her hands, moaning in a low and stricken way. Upon reaching the prison, she was placed in the condemned cell, where she sat in the corner and sobbed bitterly – finally giving way to an outburst of grief.

After a short time, Martha became calmer and began to speak to the female warders watching over her. By the next morning, she had moved out of the corner and was much more composed, even though it was also evident that she fully realised her awful position. Martha would need to get accustomed to the company of warders. From now on – consistent with prison regulations – she would be watched day and night by warders working in pairs.

There would be no more fancy clothes for Martha. As a convicted person, she now had to permanently wear the drab garb of a prisoner. She would be physically searched before dressing and was kept largely isolated from all other prisoners – spending any time in the exercise yard alone, except for the ever-vigilant warders. On her way to and from the exercise yard, she would be marched passed the gallows, an ominous-looking platform of iron and wood that occupied the landing of the middle tier of cells.

Her culinary selections were now restricted to daily prison rations, which consisted of 6 ounces of porridge, bread, meat and potatoes, with a dash of sugar and salt. Martha's food needed to be cut up for her, with the only cutlery provided being a spoon. It was planned that her death would occur with the endorsement of State authorities, so there would be no opportunity for it to occur at her own hands.[133]

The Newspapers: Extra Extra!!! - Read All About It

Since Martha's arrest and throughout her sensational trials, the newspapers had acted prejudicially towards the 'Black Widow'. Reporters and editors were not particularly enamoured of her undiplomatic counsel, Gaunson, either, given that he had scathingly criticised their every move.

So now that Martha had actually been found guilty of murder, the newspapers mercilessly unleashed like never before. The reviews they provided were not the type that Martha would want to cut out and keep in a scrapbook. The *Sydney Morning Herald* and *Argus* simply said that the verdict was 'as anticipated', while the *West Australian* likewise extolled that everything had gone 'as expected'.[134]

After a further day of reflection, the editor from the *Argus* upped the ante even further by stating: 'It is impossible to see how the jury could have arrived at any other conclusion'. Turning to the question of 'motive' – and, it seems, a little bit of amateur psychology – the *Argus* editor assured his readers that in such cases it was not 'indispensably necessary' to determine motive at all. Nonetheless, he was equally determined to provide Martha with some constructive criticism:

> The mental process by which a nature abnormally vindictive, unscrupulous and callous nerves itself to the commission of revolting crime can be little more than guessed at. Passion and avarice have been the most frequent and potent prompters in such cases, but neither can be held to thoroughly account for

284

the facts elicited in the Needle trial ... She appears to have been a woman fierce and vindictive in temper, albeit weak in body, and the frenzy of resentment of which she was capable at any thwarting her plans was instanced by the threats she freely uttered ... The fact that the crimes were committed systematically, and with cool and deliberate treachery, removes her from the category of ordinary criminals.

But it was South Australia's *Advertiser*, the most prominent publication from Martha's old home town, which led the most ruthless charge by immediately reporting:

There is nothing in Mrs Needle's case that can arouse the smallest particle of sympathy. The exceptional nature of her crimes – for the murder of Louis Juncken does not stand alone – is what has set everyone talking. It is no mere conjecture that attributes to her the murder of her husband and two children, though in the case of Juncken alone was the crime fully sheeted home. With her, poisoning seems to have become a kind of passion, and as the evidence showed it was little more than accident that saved his mother and brother from Juncken's fate ... a more atrocious miscreant never mounted the scaffold, nor one whose guilt was more completely and conclusively ascertained ... The author of these inhuman and perhaps unparalleled crimes is a monster on whose character and motives it is best not to linger.[135]

CHAPTER 24

Pleas to Save Martha

As Martha sat in the condemned cell, she was under no illusions whatsoever about her likely fate. The noose was regularly employed in those times. Martha knew that she would probably soon feel the coarse rope around her dainty neck.

But the administrative process prior to execution still had one final step to go. Martha's case would need to be considered by the State Cabinet – then usually known as the Executive Council – and a final decision about whether clemency would be granted would then be made. Submissions could be heard from the trial judge, the prisoner's lawyers or any other parties who could provide relevant information.

It was expected that the Executive Council's decision would be made within a few weeks. This was Martha's last flicker of hope – but the prospects looked faint. The Executive Council was a close-knit group of male conservative politicians, all under immense political pressure due to the harsh economic conditions of the day. They were surrounded by unsympathetic public officials and were operating in a 'get tough on crime' atmosphere. Even though history showed that patriarchal decision-makers were much more likely to reprieve a woman, the decision about Martha would be made in desperate and changing times.

Martha's signature on the suffragette petition way back in 1891 now looked strangely ironic. She had faced a justice system with an all-male jury and all-male judges. Now a committee of all-male politicians would decide her final fate – and the changing tide of politics would always play a role in such decisions.

In light of the publicity surrounding Martha's case, all the politicians forming the Executive Council were also well aware that public sentiment would be in favour of executing her. While it is said that life is all about experiencing the journey and not the destination, in Martha's case the politicians were clearly focusing on the end of the line.

Although most citizens could probably reconcile this young woman knocking off her difficult brother-in-law and domineering old man, such thoughts did not extend to the ruthless murder of her own children. These crimes were not just acts of peculiar abhorrence – they went way beyond the natural order of things; they shattered notions of trust, unconditional love and care towards the young and vulnerable. It conjured up images of Martha slowly exterminating her own, condemning them to agonising deaths as she watched on, unmoved.

Head of the Executive Council table was the new Victorian Premier, George Turner, a 43-year-old former solicitor who already had his work cut out trying to close the loopholes that had led to scandals during the land boom era. It would be fair to say that the philosophies underpinning capital punishment were not among his primary interests.

The Executive Council set a date to consider Martha's case: Wednesday, 10 October 1894. In the meantime, something extraordinary would need to happen to convince them that enough special circumstances existed in the matter to avert the hanging.

Martha did have some passionate supporters in the community, most expressing the view that there was a moral wrongness associated with executing a member of the fairer sex. Some were simply against the thought of executing anyone, considering such a sanction to be an example of barbaric, State-endorsed murder that had no place in a civilised society. Others believed that Martha was clearly insane and therefore didn't deserve to die for her actions.

Martha's most ardent advocate was crusading Irish-born solicitor Marshall Lyle, a man who had shot to prominence only a few years before as the legal representative of the doomed murderer Deeming. A fierce opponent of the death penalty and a man with a great interest in the emerging studies of mental illness, Lyle would take it upon himself to fight like no other to try to save Martha's life.

From his cluttered legal office, the 33-year-old Lyle also voluntarily did most of the secretarial work for the Victorian branch of the Howard Association for the Prevention of Crime. This association had some lofty aims, desiring to 'promote the most efficient means of penal treatment and crime prevention' and to bring about 'the abolition of capital punishment'. The association still exists worldwide today, although it is now known as the Howard League for Penal Reform and is considered to be Britain's largest organisation of its type.

An unrelenting correspondent, radical thinker and fearless debater, Lyle was prepared to put his reputation on the line to campaign for Martha's life. He also knew that there was little time left to lose.

As had been the case with Deeming, Lyle firmly supported the view that Martha had been insane at the time of her crimes and therefore should not have been condemned to die. He would not try to steer away from the outrages that Martha had committed or try to suggest that she was innocent or that the evidence did not line up. Instead, he would simply focus on her mental condition.

He began to track down and write to Martha's old acquaintances – including several men who had previously featured in her life – to see if they could offer any additional information from her past that might indicate an impaired mental functioning. None appeared to be in a hurry to become involved.

Only a few days after Martha's trial had ended, Lyle wrote to the Victorian Governor, the aristocratic Earl of Hopetoun, on behalf of the Howard Association. His neat and cursively handwritten letter indicated that a petition signed by those wishing to see Martha's life spared would soon be sent. In the meantime, Lyle wanted to make some preliminary comments of his own.

While clearly conceding that Martha belonged to the 'woman poisoner class', he implored that 'the mental condition of such criminals is always deserving of scientific inquiry'. Lyle believed that Martha's actions clearly demonstrated she was insane. 'This woman has committed an act which is utterly revolting and opposed to the natural instincts of women', he wrote. 'As a mother, she has murdered her children whom she loved very much and treated affectionately,' he continued before adding, 'I maintain that it is far more rational to assume that when a kind mother murders her children she is insane, and that any sane woman could not do such an act'.

He also stated that he had received 'further information' that would indicate Martha's case was ripe for reinvestigation but he did not disclose the nature of this information.[136]

The aloof 35-year-old Governor did not want to buy into the argument at all, nor challenge the powers of local politicians. He scrawled in pencil across the top of Lyle's correspondence 'Preferably direct to His Excellently the Hon Attorney-General' – which is where the letter was sent. Victoria's Attorney-General at the time was the ambitious 39-year-old Isaac Isaacs, a man later destined to become Governor-General of Australia. But Isaacs was also in no mood to entertain Lyle's suggestions.[137]

As promised, Lyle then forwarded a petition from the Howard Association, again duly sent to the Earl of Hopetoun.[138]

Although politically awkward, Lyle was clearly a man ahead of his time and not afraid to oppose the popular views of the press. His eloquently composed letter accompanying the petition revealed an extraordinarily progressive view of the issues involved and would compellingly stand up in the modern era. Traversing the whole question of crime and punishment, Lyle was more interested in addressing the *causes* of criminal conduct, rather than indulging 'the criminal spirit and brute passions of the mob' by utilising the punishment of execution. One of his primary concerns was the apparent ineffectiveness of the death penalty when trying to address one of the Howard Association's primary aims, namely the deterrence of similar criminals.

Lyle also did not want to let the politicians off the hook, reminding them that their decision-making process could leave blood on *their* hands. 'We deny that the Melbourne politicians have any moral right to wantonly strangle any criminal in their hands' he declared in the petition.

Lyle's creative writings did not particularly impress any of the hard-nosed government officials to whom they were ultimately forwarded. To them, Martha Needle was simply a ruthless, evil and sly child killer – and public sentiment was against her. In reality, Lyle had probably been wasting his ink and his time from the beginning – Martha's fate had been preordained. The male politicians who held her life in their hands had already decided that the world could do without this dangerous and downcast woman from low-rent Richmond.

The Bureaucratic Jungle

The first to respond with a managerial sidestep was the increasingly impatient Isaac Isaacs, who ridiculed the suggestion that Martha's case urgently required reconsideration. His handwritten reply to the Governor was brief and pointed: 'Mr Lyle states he has received information which shows that the case is one for enquiry but does not submit it for examination. As the prisoner was defended by able counsel and the defence of insanity was not raised … I do not see any reason to recommend that the request be complied with.'

Likewise, Premier George Turner wrote on the front of the petition,

'In my opinion this petition does not disclose any facts calling for further action' and returned it forthwith.

Lyle remained defiant. By this time, he had also resorted to divulging to the eager press all of his correspondence to government officials, complete with their terse replies. Since Martha's last court appearance, reporters had been scrambling for the slightest bit of news about Martha – and Lyle's work again helped to keep the newspapers full.

Before sending the petition, Lyle had already written to the Crown Law Department's permanent secretary, 58-year-old A.P. Akehurst. The purpose of the letter was to implore the Department to organise for Martha to be examined by competent medical men regarding her mental condition, before it was too late.

A consummate public servant, Akehurst submitted the letter to the Premier before forwarding a bland reply. He pointed out that the Premier considered no evidence had been presented at Martha's trial to 'furnish any ground for a suggestion of insanity'. And the 'further information' alluded to by Lyle still hadn't been sighted.

Lyle reacted angrily, believing that the question of insanity *had* been raised in the trial (although, in fact, this had only been raised in a belated and patchy fashion by Gaunson) and that it was the Department's 'greater duty' to investigate the sanity of a prisoner in their possession.

If anything, the firebrand Lyle was now getting heavily offside with the government officials he had initially tried to influence and he was making Martha's case worse – if that was even remotely possible. His reply was fully published by the *Herald* newspaper. Although this publication had never shown any mercy whatsoever to Martha, the editor guardedly noted that Lyle's response 'spoke for itself' when he wrote, 'You have the criminal safely secured in your possession and could ascertain the facts as to her mental condition if you cared to do so ... You ignorantly assume that this criminal of the motiveless crime is perfectly sane and you will assassinate under this assumption without a particle of evidence to support you.'[139]

Akehurst was insulted by the increasingly objectionable tone of Lyle's letters and did not reply. Neither did anyone else representing the government. Lyle had well and truly done his dash and the Crown law authorities would not be inquiring further into the mental state of the condemned woman.[140]

Feeling the Heat

One of the final recorded pleas on Martha's behalf came from an unlikely source. While her former star boarder at Cubitt Street, Arch Martin, had long ago hightailed it to Wellington in New Zealand, this had not prevented him from following Martha's sorry story from afar. He was so moved by what was taking place, he responded to Lyle's initial query with a theory of his own.

Martin suggested that the sunstroke Martha had suffered in South Australia before her marriage had sent her loopy. 'People who have suffered from sunstroke never properly recover from its effects' he offered, 'and those fits to which Mrs Needle appears to have been subject, you may be sure, are one effect of her trouble'. The contrite Martin further pleaded, 'I am afraid the case is too black and clear to admit of any doubt ... I am awfully sorry for her and yourself, too. But surely nobody could believe a sane person could plan and commit such crimes. I believe that Mrs Needle was not responsible for what she has done and that this point should be taken into account before it is too late.'

While it was never made clear whether Martin's theory about sunstroke constituted the 'further information' to which Lyle had once alluded, in an act of apparent desperation he immediately handed over Martin's letter to the press. A few of the newspapers even saw fit to publish it, with the Melbourne *Age* now dropping all polite pretences and simply referring to Martin as Martha's former 'admirer'.[141]

The sunstroke defence was never seriously taken up by those in power and this line of conversation came to an abrupt end. [142]

Wishing to keep Martha's story going, a reporter approached David Gaunson in the street. Gaunson had moved on with his life and was now accepting other briefs. He would provide the reporter with no headline, simply stating that he had been given to understand that Martha wished to die. He would not entertain talk about sunstroke and petitions, preferring to stick with legal realities. In his opinion, it would now be useless to take any further action in the case.[143]

While Lyle was busily trying to gather more signatures for another fruitless petition, the Victorian Executive Council met on Wednesday, 10 October 1894 to consider Martha's case. Unsurprisingly, it was decided that the law should take its course and the date of the execution was fixed for Monday, 22 October. With no appeals, recourse, reprieves or remissions pending, Martha now had 12 days to live.

The legal system of the 1890s worked with remarkable speed and efficiency. Martha would be hanged less than a month after the conclusion of her trial and only a little over four months since her initial arrest. If they were conducted today, her committal and trial proceedings alone could have taken years to complete. And, of course, lawyers in those days had yet to learn how lucrative an appeal process could be.

Although Martha was aware of the efforts of Lyle and other supporters who were trying to avert her execution, she didn't appear to place too much faith in the likely success of such campaigns. While still adamantly maintaining her innocence, she also routinely expressed a preparedness to die. Resigned to her fate, she wanted to get it all over with. Martha had never placed a great value on human life – and this apparently extended to her own.

It was left to the 40-year-old Governor of Melbourne Gaol, the grandly named Captain Robert Burrowes, to inform Martha of the Executive Council's decision.[144] As was becoming a recurring trait,

Martha received this news stoically that night and was said to maintain 'the greatest composure'. She simply said, 'Thank you – that was what I expected' and rather disconcertingly went back to what she was doing. She now appeared to agree with her detractors that her life wasn't worth saving.[145]

CHAPTER 25

Preparing to Die

While waiting for the inevitable early end to her life, Martha continued to eat well and did not outwardly display any particularly distressed emotions. She always appeared grateful for any little attentions shown to her by the female warders overseeing her grim daily existence.

She also appeared to sleep relatively well, although this was not always of a totally restful character. In his capacity as the Governor of Melbourne Gaol, Robert Burrowes would often enter her cell late at night to check on her progress with the female warders. On one occasion, he remarked to them that she was fast asleep, only to have Martha turn her head and quietly say, 'No, I am not sleeping'.

Although illogically maintaining her innocence, Martha wanted to hear no more talk about a reprieve. In her conversations with Burrowes, she made it clear that she would prefer to die than be imprisoned for life or be incarcerated forever in a mental home. In light of the ghastly conditions then existing in these institutions, her views were perhaps understandable. In a reversal of logic, she told Burrowes, 'I freely forgive all who have injured me' before also adding the postscript, 'If I had been condemned to imprisonment for life, I would not stand it long. I would poison myself.'

Bible Bashing

Whether stubborn Martha really wished it or not, outside attempts to provide her with religious solace would dominate the remaining few days of her life. The 54-year-old Reverend Henry Forde Scott was the long-term Church of England chaplain at Melbourne Gaol but he was not always an example of God's finest work himself. Scott was not only an overly active busybody but he always treated the religious destiny of people in Martha's position as some type of personal crusade.

Only ten months earlier, Scott had convinced Frances Knorr to confess her sins on death row so that she could fully repent. But while Knorr had gone completely overboard with her new-found religious fervour and would walk to the gallows reciting hymns, trying to bring about the absolution of Martha's sins would ultimately prove to be an impossible assignment.

Courtesy of the prison authorities, Martha was provided with a complimentary prayer and hymn book. She occasionally scanned a few passages of these publications in a reasonably indifferent manner and scribbled a couple of pencilled notes in the margins. Once she began writing her final letters to her associates, she did thumb her way through these references to quote some of the selected sections but she always politely avoided any serious religious discussions. She probably figured that she wouldn't be queuing up at Heaven's gates anyway.

Martha was permitted to have selected visitors for a few hours on Tuesdays and Fridays. While she was never overwhelmed with wellwishers, she had a few regulars who became very important to her. Although some, like Eliza Martin, had known her from her Richmond days, most followed a religious theme. One permanent presence was a 'soft-hearted little lady' identified as Mrs Hutchinson, who was prominent at that time for her reserve work in prisons with the Salvation Army. Martha always felt very calm and sedate in her company.

Likewise, Martha appreciated spending time with Sister Esther of the Church of England Mission and had also struck up a close acquaintance with another religious woman, Mrs Ada Owen, from the Melbourne suburb of Auburn. The latter had visited Martha in prison since she had first been arrested and had continually written letters of support to both Martha and Otto. Mrs Owen also provided Martha with a miniature volume of the New Testament. Although Martha scrawled her name inside the front cover of the Good Book, she only spasmodically flicked through the 300 pages of contents.[146]

Martha always appeared to take a respectful interest in talking to these women, as long as the conversation did not bear too much upon her spiritual welfare. Once or twice she talked for an entire hour, setting forth the reasons why she was innocent. All who had contact with Martha noted that while the power of argument may have been lacking in her, she had a ready wit and an engaging, pleasant manner with which she could effortlessly gloss over any point that might be made against her. She was fiercely intelligent but factually negligent.

By far the most important visitor in Martha's eyes was her 'fiancé', Otto. He had let her know that he still resoundingly believed in her innocence, which was enormously important to her. She hung on to this belief tenaciously. Whatever the rest of the world thought of her, Martha was satisfied that the man she loved was still supportive of her stance.

Crime No Longer Pays

There were also grim practical matters that needed attending to. Only ten days before she was destined to meet her maker, Martha summoned her lawyer, Gaunson, to help draw up her will. By this time, she had well and truly blown all her insurance money. Her belongings were of trifling value but she left everything she had to Otto. Included in the scant haul were a few sticks of furniture, some cheap items of jewellery and the relatively worthless blocks of land in Birkenhead that her late husband had optimistically purchased in more hopeful times.

Martha's 'estate' also showed that she had not lost her eminent appreciation of insurance. Prior to her arrest, she had taken out a £50 policy on her *own* life with the Citizen's Life Assurance Society but as the policy had not yet been in existence for 12 months, only £25 of that amount would be payable. It was a hard way to make £25. According to the strict interpretation of the law, the property of a condemned felon was forfeited to the Crown – but this forfeiture was not insisted upon in Martha's case.[147]

Picking Up Her Pen

Prisoners residing at Melbourne Gaol were expected to follow strict conditions about any correspondence they sent to or received from the outside world. Everything was heavily censored and harsh limitations were placed on how often a prisoner could communicate – usually one letter upon arrival and then one every three months. Under such levels of scrutiny, any romantic notion of prisoners smuggling out their memoirs or critiques of their oppressors was rendered highly unlikely.

Given that the condemned Martha only had days to live, such conditions now made little sense and the authorities didn't apply them to her special case. This meant that Martha was able to freely correspond with others as she wished – a feature that gave her some comfort.

Throughout her brief lifetime, Martha had often turned to writing letters in moments of distress or need, not always with positive outcomes. And although her erratic spelling and punctuation had not noticeably improved, she now adopted a much humbler and more appreciative tone, gently thanking those with whom she had formed friendly associations. But her ego was never too far from the surface and she often commented on how distressed everyone would surely be at the time of her demise.

On 16 October – less than a week before her scheduled execution – she wrote her final farewell to her new-found acquaintance, Ada Owen:

My kind and dear friend

You must not think me forgetful for not thanking you to day for all you have done for me during the last fore long and uneasy months for I have not forgot aney ones kindness to me now or at aney time, dear friend I hope you all will try not to grive too much for me hard as I know that will be for you all, you asked me to day if you Could do aney thing for me the only thing you Can do is to be as good a friend to Otto, as you have been to me ... dear friend I must bide you a last and found good by from your ever Loving friend.

Martha Needle [148]

The 'Art' Of Hanging

Those who still subscribe to the death penalty would be well advised to study its ghastly machinations first. By any measure, capital punishment is a barbaric act.

While Martha was counting down her remaining few days and writing letters in her condemned cell, the usual ghoulish arrangements were being made by the authorities to precisely bring about her timely dispatch to the afterlife.

The first thing to organise was an executioner, a job with very specialised selection criteria. It has been said that 'No man can destroy another, without at least destroying part of his own self' – a very apt phrase when reviewing the motley rollcall of Victoria's past hangmen.

It always took a certain type of person to be an executioner, the primary attribute being the mindset to methodically take another's life. The natural-born enemy of an executioner was compassion. Accordingly, these barbarous ghouls were generally drawn from prisoner ranks – most with violent histories and no recognisable displays of conscience. Some had been convicted of child molestation and almost all displayed traits of alcoholism combined with a mixture of ruthlessness bordering on sadism. To preserve their anonymity, many adopted aliases and even wore heavy theatrical disguises during executions.

The method of judicial hanging routinely adopted in all Australian States was the technique known as the 'long drop'. It would require the hangman to carefully weigh the intended victim, calculate the intended drop distance and speed of the fall and then provide the correct length of rope and appropriate knot to break the subject's neck immediately. The hangmen would invariably approach this task with macabre mathematical and scientific precision, aware that the hallmark of a good executioner was the speed with which their subject died.

In Victoria, the details of each hanging were listed in the Particulars of Executions Book housed in the prison. To assist executioners, a helpful chart in copperplate handwriting had been compiled and placed inside the front cover, meticulously recording the preferred table of drops, weights and measures. If a hanging were successfully carried out, a hangman would often be praised in the Executions Book for his professionalism in achieving a 'good' result.

But frightful bungles were also commonplace. If the distance or weight was miscalculated, or some other factor missed the mark, the subject could either be decapitated or left to strangle to death. Such scenarios often occurred throughout the gruesome history of Australian hangings.

The Executioner

Martha's executioner would be Thomas Pauling, a thickset former policeman. Born in Scotland, he would only be 31 years of age at the time he would be legally sanctioned to pull the lever to end Martha's life but he had already lived a chequered existence. The son of a wealthy manufacturer, he had been shipped off to Melbourne with several thousand pounds to start a new life but had quickly and wastefully sent these funds down the gurgler. This forced him to work as a wool weigher and tea hawker. He had then taken the next step in his blossoming career by becoming a Victorian police constable and, on the surface at least, had forged a reasonably uneventful stint of service – although records show that he had been fined twice for being absent from his beat. Next, Pauling accepted a position as a temporary prison warder and gleefully volunteered to assist the incumbent hangman perform his duties.

Even though Pauling had also been the primary executioner in the case of Frances Knorr, his 'promotion' to 'Public Hangman and Flagellator' had quickly arisen in grotesque circumstances. He had been a last-minute replacement to hang Knorr, taking the spot of veteran hangman William Walker, who had dramatically made himself unavailable at short notice.

To cut a bad story short, 45-year-old Walker had been considered the doyen of hangmen, despite his shady past. A convicted child molester, he had also served a three-year sentence for receiving stolen property. His big 'break' (pardon the pun) came when he was appointed to succeed the abominable hangman Elijah Upjohn, who had completely botched several hangings during his five-year stint in the gory job. As part of his punishment, Walker had at one time been flogged by Upjohn, before he became Upjohn's 'assistant'.

Walker found his gift in his new position – hanging fifteen men and flogging many others during his nine years of esteemed public service. But his downfall arrived when he was listed to execute Knorr, the first woman to suffer this fate in Victoria in 31 years. Walker began to receive 'constant annoyance' from his neighbours about the prospect of killing a member of the fairer sex and then his wife, Elizabeth, threatened to leave him if he followed through with the deed.

The veteran hangman began to drink even more heavily than usual and could not sleep at night. Becoming increasingly hysterical, Walker went to see the Governor of Melbourne Gaol, Robert Burrowes, and informed him that there was an 'echo' around his house telling him, 'if you hang Mrs Knorr, you will suffer'.

Under the regulations of his employment, the hangman was required to spend the final week housed in the same prison as his victim, fundamentally to ensure that he would not get drunk or simply abscond before the execution day. Walker duly shifted into the hangman's quarters of the prison, complete with the disguise he would don for the hanging, which included a false beard and darkened spectacles. But once locked in his room, he committed suicide by slashing his throat with a razor. Walker had chosen to take his own life before taking that of a woman. The coroner's jury would ultimately deliver a verdict of suicide while of unsound mind.

In those times, a plaster death mask was cast from the head of each executed person at Melbourne Gaol immediately after their death. While this undoubtedly satisfied some ghoulish curiosity, it was primarily done for the purpose of studying the emerging 'scientific' theories associated with phrenology and genetic indicators. The proponents of this quackery believed that it was possible to predict criminal tendencies by simply studying cranial features and bumps on a person's head. Because he died inside the prison, the remains of Walker also underwent this ultimate indignity. A death mask of his pained face was cast and still sits on display today among those of many victims he had personally executed.

On hearing of Walker's suicide, Pauling eagerly volunteered to replace him. His offer was gratefully accepted, with Captain James Evans, the Inspector-General of Prisons, commenting on the 'relief' of finding a new appointee who had 'not hitherto been a prisoner'. Clearly having no issues about executing a woman at all, Pauling was rewarded with a wage increase to 7 shillings per day. In the short time that was available, Pauling adopted the alias surname of 'Roberts' to protect his identity and settled into his new role by flogging a couple of male prisoners.

Although he had no training in execution whatsoever, Pauling made up for this with raw enthusiasm. He studied the subject of hanging, paying particular attention to the thickness and length of rope needed, in addition to the types of knots that were most efficient. His preferred 'technique' – later heartily praised – was to adjust the knot to the side of the neck. At the drop, this knot would switch around to the back and tighten precisely over the spine, severing the vertebrae immediately.

A Catalogue of Hits

On 15 January 1894, Pauling clinically executed Knorr without incident; the new hangman was praised for doing 'his work well'. Prior to being appointed to do the job on Martha, he also executed two other convicted murders – namely Ernest Knox on 19 March and Fred Jordan on 20 August. He was clearly a fiendish man who enjoyed his work.[149]

But Pauling was also an incredible shifty character and his appointment to replace his ill-fated predecessor had not been totally random. He had not only taken Walker's job – he had also previously moved in on his wife, Elizabeth.

The whole story came out in late April 1894, when Pauling, Elizabeth Walker and a woman named Maud Willow were arrested and charged with stealing a gold watch valued at £10.

Only a few months after her husband's suicide, the lovely Mrs Walker appeared in Fitzroy Court alongside Pauling on 21 April 1894. The court heard that four days earlier a man had been accosted by the prostitute Willow and invited back to nearby premises, where he also met Pauling and the widow Walker. All of them drank freely and, upon leaving the house the next morning, the victim noticed that his gold watch had been removed from its chain and replaced with a brass one that had belonged to the late hangman Walker. Pauling was arrested, later being granted bail on the sizeable surety of £50. Walker's widow was not so lucky. She was additionally charged with neglecting her eight-year-old son, Alfred Walker (the son of the late hangman) and remanded for seven days.[150]

This after-work indiscretion did not impede Pauling's public service role as executioner. He remained fully endorsed to undertake the task of dispatching Martha to the next world.

The Able Assistant

The executioner was usually allocated an enthusiastic offsider for each hanging and Pauling had a ready-made one – 43-year-old sexual pervert Robert Gibbon, alias William Smith. Born in England, Gibbon had firstly immigrated to America before venturing to Australia. America's loss did not turn out to be Australia's gain. Always considered to be a pea in the whistle of life, Gibbon was heavily tattooed with cheap images of young girls. He had already volunteered to assist Pauling in the hanging of Knorr and was now waiting in the wings to assist with Martha. Eyeing off Pauling's job, Gibbon was aware that such a role would add to his already bulging curriculum vitae.

The Final Days

With Martha due to be hanged at 10 a.m. on Monday, 22 October, prison authorities ceased most visitor access during the preceding weekend. The time for Martha to say her 'final goodbyes' had ended.

Apart from prison officials and her religious attendants, the only other person who was permitted to see Martha on the preceding Sunday was Otto. The pair sat and chatted for a considerable time, before their final visit was brought to a close. Although Otto had frequently seen Martha in her cell, this time the final parting was said to be a most painful sight for those in attendance.

As Otto left the prison that day, he knew he would never see Martha again. Although he still resided at 137 Bridge Road, he had already begun to tentatively move on with his life. After a new proprietor had taken over the saddlery shop, Otto had renewed his employment as a builder, again working from the shop of Mr Clements Langford in the same thoroughfare at 151 Bridge Road. His boss was happy to describe him as one of his most industrious and capable workmen.

On the previous day, Otto had declined to take the usual half-holiday then allocated to a Saturday and insisted on working until 5 p.m. in order to finish a job. He then told the firm's accountant that he might not be able to turn up for duty for a few days. In light of the painful circumstances under which this request for time off was made, it was 'sympathetically agreed to'.[151]

Hanging Business

By this time, Martha's executioner, Pauling, and his demented assistant, Gibbon, had taken up their quarters in the prison and commenced their necessary mathematical rituals. For the petite Martha, there would be no moments of modesty left. She was weighed and measured, it being systematically noted in the Executions Book that she was 5 ft 2 in (157 cm) in height and 8 st 6½ lb (55 kg) in weight. As evidence of her healthy appetite for prison food, it was dispassionately reported that she had managed to gain 1½ lb (0.68 kg) since her incarceration.

Martha would be hanged while wearing a brown, wincey dress. To avoid the final indignity of the dress ballooning up over her hips as she fell through the trapdoor of the gallows, the dress required some last-minute adjustments. Lead was fitted into the bottom of the dress and fixed with a drawing cord by an unemployed woman who had given herself up a few days earlier and asked to be arrested as a vagrant. Pauling diligently added an extra 1 lb (0.45 kg) to his calculations to allow for the additional weight of the lead, before determining that the length of rope needed to successfully execute Martha was 42 ft (12.8 m) and the 'drop' would need to be exactly 8 ft 5 in (256.5 cm).

Like each person executed at Melbourne Gaol before her, Martha would have the final indignity of being fitted with waterproof underclothing for her hanging. When death occurred, the body could lose control of all functions, including those of the bowel and bladder.[152]

Martha's curly locks were also closely cropped, so as to offer 'no impediment to the discharge of the hangman's office'.

A Final Tantrum

All along, Reverend Scott persisted obsessively with his desire to have Martha confess all her sins. His firm religious view was that if she did not acknowledge guilt for her crimes, she could not repent and was therefore unlikely to trouble the gatekeeper at the Pearly Gates. Scott was aware that Martha was still clinging to the notion that Otto believed in her innocence. With only a scant regard for the ethics involved, he set about trying to drive a wedge between the pair.

He spoke to Otto privately. During the conversation, Otto confided in him that while he had certainly formed the view that Martha *had* committed the crimes of which she was accused, he further believed that she must not have been mentally aware of what she was doing at the time. Otto would allow Martha to go to her grave believing that he did not think she had committed these crimes. After all, this was just about the only positive thought she had left and she appeared to gain a great deal of solace from his support.

Scott did not maintain Otto's confidences. Instead, he visited Martha in her cell that night and blankly told her that Otto had told him he believed she was guilty. In such circumstances, he suggested that she should now simply confess to her crimes.

Martha did not appreciate Scott's awkward attempts at conflict resolution. Upon hearing Scott's words, she flew into a sudden rage, the ferocity and uncontrolled anger of which shocked the prying Reverend and the warders passively looking over her. Forming the view that Scott was trying to trick her into confessing, she completely blew her stack and shrieked at the top of her voice, 'It's a lie! It's a lie!' while violently stamping her feet. The berserk Martha then demanded that Scott leave her cell. Such was her terrible anger that he did so immediately under a hail of abuse.[153]

Martha later calmed down and continued to chat with her keepers in her normal, restrained manner – but she would have little to do with Scott or his spiritual advice again. Those overseeing Martha had seen a final and frightening glimpse of just how quickly and fiercely she could erupt if something didn't go her way.

CHAPTER 26

Facing the Noose

'My darling … we shall meet again where there is no parting.'
– Martha Needle to Otto Juncken, on the dawn of her execution

During her final night, Martha slept reasonably well. But she awoke at 4 a.m. and soon became a woman on a mission. She still had one last letter to write to Otto and she set about the task quickly.

This letter followed the themes of most of her others – how she would find some relief to her troubles through death and how others would experience suffering at her demise. She also made her customary bizarre reference to her children.

In order to put the letter in its most presentable form, an unknown editor later corrected all the inevitable spelling and grammatical mistakes before it appeared in its modified state:

> Melbourne Gaol
> Monday, 4 o'clock
>
> My darling – As you wished me to write I will do so, but truly I do not know what to say to you on this my last morning on earth. In a few hours, I shall be free of all sorrow, but

you, dear Otto, must live on for a time. It may be a very long time or it may not, but whichever way God wish, it will be; but never mind, try to bear up under the very sad blow. Rest assured we shall meet again where there is no parting. Your good father, also poor Louis, and my dear little ones will welcome you. You know dear Elsie and May loved you on earth. They will do so in Heaven. Think how they will all welcome you to our happy home on high. I must ask you not to think unkindly of me for saying what I did last night to Mr Scott. I think it right that you should know what that man did say about you, but I want you to thoroughly understand that I did not believe that you ever did say so to him, and I told him so. You must not think what he said upset me, for it did not; only it annoyed me to think that such a man would tell an untruth. True, he may think he was doing right. We must hope that he did think so.

Now, you will want to know what sort of night I have had. Fairly good. You and all dear ones have been in my thoughts and prayers. Dear Otto, please read the 139th Psalm from the 7th to the 13th verse. As I have asked God to forgive me anything that I have done to displease Him, and trust to His forgiveness, so do I forgive all that have ever done me any sort of unkindness. For I know that they are very sorry for me, be the wrong little or big. Give my everlasting love to all inquiring friends. I must now say good-bye to you for a time. When you receive this, you can think of me as being in a happy home with my loved ones, waiting and watching for you. I know, dear Otto, that you will get ready for that happy meeting with us all. With love and sympathy, from your loving Martha.[154]

The passage in the Psalms selected by Martha for Otto's reading had been chosen after much searching through her bible for something she deemed appropriate. It turned out to be a Hebrew prayer for days of sorrow.

A few hours later, Martha was back writing again. This time she copied a few verses from her hymnbook, which commenced with the words, 'Farewell, faithful ones, I must bid adieu to the joys and the pleasures I've tasted with you'. Martha marked these hymns, 'Monday, 6 o'clock' and again addressed them to Otto.

Martha then began a third communication. It commenced, 'This will be my last prayer and thought' and she then copied out a series of short prayers of the Church of England. Martha finally put her personal letter to Otto plus her selected hymns and prayers into one envelope, expressing satisfaction at having completed her tasks.[155]

At 8 a.m. Martha was offered her last breakfast and she ordered her usual signature dish – a meal of bacon, eggs, bread and butter. Somewhat ironically, she was also given a cup of tea, although it was clearly devoid of any traces of arsenic. Her appetite was not impaired even though, in racing parlance, the end of her life was now in the shadows of the post. Her watchful attendants noted that she ate with some heartiness.

Some people still entertained the possibility that the gritty Martha might break down at the last moment and that alcohol (then politely called 'stimulants') would be required to sustain her throughout the dreadful final hours. But this 'poor piece of humanity' and 'stricken monster' (as the *Herald* and *Age* newspapers described her) appeared to suffer no nervousness. Although brandy had been kept in her cell, she had always refused to touch it. When offered some on her last day, she again unwaveringly declined, preferring a glass of cold water, with which she moistened her lips.

Martha's main visitor from early that morning was the Salvation Army's Mrs Hutchinson. She found Martha to be in a calm state, describing her as 'softer than she ever had been since she was arrested'. One newspaper provided a different interpretive slant by observing, 'Mrs Hutchinson's kindliness and womanliness seemed to soften the heart of the worthless creature, for she paid deep and close attention to all that was said to her'. As the hanging drew near, Mrs Hutchinson departed and left Martha in the care of the less-favoured Reverend Scott. Martha displayed genuine grief at bidding her final farewell to Mrs Hutchinson and began to take more notice of her approaching demise than she had previously shown.

The morning moved by quickly as the prison was prepared for the dreaded hour of 10 a.m. Martha was relocated to what was known as the 'scaffold cell', which sat directly next to the gallows. From the small doorway of this cell, Martha could clearly see the noose dangling. The hangman and his assistant, both cheaply disguised like a pair of stage villains, could also be seen in the cell directly opposite, peering out, as if eager and impatient to get on with their dreadful work. Martha had already heard them release the trapdoor for several practise attempts.

There had been a large demand for tickets to personally witness the execution but the sheriff, Louis Ellis, wanted to keep the function as private as possible. Ultimately only 13 men – mostly Justices of the Peace and a few members of the metropolitan press – were given 'right and title' to be present. A few minutes before 10 a.m., these ticket holders assembled outside the prison gate and were then ushered by a stalwart warder across the courtyard to the prison proper. They passed along a musty corridor to the scaffold, in front of which they solemnly took up their position to await the arrival of the condemned woman.

Outside the main prison gate in Victoria Street, a crowd estimated at a few hundred people of the 'usual motley throng of loungers and gazers' had gathered for the execution. None had ever been considered workaholics. Since the executions at this very prison of Ned Kelly and Frederick Deeming, large congregations outside the gates on these occasions had become a rarity because there was little to see to satisfy the curiosity of attendees. By this time, the customs of hoisting a black flag when the execution was completed or tolling a bell as the soul of the condemned person passed away were no longer in operation.

The mood inside the prison was vastly different and all prisoners remained locked in their cells. Although a bleak sense of gloom would usually settle over the place on the mornings of executions, this time the feeling was particularly marked. Scarcely a sound could be heard to break the sacred stillness. Even though some prisoners strained to hear what was going on, no whispering or sobbing could be heard coming from the proximity of Martha's cell.

For Martha, the end was clearly at hand. Just before 10 a.m., a white death cap was placed and fitted on her head. Sheriff Ellis, prison Governor Burrowes, physician Andrew Shields and Reverend Scott were heard approaching the scaffold cell. Keeping with protocol, upon reaching the cell the sheriff declared, 'I demand the body of Martha Needle'. This grim order was acknowledged by Burrowes, who relinquished the prisoner to the executioner and his assistant. They roughly seized Martha and immediately pinioned her wrists behind her back, or as one report more dramatically put it, 'her hands, which had done such mischief in the world, were strapped down and rendered powerless for ever'.

A compulsive shudder passed through Martha's slight frame as the cold hands of the grim servants of the law first fell upon her. She even seemed to slightly falter but was then steadied by the hands of 'Roberts', the hangman, and the physician Shields. She then fully composed herself and without any assistance strode purposefully towards the fatal spot under the shadow of the noose. As soon as Martha reached the 'drop', the hangman slipped the hempen noose over her head and, with a deft rapid motion, adjusted the knot.

'Have you anything to say?' asked the sheriff, as those soberly assembled below strained their ears to try to catch the condemned woman's last words. Speeches at the gallows, of course, are the stuff of legend. It was in the very same spot that Ned Kelly had allegedly uttered 'Such is life'; other condemned prisoners had traditionally used this opportunity to either confess their sins, plead their innocence, praise their God, decry their enemies or thank their loved ones.

But this was never going to be the case with the resolute Martha. She would give no last-minute confessions, nor concede any ground. She turned her pale face and restless eyes full upon the sheriff, shook her head and then in a voice that was almost a whisper said, 'I have nothing to say'. Martha then muttered one further comment but her whispered voice faded away so quickly that it was inaudible to those near the scaffold, let alone those standing below.

Martha then seemed to become dazed. She shut her eyes and compressed her lips, leaning back to get some support from the parapet alongside the trapdoor.

But the last that was seen of Martha's face showed an expression of grim determination. It would be the enduring memory of those in attendance. A reporter from South Australia's *Advertiser* standing below would later recall, 'She moved not a muscle and awaited death unflinchingly'. Another report indicated that she had subjected her morbid onlookers below with one final glare 'that scorched them'.[156] Either way, Martha had maintained her impenetrable demeanour to the end – and she would not die a coward.

An instant afterwards, the sheriff gave the necessary signal and the hangman pulled the death mask over Martha's face. In a rapid movement, he then drew the bolt and, with a sharp click, the trapdoor opened under Martha's feet and she fell through with her fists clenched. There was a terrible crashing sound. The long rope unravelled and straightened, violently checking the fall of Martha's body, which was left dangling from it and swaying to and fro. Simultaneously, a screen fell between the spectators and Martha's body, the convulsions of which were only seen to last a brief moment. Death appeared to have occurred instantaneously.

As far as hangings went, this would be considered a successful one.

Martha was only 30 years old at the time of her death, the end of a short and very destructive life. Some would suggest that she had singlehandedly ruined the theory that only the good die young.

Under regulations, the official spectators to the execution were not allowed to depart the prison for at least a quarter of an hour after the event. It was therefore some time before they walked past the crowd still assembled outside the prison and faced the usual lines of inquiry, such as 'How did she go off, sir?' The meagre replies received by the curious mob indicated that all had gone as planned.

In keeping with usual practice, Martha's body was left to hang for the customary period of one hour, before Shields performed an examination to confirm that there were no longer any signs of life. A more formal autopsy was then performed by Dr Richard Youl, confirming that Martha had been 'judicially hanged', before her death mask was cast.

As a condemned person, Martha's remains would be buried in the precincts of the prison in an unmarked grave. For a person who had attended so many funerals, Martha's own interment would be completely devoid of any sense of ceremony. A hole was roughly dug in the area of ground directly along a bluestone wall reserved for such disposals; at sunset, Martha's body was buried in a casket filled with a few shovels of quicklime. The only marker was 'M.N. 22.10.94' roughly carved into the bluestone that sat immediately above the mound of dirt containing her body.

Following Martha's burial, there were congratulations all round.

The *Brisbane Courier* informed its readers that 'the arrangements were perfect and carried out without a hitch'. Likewise, South Australia's *Advertiser* explained, 'The execution was faultlessly carried out' and 'Mrs Needle … took her place under the noose with as much calmness and self-possession as a martyr'. Perhaps in her mind, she believed she was.

The sheriff, Ellis, expressed relief that 'no show' had been made on the scaffold, while Robert Burrowes rather proudly entered all the details in the institution's Particulars of Executions Book. Under the heading 'Remarks as to Result', he clinically wrote:

> Death was instantaneous.

> There was not the slightest movement of the body after she dropped. Whilst hanging a measurement was made from the floor level of the drop to her heels and it was found she had dropped 9 ft. This is accounted for by the stretching of the ligaments and the forcing of the rope under the jaw.

> An autopsy was made and the neck was found to be broken. The skin under the rope was slightly abraded. The large muscle under the skin of the neck called sternomastoid was cut through on the right side. The windpipe and gullet were also cut.

> The execution was perfect.

The Aftermath – 'An Abnormal Woman'

Even on the day of Martha's death, the press was in no mood to respect her memory. A great deal was made of her refusal to confess her crimes, her cool attitude while facing death and her failure to seek religious penitence. In between describing her as 'a heartless, wretched woman', 'a monster in human guise' and 'the cruel destroyer of husband, children and friend', the *Herald* went on to declare that 'prison officials have never had a more callous, indifferent criminal under their care' and that her crimes stood out as 'the most awful, if not the very worst, in the records of crime'.

One particularly uncharitable article clearly reflected the prevailing theory that criminal conduct was genetically linked. Noting that Martha had wiped her progeny off the face of the earth, the writer expressed some relief that this may prove 'kind to humanity' in the long run because it would prevent 'the extension of hereditary tendencies to crime'.[157]

Those who were with Martha to the end were eagerly sought out for press interviews. Most prominent of all was Reverend Scott, who revelled in the limelight. Scott had never concerned himself with whether or not he was breaching any prison regulations by passing on statements made to him by a prisoner, nor did he appear to place any weight on confidentiality. He wasn't in any mood to pay homage to Martha's character either, working on the assumption that she 'had destroyed the fruits of her womb'.

Still smarting over his failure to draw a confession, Scott was even willing to assume the role of armchair expert in the emerging fields of psychology and criminology. When asked by a reporter how he would 'classify' Martha, he declared, 'In my opinion she was an instinctive criminal … Her environment, at the time her character was being moulded, was against the development of a high moral tone, even supposing that possible in her case'.

While on a roll, the good Reverend continued his amateur personality analysis:

> She exhibited marked indications of moral insensibility or imbecility, and from the time I first saw her I considered her an abnormal woman. She had a masterful will, a vast fund of vanity and a passionate nature. I never could imagine her to have been a loving or lovable person. It is possible that a strong attachment, based on passion, may exhibit outward tenderness, but it is liable to evaporate and leave the nature more frigid.

> ... Martha Needle was a psychological conundrum, and as
> such was well worthy of the close study of mental scientists,
> moral philosophers and students of criminology ... The
> question arose: How came she so? Were the horrible qualities
> attributed to her inherent and hereditary or were they
> contracted, cultivated and made potent by environment?

And given such abnormalities, how had Martha managed to survive
so long? Scott offered, 'She was uninstructed but had a good deal of
native tact and kept her ignorance from being apparent by a ready wit,
an agreeable manner and the fascination of a not uncomely person'.

Whether Scott, as a religious supporter, should have been offering
such unqualified opinions to the newspapers was ethically debatable
– but his words were perceptively accurate. Martha had indeed been
a 'psychological conundrum' and debate would always emerge about
how far she had been the product of heredity versus environment.
And at the times of her crimes she had been young, good-looking and
blessed with engaging manners and an overmastering sentiment of
vanity – not the type of person to necessarily arouse much suspicion in
ghastly circumstances but one fully equipped to deceive medical men
and others around her.[158]

The Media Stoush

Due to the ramblings of Reverend Scott, the public humiliation was
still not over for Otto Juncken. Even though Martha's body was now
buried cold in the ground, Scott and Otto remained at loggerheads over
whether or not Otto had expressed to Scott his belief that Martha had
committed the crimes of which she was accused. In Scott's view, Otto
had been Martha's false human prop. Just as he had not let Martha's
memory rest, Scott appeared determined not to let this matter slide
either. It would end badly for Otto.

Scott repeated his claims in the press – Otto had told him that he did not believe in Martha's innocence. In response, Otto sent an open letter to the newspapers, emphatically denying that he had ever said such a thing. 'Evidently the reverend gentleman knows my mind better than I do myself', he wrote indignantly.

The ever-helpful 'reverend gentleman' was only too happy to explain his comments. He again turned to the newspapers, publishing a lengthy letter in which he pointed out that Robert Burrowes had also been present when Otto had made his statements and he now had permission from Burrowes to quote him as an authority.

Then, out of the blue, Scott gained another unexpected ally. Otto's mother, Margaret Juncken – certainly no fan of Martha – had been following the argument in the newspapers and joined in the debate. She forwarded to South Australia's *Advertiser* private correspondence that her son, Otto, had been sending her throughout the ordeal.

Old Mrs Juncken stated, 'As there have been so many untrue and contradictory statements published relative to my son Otto's belief in Mrs Needle's innocence, will you kindly publish the enclosed extracts from letters I have received from him which will clearly show that he believes in her guilt'. Much to the embarrassment of Otto, the newspaper had no hesitation in publishing the correspondence, which was then requoted in all the other newspapers.

Otto's words clearly showed that he *had* believed Martha committed her crimes. The most significant letter of all – now published for the whole world to see – had been written well before Martha had even been convicted, shortly after arsenic had been detected in the remains of her late husband and two children.

In his correspondence, Otto was particularly anxious to dispel any impression whatsoever that his sympathies rested with Martha in preference to his family, telling his mother, 'It grieves me beyond expression to think that I did not follow your sound advice and judgement at the time you first gave it and before any harm was done … That you were right in your estimation as to her true character no one can ever doubt, only that your estimation as to the evil in her nature fell well short of the mark'.

The deaths of Elsie and May had affected Otto the most, as he informed his mother:

> Is it not terrible to think that those two dear little girls should have met their deaths in such a cruel manner? This is the most diabolical thing of all. In the other two cases, I mean that of the husband and our poor Louis, there may have existed a certain amount of ill-feeling, but for those two innocent little children there could not have been any such thing … If she [Martha] is not a maniac, her mind must be so utterly depraved that she has no ordinary feeling of the human being. … Terrible as those revelations have been, they must bring a certain sense of relief … It proves clearly to the world that this evil was in her before she came into contact with anyone of us.

But, most tellingly of all, Otto revealed a fear for his own safety:

> I would eventually have followed the two little girls. Whether she loved them or not she appeared to do so, and always manifested the deepest affection for them, and if she could take their innocent lives, whatever her feelings for me, in time I don't for a moment doubt that I should have suffered as well. It is certainly hard that poor Louis should have had his life sacrificed, but we must be thankful that it has stopped there. One thing we must be thankful for is that she should have fixed on Herman instead of me. Had it been me the chances are that she would have again succeeded. I would not, like Herman, have left the house, and in many other ways her chances of success would have been much greater.

So bad as things are for you all, my dear mother, they may have been worse.[159]

Otto's words were coming back to haunt him and they were illustrative of a man caught in a conflicted position between his family and his previous love.

They also highlighted the personal tragedy of Martha. All along, she had pinned her hopes on her man, Otto, and his faith in her. And all along he had been discreetly distancing himself from her and siding with his family. What's more, he clearly considered Martha to be dangerous and feared the things of which she was capable.

With his truthfulness being openly questioned in the press, Otto finally felt the need to clarify his contradictions – in modern speak, he did a 'backflip'. He emphasised that the letter he sent to his mother was never intended for publication, before agreeing with reporters that he *had* told Scott that he *did* believe Martha had committed the misdeeds. But he went to great pains to re-emphasise his thoughts that Martha was not fully conscious of what she had done. In many respects, he was putting forth the type of criteria that would now be advanced in a modern case involving insanity.

Throughout the entire saga, Otto had been repeatedly portrayed as a remarkably honourable citizen and in many respects this assessment was justified. But behind the public veil of integrity, he was far from perfect – he was just as capable as anyone else of running with the hares and hunting with the hounds.

He had also paid some of Gaunson's bill but didn't want his family to know about this. Once again, a letter would unexpectedly surface confirming his dilemma. The relevant correspondence was from Otto to Ada Owen, the woman regularly visiting Martha in prison. He urged Mrs Owen not to mention this payment to the 'Adelaide folk' because they were very fond of gossip and, should his mother hear about it, such a revelation would be 'a great sense of trouble to her'.[160]

Otto's letter to his mother not only doubts Martha's stories but it also displays a certain sense of emotional betrayal. And this was from a man who had privately treated Martha as a bit of a crank in many ways. He had continually distanced himself from any suggestion that he had engaged in any form of sexual relationship with Martha (assuring the court repeatedly that there had not been 'anything wrong' between them) and he had also sat with Martha drafting letters about her mythical 'inheritance', even though he did not believe for a moment that such an inheritance existed.

In retrospect, Martha's cynicism of the male gender may have been well justified. After all, a lot of the time she *was* being emotionally deceived, including by the love of her life, Otto. And the newspaper articles being beamed around the world – all written by men – always painted the males in the story, including her late husband Henry and the doctors falling for her engaging sweet-talk, in the most noble, chivalrous and forgiving light possible.

With Otto's confessions now publicly aired, the press called a truce and started to leave Otto alone. This allowed him to gradually put this incredibly painful episode behind him and move on with his shattered life – something he would ultimately do most successfully.[161]

CHAPTER 27

How Many More?

The luckiest serial killers are always the ones that no-one initially suspects. Such people are afforded an unimpeded run while committing their misdeeds. On the very day of Martha's execution, it was the *Herald* newspaper that prominently provided the editorial opinion that Martha was simply 'a cool, calculating, deliberate murderess, unrelenting, implacable, merciless'. After revealing such character traits, the newspaper then went a step further:

> The technical view − that the woman was convicted only of the murder of Louis Juncken and must not be held guilty of other crimes − can at this stage be insisted upon only by the hypersensitive … There is little reason to doubt that Martha Needle killed four people and attempted the murder of a fifth. She had killed with a strange impunity … but the community is rid of a positive peril to the lives of all who came within the baneful circle of her influence.[162]

The editor of the *Argus* newspaper chose different wording, preferring to speak about Martha's 'black catalogue of undetected atrocities'. The paper further informed its eager readers, 'There is too much reason to suspect that the wretched woman … had acquired a fearful familiarity with crime of this nature, and that repeated immunity had inspired her not only with an almost incredible contempt for human life, but with a recklessness that led to her undoing'. The *Argus* editor continued: 'The evidence pointed to a series of heinous crimes extending far beyond the immediate issue which the jury had to try'.

Such opinions had been indirectly supported by Martha herself, who had indisputably commented to Whitney and Fryer while incarcerated, 'So they found arsenic did they? A few more of my friends have died lately, I can give you their names. Would you like information about their burial? It would be useful if you wanted to dig them up'.[163]

According to the evidence given in court, these comments were made with not even the slightest hint of jocularity. Coming from such a tight-lipped murderer, Martha's words should not have been taken lightly. Her career as a prolific poisoner had commenced long before she was caught. And given her heartless and deceptively subtle methods of human destruction, the likelihood that she claimed other victims is exceedingly high. One would need to suspend belief considerably to ignore such a possibility.

While an unusual dose of coincidence may be involved, an uncomfortable reality is that wherever Martha went, people died before their time – often squirming in agony and suffering from a sudden and unexpected onset of unusual symptoms that failed to respond to normal medical treatments. And a number of these people had the definite potential to stand in Martha's way or annoy her.

Although Martha lived in an era when life expectancy wasn't as high as that enjoyed today, the rollcall of those within 'her baneful circle of influence' who met a suspicious and untimely demise is considerable and over-represented.

Given the urgency and emotion surrounding Martha's murder trial and execution, and the scarcity of information then available, much of the evidence relating to these cases was not considered, accessed or examined contemporaneously. While there were plenty of whispers and rumours, the overworked and undermanned police force could not expend any further energy on a murderer who had already been hanged.

It is only through the cool passage of time, and with more analytical information available, that these probabilities can be afforded their due consideration. And, for the purposes of justice and the potential victims involved, this needs to be done.

Mabel Needle

We already know that Martha's first child, the previously healthy Mabel, began to fall ill with vague symptoms towards the end of 1885 – the first year that Henry and Martha moved to Richmond. Martha would later comment that the child simply began to 'fade before her eyes'. The matrimonially distracted Dr Frederick Elsner regularly treated Mabel for fever, vomiting and stomach spasms, all occurring for short bursts of time, but Mabel's short life of three years and seven weeks came to an end on 28 December that year.

In light of Martha's later crimes associated with her other two daughters, Mabel's death has always been treated with maximum suspicion, with many presuming outright that Mabel was another of Martha's poisoning victims – perhaps even the very first. Much of the existing literature about Martha, both then and since, has simply listed Mabel among her victims, even though this was not verified by searching for arsenic.

When assessing criminals, it is largely a true theory that the best predictor of their future behaviour is most likely to be their past behaviour. Here, the reverse of that theory could be applied: namely that Martha's future behaviour could be a strong indicator of what she had already got away with previously.

So, do the facts suggest that she also murdered her daughter, Mabel? Did she systematically and slowly poison that child in the same manner she employed to dispose of the other two? Or was the demise of Mabel simply an unavoidable tragedy that set her heartbroken mother down a path of despair and criminality? A close examination of the facts, particularly the recorded medical opinions available, provides no comfort about Martha whatsoever.

It is clearly rational to presume that Martha followed similar methods throughout her path of human destruction. Once she found a poison distribution system that worked (and one that hadn't raised undue suspicion), she would have been very unlikely to change it. It follows that a certain measure of consistency would also be observed with the symptoms being displayed by her youngest arsenic victims, all little girls.

Each dying young girl was attended to by a different doctor – Mabel by Dr Elsner, Elsie by Dr Hodgson and May by Dr Payne – with all of these doctors working independently of each other and with no thoughts of linking the cases together. Yet, the symptoms endured by all three of Martha's daughters before their untimely deaths (which were subsequently recorded by the treating physicians) bore striking similarities.

Rather than pointing out a specific diagnosis for death, in each case the doctors noted generalised physical failings and a decline in health. Each was puzzled when their customary, trusty treatments would not work and noted that the health of the patient in each case would seem to rise and fall. But the key feature in all three cases was the unexplainable and continued vomiting being displayed by each patient, despite all the usually reliable medical interventions being applied to stop it.

Although he couldn't nominate one specific ailment that took the life of little Mabel, Dr Elsner particularly noted that she appeared to be experiencing 'cerebral' irritations and 'cardiac paralysis'. On the official death certificate of this child, he was satisfied enough to note the cause of death as 'cerebral tumour (congenital)' and subsequent respiratory and cardiac bronchitis.

It appears that Martha was more than content with this diagnosis. In the poorly spelled death notice she placed in the *Age* newspaper a few days later, she made specific note that Mabel had died 'after a short illness, of tumor on the brain' and would cite the same information in other documents in the future.

Move forward less than six years and the late Mabel's younger sister, May, was displaying uncannily similar symptoms. Dr Payne noted that he believed the symptoms were pointing to 'irritation of the brain'. Although, as with all of Martha's dead children, no official autopsy was conducted upon May's mysterious death, Payne was confident enough to write out the death certificate, citing the official cause of death as 'tubercular meningitis' – but he also clearly took the time to officially point out in writing the symptoms related to obstinate brain irritation and vomiting.

In light of the similar symptoms displayed by Mabel and May six years apart, it is certainly more likely than not that Mabel was also a victim at her mother's hand. This development would also add another ugly entry to Martha's dishonour board – it would make her the only Australian woman to have ever poisoned her entire family.

Mabel's body was never exhumed and her remains still rest in her lonely grave – Plot B0881 in Boroondara General Cemetery – about 50 m away from the once world-renowned gravesite of her other relatives.

Thomas Gilroy - 'A Startling Development'

One morning in late 1892 (more than 18 months *prior* to Martha's ultimate arrest), her former 'fiancé', Thomas Gilroy, reported for duty at Moloney's Drapery Store in Swan Street, Richmond. The usually chirpy 34-year-old had reliably worked at the shop for nearly seven years – but this would not be a normal day. Shortly after starting work, Gilroy began to complain to his boss, James Moloney, about feeling ill. His condition was so extreme that he uncharacteristically asked to be released from duty and Moloney immediately granted the request.

Gilroy's health deteriorated quickly, so his concerned friends rushed him to the nearby Alfred Hospital, where he was urgently admitted with severe abdominal pain, retching and an apparently high temperature. It was first thought that he might be suffering from the dreaded typhoid but, upon proper examination, it was discovered that this illness was definitely *not* present and the medical men examining Gilroy eliminated this possibility completely.

Nonetheless, Gilroy's young life came to an abrupt and unexpected end a few days later on 4 December 1892.

The doctor providing Gilroy's death certificate, the Chief Medical Officer of the Alfred Hospital at the time, Dr Anderson, officially listed the cause of death as ulcerative endocarditis – the very same curious ailment that came to be incorrectly cited as the primary cause of death for Louis Juncken less than 18 months later. It was certainly a peculiar diagnosis, particularly as the very astute Dr Boyd would later agree in a packed courtroom that ulcerative endocarditis was indeed a *very rare* disease.

After Martha's arrest, the circumstances related to Gilroy's premature death came to be viewed retrospectively and stories about his rapid demise were extensively circulated. There were even a few press reports about it. Under the heading 'Remarkable Coincidence', a *Herald* reporter saw fit to ponder publicly:

> The whole matter is certainly remarkable, affording as it does, two most singular coincidences. In the first place, as is known, Louis Juncken, who was opposed to a matrimonial engagement that his brother Otto had entered into with Mrs Needle, died under exceptional circumstances, and the cause of death was certified by his medical attendant, Dr McColl as being gastritis and endocarditis. Thomas Gilroy, who was for a while engaged to Mrs Needle, is certified to have died from

the same disease as was certified to have killed Louis Juncken.

The editor of this newspaper thought enough of this story to dispatch a reporter to interview Dr Anderson, who by this time had long left the employ of the Alfred Hospital and was operating a private practice in Prahran. When unexpectedly approached in the street, the reticent Anderson was initially very reluctant to talk about the Gilroy case, even though he said he remembered it 'perfectly, owing to its peculiarity'. He expressed surprise when the reporter began to raise the Needle case and then flatly refused to discuss the Gilroy matter further. Once the words 'Martha Needle' were mentioned, the medical fraternity now routinely clammed up.

But feeling the need to fill some of the void of official information, Anderson did let slip some general details prior to departing. He told the reporter, 'First typhoid was thought to be the cause of the trouble but the idea was soon dispelled and it was determined upon examination that ulcerative endocarditis was the mischief'. The doctor recalled that Gilroy's medical history had only revealed a bout of rheumatism a few years earlier, before he suddenly presented at the hospital's admissions with retching and a loss of appetite.

By the time that he arrived at hospital, the distressed Gilroy was desperately ill and the doctors gave him little hope of recovery. Anderson claimed that a post-mortem examination had taken place 'in accordance with the usual practice', which confirmed the hasty diagnosis, even though no official report of such an autopsy has ever been found. Even more curiously, although typhoid was definitely not detected, Anderson could still clearly recall 'there had been some changes in the intestines' of Gilroy.[164]

The 'Gilroy Story' initially broke around the time that Martha's proceedings were commencing in the Police Court. Sensing that the matter needed to be addressed, Martha's lawyer, Gaunson, ensured that the issues were raised in the court hearing itself and he called upon draper James Moloney as the reluctant witness to do so.

Gaunson went on to completely mock thoughts that Martha had caused Gilroy's sudden death and did so on the back of a single proposition: namely that Martha was in South Australia around the time that Gilroy had died – in fact, according to her lawyer, she was appearing before an Adelaide court.

Like most Richmond residents, Moloney had little desire to be involved in giving evidence in Martha's case but he now found himself in the witness box, facing Gaunson at his sarcastic best. Moloney hesitatingly commenced by agreeing that he knew Martha – she had even deposited a cheque of over £2 into his business account on 22 August 1891, which happened to be only five days before her daughter, May, had died.

Then Gaunson introduced the topic of Gilroy.

Gaunson: Did you know a man named Thomas Gilroy?

Moloney: Yes.

Gaunson: When did Gilroy leave your service? I have to trouble you because one of the papers has suggested that the accused also caused his death. Did you ever hear of any alleged love passages between the accused and Gilroy?

Moloney: I had it reported to me in the shop that she was 'sweet' on him.

Gaunson: Did Gilroy take ill in your shop?

Moloney: On a Monday morning shortly before his death he told me he felt very unwell and asked to get off for the day. I think it was in the month of December 1892. He died on the following Monday.

Gaunson: Did you know at that time the accused was in Adelaide?

Moloney: No.

Gaunson: Wouldn't it be surprising if she were that she could have caused his death?

Moloney: I don't know anything about it.

Gaunson: And you heard it reported that she was 'sweet' on him or he on her?

Moloney: They were sweet on each other, I heard.

Gaunson: Had you heard that Gilroy had ceased visiting the accused's house for months before he was taken ill?

Moloney: No.

Gaunson: Had you ever seen them in company?

Moloney: No, except when she came into the shop to make purchases.[165]

Based on this cross-examination, the newspapers eventually lost momentum with the 'Gilroy' matter and the story began to fade from the public's attention. With the extermination of Martha's family members and her one-person attack on the Junckens, the newspapers and police already had enough fodder with which to work.

In any event, it appeared from Martha's clear instructions to Gaunson that she was in South Australia around the time of Gilroy's death. It was also being implied that December 1892 was when Martha was being sued by her vexatious mother for maintenance and was seated in an Adelaide courthouse. But this had all been a big, fat lie.

A proper examination of the available records indicates that Martha was actually in Richmond at the time of Gilroy's death and had been there for a considerable number of days before the death occurred. And the South Australian court case dealing with her mother's writ had occurred in *January* 1892, not *December* 1892.

Martha was not to know that a bored court reporter had been in the Adelaide court on 6 January 1892 and, on an obviously slow news day, had seen fit to file a report on her unusual case with her wretched mother. This report ultimately found its way onto page six of the *South Australian* newspaper that afternoon. It read:

Police Courts

Adelaide: Wednesday, January 6 1892

[Before Messrs. T.K Pater, P.M. and Von Dittmer]
John Forran [sic] and Martha Needle (a widow), the former
of whom was represented by Mr V.F. Smith, were accused
by their mother of not providing her with adequate means
of support. From the evidence of the complainant, Mary
Forran [sic], it appeared she was destitute and weakly. Both
defendants denied their ability to contribute anything towards
the support of the complainant, the son stating that he had
been out of employment for some time and was living with
a friend: whilst Needle gave evidence that she had no means
of her own and was also living with a friend at Birkenhead.
Information dismissed.[166]

So, although Martha had spent some time in South Australia in 1892,
this had *not* been in a courtroom at the time of Gilroy's death. Her
return to Victoria in *January* 1892 was also verified by Otto in his
Supreme Court evidence, when he indicated that Martha returned
to Victoria and started as the resident housekeeper at Bridge Road on
'23rd January' that year.[167]

Another witness in the matter was Georgina Lillis, who became
one of Martha's closer companions while living under the same roof
at Bridge Road. Lillis' evidence to the Police Court hearing about
December 1892 was relatively clear: 'I attended at the cemetery with
Martha Needle when a man named Gilroy was buried. She returned
on the Friday and on the Monday or Tuesday Gilroy died. She had
been in Adelaide for five weeks prior to that time'.[168]

While the witnesses were struggling over some of the details, it
remained understandable that Martha would keep distancing herself
from the Gilroy situation. After all, on the facts, there were some close

links with her other dirty work and it didn't look good for her. But it was never contested that she had been close to Gilroy, that she had seen him regularly and that at one time she had been 'engaged' to him. Nor that he had then died suddenly and unexpectedly, displaying similar, rare symptoms to those experienced by her other murder victim, Louis Juncken. Nor was it questioned that Martha had actually attended his funeral.

Martha's sole alibi – articulated through her aggressive mouthpiece, Gaunson – rested on the proposition that she wasn't in Victoria around the time Gilroy died but this was clearly incorrect. And Gaunson could only possibly have been acting on Martha's instructions – it was Martha who sat back while one wrongly asserted statement after the next was aired. At no point did she move to correct any of them. Why did she allow this string of inaccuracies to continue unanswered?

In many respects, Martha was being advantaged by a mixture of the passing of time, misinformation, careless reporting, blurred recollections and the reluctance of witnesses, who did not want to become too fixed on the facts and therefore risk being pulled into the case.

The witnesses Moloney and Lillis were belatedly asked to recall details about Gilroy's death many months after it had occurred and they understandably began to offer a maze of dates, days and times when things may have taken place. And it needs to be remembered that at the time of Gilroy's death, Martha was operating under no suspicion whatsoever – therefore, there was no reason for Moloney or Lillis to fix in their minds dates and times to seemingly unconnected events.

Yet to the best of Moloney's hazy memory, he would initially suggest during his court cross-examination that Gilroy had left for hospital on a Monday morning. An *Argus* newspaper reporter would then incorrectly report Moloney's vague suggestion that Gilroy had also died on a Monday. But this had been misheard. In the court transcripts diligently produced by the clerk of courts, J. Pennefather, Moloney is clearly quoted as saying Gilroy died on a *Sunday*.

Meanwhile, the *Herald* newspaper would later suggest that Gilroy fell ill and was hospitalised on 1 December (which was actually a Thursday) and Dr Anderson would also recall that Gilroy was only in hospital for a short time before passing away.[169]

The Known Facts

Gilroy's official death record clearly shows that he died on 4 December 1892.[170] This day was a *Sunday*. This confirms the information uttered by Moloney in court about the day of Gilroy's death but contradicts Lillis' memory that this had possibly occurred on a 'Monday or Tuesday'.

But Lillis could not be wrong about Martha attending Gilroy's funeral. From the funeral notices appearing in the newspapers, it can be definitely ascertained that this occurred on Tuesday 6 December.

Lillis' recollection that Martha had returned to Richmond from South Australian on a Friday *before* Gilroy's death also appears to be reliable. While she did not have enough clarity of thought to specify a date, this was most likely either Friday 25 November or Friday 2 December.

Then in the evidence he gave before the Supreme Court, Martha's previous best ally Otto crucially let slip, 'From May 1892 till November of the same year when Martha returned from Adelaide, we got on happily enough in the household – the only thing was she suffered very much in health'. This testimony clearly supports the view that Martha was back in Melbourne by Friday, 25 November at the latest. And it must be remembered that by the time he was giving evidence in the Supreme Court, Otto was well prepared. He had been afforded plenty of time to recheck all the relevant dates and facts.[171]

Regardless of whether the Friday on which she returned was 25 November or 2 December, Martha would easily have had sufficient time to access Gilroy. And even if Lillis happened to get the day wrong, the proposition that Martha returned to Melbourne well before Gilroy's death was crystal clear.

In terms of motivation, there could have been many reasons why Martha may have felt the need to have Gilroy eliminated, at least in accordance with her damaged moral compass. Just as she had regularly corresponded with her other contacts, she would have kept up her writing to Gilroy. While she was in Adelaide, he would only have needed to annoy her sufficiently to have her storm back to Melbourne in a rage with the intention of doing him harm as soon as possible.

With her new fiancé, Otto, now tenuously in tow since May 1892, was her old one starting to become troublesome? Or was he beginning to uncomfortably comment about the destruction of human life around her? After she had become engaged to Otto, Martha had said she could not marry him immediately due to 'the delicate state of her health'. In reality, was this because she needed to deal with Gilroy first?

We know that Martha would only have needed a very hasty meeting with Gilroy, such as for a quick meal or the sharing of a refreshing cup of tea, to bring her plans into fruition. And, most significantly of all, we also now know that, for some reason known only to herself, Martha had chosen to be less than truthful and transparent about her whereabouts at the time of Gilroy's demise.

In any event, Martha could not legitimately claim a detachment from Gilroy. Of all the places on Planet Earth, his gravesite is plot B2419 of the Church of England section of the Boroondara General Cemetery. Remarkably, this plot rests only about 15 m from the very place where Martha's late husband and children, Elsie and May, were buried.

This is not only a chilling coincidence – on all those Sunday afternoons that Martha had visited the gravesite of her children to mourn, she would have been also treading directly over the remains of her former fiancé, probably with a degree of contempt. Likewise, the party disinterring Martha's family would have been hovering over this site the whole time they were working at the cemetery.

In light of the circumstances of Thomas Gilroy's sudden death, and the associated symptoms, there was only one way that Martha's involvement could have been either confirmed or eliminated – and that would have required the human remains in Gilroy's plot to be tested for traces of arsenic.

And, as was the case with Mabel Needle, there appears to be a high likelihood that arsenic would have been detected.

Annie Robinson

Martha had always remained strikingly close to Robert and Annie Robinson, her former neighbours from Wellington Street. This relationship had commenced from the moment Martha first moved into Richmond and continued even after the Robinsons left the area and relocated to the small Latrobe Valley township of Morwell.

After the deaths of her husband and children, Martha would still embark on curious examples of tourism and regularly visit the Robinsons, staying for several weeks at a time in their humble residence, rented from Robert's employer, Victoria Railways. The Robinsons would also occasionally return to the Richmond area and the first person they would seek out was usually Martha. While Robert had always been entranced by Martha, Annie became much more wary of her. Whether or not this was simply the case of a woman's instinct is unclear, although Annie was able to maintain much more objectivity about Martha than could her starry-eyed husband.

After all, Martha was a woman who had suddenly lost her husband and three children all within a short space of time – yet, to Annie at least, this fickle widow seemed more interested in pursuing new opportunities than mourning their loss. And the final clincher for Annie occurred the day at Morwell when she tried to console Martha over the death of Henry, only to have Martha blurt out, 'If he walked in through that door, I wouldn't speak to him'. Annie was left openly incredulous by that utterance and her friendship with Martha soon cooled considerably.

Annie was therefore another cynical person whose scepticism and suspicions could make life uncomfortable for the ambitious Martha. And she had viewed all of Martha's reactions at close range, which gave her considerable knowledge and power.

In October 1893, the previously healthy Annie was a few months pregnant with her third child, when she suddenly fell violently ill. Despite being under the best medical care of a local doctor, she just could not stop vomiting. After battling on for a week, Annie lost her unborn child and then died on 7 October 1893 at just 27 years of age. She was uncontrollably vomiting to the end.

Her official death record provided an unusual primary cause of death, even by the standards of 1893, namely 'Vomiting/Pregnancy'. This was supplemented by the later suggestions 'gastro intestinal influenza' and 'exhaustion'.

It is not fully recorded whether Martha had access to Annie at this time or whether she had been recently staying with the Robinson family at Morwell. And the 'Martha-friendly' Robert was never likely to be too reliably fixed on these facts, offering the usual hazy lists of poorly remembered dates. But in his court testimony, he did openly concede that Martha would often stay with his family for considerable periods of time.

Of course, Annie Robinson wasn't the first woman to die during pregnancy in this era but the symptoms suddenly overtaking her were eerily and suspiciously similar to those suffered by Martha's other victims – and her death on 7 October 1893 fell at a time when Martha was in fine form with her application of 'Rough on Rats'. It was only about two months after Martha had first begun to poison Louis and approximately seven months before she finally killed him.

Annie was greatly mourned by her two surviving children and extended family. Her passing was also said to have been 'deeply regretted' by Robert, her husband of eight years. Despite enduring a great deal, including the untimely death of Annie and the need to stand by Martha in court, Robert was to recover and quickly find love again, marrying a younger woman only 16 months later.[172]

As the eldest daughter of Brighton minister Thomas Stone, Annie's body was transported to Melbourne and she was laid to rest in the Stone family grave at Brighton Cemetery on 9 October 1893. No doubt, Martha attended this funeral and offered her full condolences to Robert.

By the time of the first anniversary of Annie's death, Martha had been convicted of Louis' murder and the extent of her other crimes had been revealed. It was also at that time the Stone family spared no expense to remember their lost loved one. Her parents offered a memorial in the *Age* newspaper for their 'dear daughter' and then paid for a poetic tribute to appear on page 1, which ended with the lines:

> But God alone, who knoweth best,
> Did ease her pain and give her rest.

Likewise, Annie's heartbroken siblings paid for another lengthy poetic tribute, which also appeared on page 1 of the same newspaper.[173]

There may have been a purposeful message behind such expanded tributes at this time. Either way, the circumstances related to Annie's death and her close connection to Martha would have rendered it very useful to have her remains subjected to a test for arsenic. Although her parents believed that it was 'God alone, who knoweth best', it wouldn't have hurt to get a second opinion.

Sophia Gilroy

Two factors led to queries being retrospectively raised about the premature death of Thomas Gilroy's wife, Sophia. One of these factors was the early and unexpected death of Thomas himself. The other was Martha's shameless flirting with Thomas while he was still married. Although Gilroy had wedded Sophia before emigrating from Ireland to Melbourne, this did not prevent Martha paying him high levels of attention.

Sophia Gilroy, the mother of a young son, died quickly on 24 April 1889, at just 27 years of age. She passed away at the Gilroy's rented house in Brighton Street, Richmond, and, like a number of other Richmond residents around that time, was buried in the Church of England section at Boroondara General Cemetery. Her treating physician was none other than the local lodge's George Hodgson, although the tried-and-true doctor had not consulted with her for over 12 days, indicating that her demise at such a young age had probably been unexpected.

Was Sophia's death at this time merely an unfortunate coincidence? Or did it point to something much darker? Was it possible that Martha had plotted to rid herself of a local love rival?

Even though Sophia's death seems to have Martha's modus operandi written all over it, the available records do not appear to directly implicate her in the tragedy. Although the handwriting scribed in fountain pen on Sophia's death record is almost indecipherable, it appears to indicate that the primary cause of death was 'phthisis' – a very old medical term for pulmonary tuberculosis. If diagnosed correctly, the symptoms related to this type of illness would have included persistent coughing and a gradual wasting away – they would, therefore, be unlikely to resemble those of Martha's known victims, even for a careless quack like Hodgson. But with Hodgson, one could never be totally sure.

Discussion of the tragic circumstances experienced by the Gilroy family would not be complete without mentioning their young son, James, who became a five-year-old orphan. He was left to face a very harsh start to his young and vulnerable life.

James and Lily Stiles

James Stiles had always been Martha's most trusted chemist in

Richmond. And it was only by a quirk of fate – namely Thomas Brittain steering her to another shop – that she had been prevented from buying the offending 'Rough on Rats' at his establishment, prior to killing Louis.

During Martha's trial in September 1894, it was mentioned that 39-year-old Stiles had died from poisoning a month or two earlier. Worse still, his wife Lily had also died from poisoning a short time later. Suicide was thought to be the reason in both cases – but this did not prevent tongues from inevitably wagging.

After all, as the trusted supplier of substances, Stiles knew many of Martha's secrets and he was in constant contact with her. Had the shrewd chemist put two and two together and confronted Martha with his suspicions? Or had he simply fallen victim to the Black Widow's wrath?

Stiles was found dead at the back of his shop on 2 June 1894. For Martha, the timing could scarcely have been more suspicious. This was only about two weeks after Louis had died, a week after she had sent a spiteful letter threatening the life of Louis' mother – and four days before she first poisoned Herman.

But a close review of the available facts seems to exonerate Martha from any direct involvement, at least this time.

Stiles had become a victim of the horrendous 1890s Depression. Poor investments had left him in financial embarrassment and he was threatened with the loss of his business to creditors. The worry was more than he could bear and it was then believed that he poisoned himself.

An official inquest was conducted on Stiles' body and it was found that he had consumed prussic acid, the term then used for hydrogen cyanide. And he had taken quite a lot – the inquest suggested he had consumed about 450 drops, whereas 50 drops would have been sufficient to kill him.

Hydrogen cyanide was clearly not Martha's poison of choice. And she would not have been likely to suddenly change her previously successful methods. Given that Stiles' death had occurred 11 days before her arrest, it cannot even be said that Stiles was publicly shamed by his previous connections with her.

The same may not be said of Stiles' wife, Lily, who also evidently opted to kill herself some six weeks later on 16 July, leaving behind three young children. Again, the culprit was prussic acid. It was Constable Joseph Robinson of Richmond Police (the old school friend of Thomas Gilroy) who was called upon to retrieve the body and poison. An official inquest found that Lily had committed suicide due to financial embarrassment. Given that Martha's story was by now entrenched across the front pages of every newspaper, Lily undoubtedly felt some shame over this involvement as well.

But it doesn't appear that Martha was directly involved – she had been locked up in prison for over a month when this poisoning occurred.[174]

Dr John Singleton

The celebrated life of the philanthropic physician John Singleton came to an end on 30 September 1891. He was 83 years old when he died and considered to be one of the greatest Australian charity workers of the 19th century. To put the time of Singleton's death into the chronology, this occurred just over a month after the passing of Martha's last child, May.

Not only had Singleton always been one of Martha's favourite doctors but he had also been closely associating with her as her husband and children all died. In his dying hours, Henry Needle had even specifically asked for a private consultation with the great doctor, only to be given the grim news that he would not survive his illness.

Although Singleton did not live long enough to see Martha arrested, is it possible that he had formulated an educated view about what was occurring? Had he mentioned these suspicions or concerns to Martha? Based on her past form, it would only have needed an errant comment or two to set Martha into action to defend her position. She was in regular contact with Singleton and could easily share a cup of tea with him during his numerous consultations and home visits.

Of course, it needs to be acknowledged that Singleton had already made it to 83 years of age – well past the average life expectancy of that era – and his advanced years and heavy workload had begun to leave him a bit feeble. But even though calls had been made on his constitution, numerous newspaper articles announcing his death reported that he had 'rallied with remarkable vigour and vitality' for a man of his age before being 'seized with a sharp attack of sickness'.

The newspapers presupposed that his death had been a consequence of the influenza outbreak then spreading throughout the city. But his death record tells a different story.

Singleton's death certificate was provided by none other than Dr Donald McColl, who less than three years later would make a frightful mess of treating Louis Juncken and misinterpret arsenical poisoning as the unlikely Riggs' disease. McColl made no mention whatsoever of influenza when citing the cause of death for Singleton. Instead, he specifically listed the causes as 'cystitis' and 'asthemia'.

'Cystitis' is a bladder infection that is more common in women than men. Although its primary symptoms include a persistent urge to urinate and pain or pressure in the lower abdomen, it can also be confused with kidney infection, the symptoms of which can include fever, chills, nausea and vomiting.

And 'asthemia' is defined as 'abnormal physical weakness or lack of energy'. At this point, it must be remembered that among the causes of death given for both Henry and Elsie Needle and also Annie Robinson was the vague term 'exhaustion'.

Singleton was buried by the ever-reliable undertaker Herbert King at Melbourne General Cemetery – yet another person who died with Martha lurking in the shadows. A number of local welfare agencies still bear his name and portraits of him are displayed at the Royal Children's Hospital in Melbourne and the Singleton Medical Welfare

Centre. His 'Free Medical Mission Dispensary' continued to operate right up until it was replaced by the Collingwood Community Health Centre in 1977.

Just before his death, Singleton published his memoirs entitled *A Narrative of Incidents in the Eventful Life of a Physician*. Had he lived long enough to know the full extent of Martha's activities, he probably would have been tempted to add another chapter or two.[175]

The Fateful Candidates

So, when Martha had fatefully uttered to detectives, 'A few more of my friends have died lately' and offered their burial details because 'It would be useful if you wanted to dig them up,' to whom had she been actually referring?

On the available evidence, she appears to be firmly in the frame for the potential murders of her eldest daughter Mabel, her ex-fiancé Thomas Gilroy and her long-term acquaintance Annie Robinson (along with her unborn child). Her involvement is less likely in the case of Sophia Gilroy and, on account of his age and failing health, Dr John Singleton could also be considered as more of a long shot. With what can now be ascertained, she can be safely eliminated as a suspect in the deaths of James and Lily Stiles.

There is no need to push reality too far or ask one question too many to reach these conclusions. Martha's possible involvement in these additional crimes can now be clearly ascertained on the evidence available, including the prevailing medical reports and death certificates.

But the only way of knowing for sure would be to test the relevant human remains, as had occurred with Martha's other victims. Analyst Cuthbert Blackett had once optimistically expressed his view that arsenic was 'indestructible' and, under the right conditions, it could still be detectable in a dry gravesite for 500 years. So, it might not be too late to check ...

The near misses must also be remembered along Martha's road of carnage. She had directly attempted to kill Herman Juncken and probably attempted to rid the world of her own mother. She had fully threatened to kill Margaret Juncken – and would undoubtedly have done so if the chance arose. She had also suspiciously issued continual dinner invitations to Herman's distant relative, Emma Jones.

And, of course, these are the people within Martha's 'baneful circle of influence' that we know about – and we are still counting … To Martha's advantage, dead people tell no tales.

CHAPTER 28

A Time for Reflection

'Mrs Needle probably was posing and acting all through her life.'
— ***South Australian Register***

G iven Martha's staunch denial of her alleged crimes right to the bitter end, is it worth re-examining her defence? Is it possible, however remotely, that she was in fact *innocent* of these despicable deeds? Was she simply a cursed victim of an outrageous travesty of justice? Was she a powerless woman victimised by a cruel, male-dominated justice system anxious to bring about a quick result? Or was she just a dreadful cook – so bad, in fact, that if she was alive today she wouldn't last through to the first commercial break in *My Kitchen Rules*?

When examining past crimes, some investigators (and many writers, for that matter) often find an inconsequential contradiction in some of the copious evidence that was presented, overanalyse it and then succumb to the irresistible temptation of presuming a person's total innocence. A process of reverse engineering is enlivened, which effectively skips over the primary matters that proved the case well beyond reasonable doubt in the first place. There is also a tendency to view those who were ultimately executed for their crimes more sympathetically.

Objectively, there is no need to embark upon such an idealistic process with Martha. The strings of evidence in her cases dovetailed together, she had no obvious defence on the facts and she appeared to have clearly committed the crimes attributed to her. In fact, in all likelihood, Martha also cold-heartedly committed a mind-boggling succession of further murders that remained concealed.

But this is not to say that her case cannot be reviewed in a modern context. According to the law that prevails today, she may have been treated very differently.

Contamination?

In the previous Louisa Collins 'Rough on Rats' case in New South Wales, a great deal of argument had been heard about the possibility of arsenic ingestion through environmental contamination. However, such arguments lacked any veracity in Martha's case. Clearly, in Martha's circumstances, the arsenic did not put itself there.

Through the admission of 'similar fact' evidence, it was shown that Martha's crimes had taken place across multiple properties and in different environments. Likewise, any arguments about the possibilities of bismuth contamination were unconvincing. Martha purchased medicines from a range of different chemists and the evidence given in court severely downplayed the likelihood of multiple contaminations.

Mad or Bad?

The most prominent question today relates to the possibility that Martha may have been insane. In fact, many have simply presumed that this was the case, based purely on the peculiarity of her behaviour and the astonishingly frightful nature of her deeds. They presume that a woman is normally expected to be a nurturing caregiver – in such a light, how could a *sane* mother ruthlessly exterminate her own children? This was all against the natural order of things. Mothers are supposed to love their children, not cold-bloodedly murder them. Martha's actions were so evil that surely no *sane* woman could perpetrate them?

But this can all be very counterintuitive and is even indicative to some degree of the type of thinking that allowed Martha to avoid suspicion for so long in the first place. In the eyes of the law, there is a vast difference between being *legally* insane and simply displaying idiosyncratic or evil behaviours.

The *legal* test of insanity, both then and now, is the trusty old M'Naghten Rule. Put briefly, the question to ask is as follows: is the accused able to understand what he or she is doing and capable of mentally determining the difference between right or wrong? In the case of Frederick Deeming, Justice Hodges had explained it in a different way by asking out loud if Deeming would have committed his crimes if a policeman had been watching?[176] The same question could be applied to Martha: would she have poisoned her victims while a policeman was watching? Not likely.

The criteria associated with the legal requirements for insanity therefore didn't assist Martha much at the time of her trial, nor do they appear to help her now. Her actions were not a 'one-off' episode of madness. She committed multiple offences at different times, all requiring a calculated approach. She gained either financially or personally from each murder. And, on each occasion, she also went to considerable lengths to conceal her behaviours and avoid detection. None of this pointed to a woman who was so crazed that she didn't know what she was doing.

This is not to say that Martha was not bizarre and unusual. The depravity of her deeds points to a warped human being with a number of psychological foibles. In modern speak, she would probably be deemed to have an antisocial personality disorder with psychopathic tendencies.

These types of people used to be labelled 'psychopaths', although the term 'sociopath' is also commonly used today. Either way, the primary characteristics displayed by these people are an incapacity to form any sense of empathy for others; a superficial charm and 'mask' of normality; a grandiose, egotistical self-perception; and a belief that they are smarter or more powerful than they actually are. Such people may also form artificial and shallow relationships, the major motivation of which is to manipulate matters in a way that best benefits themselves.

Unsurprisingly, an antisocial personality disorder is a very common trait among many murderers and those finding themselves in prison, which to a large extent explains how they came to be there in the first place. But according to the law, this is not the same as being 'insane'.

Nonetheless, a plea of 'insanity' may have provided Martha with her best chance of escaping the noose. But this possibility was only raised very belatedly towards the end of her Supreme Court trial and dismissed almost as quickly by the presiding Justice Hodges. Martha's lawyer, David Gaunson, faced a two-edged sword in this regard, because all along his client had resolutely refused to admit or concede her deeds – a helpful precursor to such a plea.

And what about the 'fainting fits' that Martha had evidently been prone to? Were these aligned to the neurological condition of epilepsy? This condition was often very wrongly misdiagnosed at the time and, even more tragically, incorrectly associated with insanity.

We now know vastly more about epilepsy than was recognised in Martha's day. While the cause of epilepsy isn't always known, it can be due to brain injury or infection, genetic factors, stroke or structural abnormalities of the brain. There are several types of seizures associated with epilepsy. In the mild range, a person remains conscious but may be confused, experiencing nausea and hallucinations. At the other end of the scale, the person may fall, become unconscious, have stiff muscles and have convulsions.

Martha's 'fainting fits' may also have been demonstrative of a psychotic disorder, the symptoms of which broadly being delusions, hallucinations and disorganised speech.

Significantly, most of those offering evidence about Martha's fainting fits – such as Otto, Eliza Martin and Georgina Lillis – all had sympathy for her cause and realised that proof of 'insanity' was her best chance to come out of her ordeal alive.

Yet, while epilepsy can be diagnosed at any age, Martha had never shown any signs of epilepsy or fainting fits during her younger years (as confirmed by her old childhood friend, Eliza Martin) – or evidently during the early years of marriage. And although it was suggested that she might have felt a bit faint a couple of times while locked up in prison, her full-blown fits were not witnessed. Therefore, her 'fits' appeared to be primarily associated with her overuse of the dangerous brew, chlorodyne. And if the sworn observations of some – such as Herman Juncken – can be relied upon, she was also capable of 'putting on' a fit when the need arose to seek pity or attention.

In any case, while committing her crimes Martha had displayed high levels of deliberation. On multiple occasions across many years, she had been required to gradually drip-feed doses of arsenic to others, while remaining careful not to poison herself. She had needed to prepare the food, apply the poison, serve it up and even organise insurance policies. These types of actions required rational and premeditated action and could not be achieved in the middle of a debilitating fainting fit.

Slow poisoning is also a cruel way of killing. Martha had not only deceived everybody by feigning affection but also through her considerate nursing of each person whose life she was slowly destroying. She even went as far as shedding tears over the graves of the children she had put to death. In each case, the victim had got in her way in some manner. And she could always blindside the judgement of men by appealing to their masculine ego. None of these actions pointed to an irrationally insane person.

Childhood Trauma and Domestic Violence

The true tragedy of Martha rested with her horrible childhood, during which she was forced to endure verbal and emotional abuse, sexual and physical assaults as well as horrendous neglect. In a modern context, this helps to explain *how* she came to be the person she was. Under such conditions, a person could not be expected to develop normally. From an extremely early age, Martha's personality had been shaped and damaged beyond repair. And she had unquestionably learned to hate.

But to mitigate these theories, such childhood factors never offer an exact science that is easy to predict. Not all children coming from similar backgrounds become serial killers – many even rise above their unfortunate beginnings and develop into outstanding citizens.

In light of the evidence given, it is also reliable to assume that Martha had been a victim of what is now known by the general term 'domestic violence'. Trapped in a loveless marriage, she became a target for whatever the bully saw fit to dish out. This was an era when a woman could easily find herself trapped in a horrendous and violent union. There was little prospect of divorce, no money or help at hand – and seemingly no way out. And the beltings didn't just hurt physically – they left scars in grudging memories.

In modern times, the law recognises that some women may have put up with years of abuse before they finally snap and take matters into their own hands. This is a form of self-defence to escape the violence.

Nonetheless, the all-male jury and judges in Martha's day had not viewed this too sympathetically. They may even have figured that if all husbands who mistreated their wives at that time could be murdered, the male population would be seriously reduced.[177] And even if Martha did hate or fear her husband, this still fails to explain why she also murdered her own children.

Childhood trauma and domestic violence would undoubtedly be raised in mitigation if Martha's case were heard today. But this would be cold comfort for Martha, who lived and died in a different era. Many youngsters of that time had an utterly bedraggled childhood and an astonishing percentage of women found themselves ensnared in frightful domestic situations – but society was slow to acknowledge the depth of such factors.

And not all victims at that time reached for a tin of rat poison to solve their problems.

The Question of Motive

An intriguing aspect of Martha's murders has always centred on the question of 'motive'. Despite extensive discussion over many decades, a single definitive motivation has never been identified. She took her greatest secret to the prison grave – what actually caused her to murder?

Unfettered greed stands as an obvious candidate, particularly in light of the insurance monies that Martha systematically collected. Then again, the sums involved didn't always appear to justify the risk (remembering Gaunson's quote of 'murder at the rate of about £62 per head') and the prosecution ultimately dropped this angle for the Supreme Court trial. Also, Martha kept killing even during times when she clearly had enough money to live off.

Martha's ambition and her need for convenience and power all stand as motive possibilities. Also, her apparent love for Otto, the course of which she did not want impeded.

However, while love between couples is notoriously one of the most powerful forces imaginable and often associated with blind acts of crime, Martha's saga was far from a story of pure romance. In many respects, it was more about maintaining control. Martha could hate in equal measure, leading to the question: did she murder for love, or did she murder for hate? Although she had killed some people to be rid of them, in the case of Otto she had demonstrated a possessive willingness to kill others to be *with* him.

She probably murdered her last two children, one by one, partly to get some insurance money but mostly to free herself from any encumbrances that stood in the way of seeking a second marriage. Her husband, Henry, was not only poisoned for his insurance payout but also from mere dislike. Likewise, Louis Juncken was doubtlessly sent to his maker due to Martha's vindictiveness after he dared to question her and impede her marriage intentions.[178]

A Product of Lucifer

Of course, another unpleasant possibility is that Martha was just plain evil. In more recent years, a number of studies have been conducted about the general trait of 'evil' that have dispensed with the usual psycho-boloney to explain heinous behaviour. Leading the way with these groundbreaking theories has been Dr Michael Stone, Professor of Clinical Psychiatry at Columbia University. After an extensive study of criminals, his forensic research has concluded that many deviants commit their awful deeds to bring about a twisted sense of personal pleasure.

These observations have prompted Dr Stone to dispense with the usual psychiatric categories and stop trying to explain all behaviours in terms of biological, psychological and social theories. Instead, he has stated: 'Such people make a rational choice to commit terrible crimes over and over again. They are evil, and we should be able to say that formally.'[179]

Suffice to say, these types of theories remain controversial. But, when faced with the sordid crimes of Martha Needle, the straight-out evil conclusion may carry some weight. It must be remembered that Martha never conceded any involvement in her crimes, nor offered any hint of remorse.

She never expressed any *genuine* pity whatsoever for her victims and her only displays of grief were publicly staged to bring about sympathy for herself. She enjoyed taking revenge on the world and worked hard not to get caught. In short, Martha seemed to get her jollies from committing her crimes.

Our perception of a crime's brutality can soften over the passage of time. It is therefore necessary to carefully consider the outrages that actually occurred. Just as some have formed a romantic view of Martha's predecessor, Ned Kelly, it may be possible to view Martha through a sympathetic lens – until we recall all that she did.

It must be remembered that Martha was a grown human who made life and death decisions. It is highly probable that her crimes stretched over a period of at least nine years before she was caught. And she exterminated her own little children.

Of course, the spirited search for Martha's *single* motive could be somewhat futile in any case. When dealing with a nefarious person like Martha, there may not be *one* obviously good inspiration at all. Such a complex personality does not lend itself to simply having the answers in the back of the book. In all likelihood, Martha acted for a multitude of reasons, including greed, control, cruelty, convenience, vanity, sadism, power, love, hate and even a lusty dose of evil – with no predominant purpose.

But what we do know is that she was an intriguing character who had learned how to maintain a smile and charm others while she murdered.

What Can Be Learned?

Even though the detectives involved were lauded and Dr William Boyd enjoyed a rise to hero status in the media of the day, there were no real winners in the Martha Needle story. But it is comforting to think that at least some worthwhile knowledge came from this frightful tale.

Martha's case came to stand as a warning to two classes of people. To the medical profession, her story underlined the principle that things are not necessarily always as they seem. For many years, Martha's murders all went undetected as trusting, naïve and charmed practitioners asked no questions and then unsuspectingly supplied death certificates adorned with the names of all sorts of ailments –

except, of course, the one that had actually killed their patients.

The second warning was to criminals who found themselves emboldened with initial success and then couldn't resist the temptation of returning to the proverbial well once too often. Because the ultimate irony of Martha's story is that, in the end, her own self-assurance brought her undone. By trying to dispatch Herman so rapidly, she moved away from her more patient modus operandi and literally attempted 'one murder too many'.[180]

She had already successfully murdered a string of other people, consigning her victims to history and the local cemetery at the same time. An old hand, she *knew* to only feed her victims small doses of arsenic – she was an efficient killing machine. While attempting to murder Herman, was she recklessly overconfident or desperate due to time pressures? The excessive dose of 'Rough on Rats' she used tends to indicate the latter.

But one thing is certain: had she not become so careless, panicked and clumsy with Herman Juncken, this book would never have been written.

CHAPTER 29

Life Rolls On

Martha's life may have ended abruptly on 22 October 1894 – but the world kept moving. And not everything progressed the way Martha would have envisaged.

Losing the Plot

Although towards the end of her short life Martha entertained visions of grandeur about being mournfully buried with 'her babies', her incarceration did not go the way she planned. Even after being buried inside the prison walls as a common murderer, she was not destined to rest in peace.

In 1924, Melbourne Gaol closed down and the site was allocated for educational purposes, firstly for the newly established Emily McPherson College and much later for the Royal Melbourne Institute of Technology. The burials of those executed within the prison walls had always occurred haphazardly and during construction work in 1929 a number of graves were exposed by a large steam shovel dismantling a bluestone wall. Edges of coffins were ripped off and a number of skeletons were exposed.

As soon as this morbid event occurred, an excited crowd of onlookers mobbed the unearthed gravesites and began to souvenir the bones. At least four skulls were stolen, including one mistakenly thought to be that of Ned Kelly. But two of the skulls had come from female bodies, their original owners believed to be Martha Needle and Frances Knorr.

The skulls were later returned and ended up being housed at the National Trust and later The University of Melbourne. All the other bones located at Melbourne Gaol were then exhumed in a disorganised manner, placed in sacks and transferred to Pentridge Prison in Coburg to be reinterred in mass graves. So, part of Martha ended up in university storage and her other remaining bits lie jumbled in a mass grave at Coburg.

Instead of resting in peace, she ended up being scattered in pieces.

The Grave Marker

Just as Martha had died during the 1890s Depression, her remains were disturbed during the world's next economic downturn. It was noted that the prison bluestones, including some adorned with the markers used for executed prisoners, had some value. These bluestones were recycled and used by the Brighton City Council to build a seawall to protect the local beach from erosion.

Although most were placed with the engravings facing inwards, a worker with a sense of occasion left Martha's stone facing outwards, with the marker 'M.N. 22.10.94' still clearly visible in the Green Point Wall. Over time, the marker came to be buried by metres of sand but it has been recently rediscovered. It sits along the Esplanade, at the foot of Wellington Street, Brighton – a mixture of mystery and fascination for passers-by.

Although Melbourne Gaol closed to prisoners in 1924, one multistorey wing remains standing and is now an extremely popular museum. Martha's death mask sits very prominently on display, a haunting reminder for the hundreds of thousands of visitors each year of the macabre time in which Richmond's infamous Black Widow

355

lived and died. It is an unglamorous and undignified memorial for the vain Martha Needle.

By accessing the best figures available, history now tells us that Martha was one of 187 offenders to be executed in Victorian prisons. Some 41 of these executions took place at country prisons, while 135 unlucky souls had their lives extinguished at Melbourne Gaol – with 15 of these following Martha. This included Emma Williams the next year. Although many women were reprieved for the ghastly murders of adults, it is worthy to note that the three women executed during that period (Knorr and Martha in 1894 and Williams in 1895) were all involved in child deaths.

Upon the closure of Melbourne Gaol, the prison's gallows beam from which Martha was hanged was transferred to Pentridge Prison, where it did the job on 11 more prisoners, including the last woman hanged, namely prostitute Jean Lee in 1951, and the last man hanged in Australia, Ronald Ryan in 1967. From there, the gallows beam found its way back to the Old Melbourne Gaol museum, where it is still on display today.

The Famous Gravesite

Given that Martha had wiped out her entire immediate family, ultimately including herself, the branches on her side of the family tree became stunted. She had stolen the future lives of her children and this effectively left no-one to tend the graves of her family members at Boroondara General Cemetery.

Over the years, the elaborate memorial Martha paid to have erected at plot B2477 was vandalised and stolen. At the time of the exhumations, this plot of land became the centre of intense attention as the most famous crime-related site in the world – but today it sits in a lonely state of neglect. If Martha's ghost still haunts this gravesite, she would undoubtedly be disappointed to observe such a downfall.

The grave of Thomas Gilroy, located 15 m away, and that of Mabel

Needle a little further down the path are in a similar state.

Martha's Richmond

While most of the landmarks and building façades around which Martha did her best work remain identifiable, Richmond is no longer the poverty-stricken area that it was in her day. Today, Richmond has developed into a more affluent and multicultural enclave that has seen industrial factories replaced by a flood of new apartment complexes.

The Bridge Road shopping precinct no longer specialises in the grocers, tinsmiths, chemists, hay stores, butchers, surgeries and photography galleries that Martha knew. Today, Bridge Road is a well-known upmarket fashion capital, specialising in outlet stores for the most iconic brands available, and it is lined with cafes and coffee shops.

The building that housed Louis' saddlery at 137 Bridge Road still stands, after being utilised over the years as a boutique, restaurant and swanky clothing store. Visitors to the area can take a 'history walk', which heavily features this building. A council-produced plaque attached to the front of the store clinically outlines the deeds that Martha committed there, a chilling reminder for the daily streams of passing pedestrians.

The Needle family's abode at 110 Cubitt Street, where Martha had performed much of her devilish work, always remained an eerie object of fascination for local residents. It eventually housed another family for several decades before becoming the first headquarters of the Melbourne Bread and Cheese Club. The building was sold in 1967 to developers and demolished in the name of progress soon after.

The Poisoning Industry

The ghastly publicity surrounding the Needle case and the legislative tightening of access to 'Rough on Rats' saw the popularity of this product as a murder weapon irretrievably wane. But some cases still emerged internationally, one of the most famous being Chicago's sinister Tillie Klimek, who was convicted in the 1920s of disposing of a series of superfluous husbands.

The decline of 'Rough on Rats' did not necessarily mean the end of poisoning cases in Australia. In fact, given the size of the population, Australia always held its own when it came to producing dangerous critters such as Black Widows. But although these monstrous women would build upon the labours of their more masterful predecessor, Martha Needle, they needed to find other potions.

In 1909, the sadistic Martha Rendell became the last woman hanged in Western Australia after killing her stepchildren with diluted hydrochloric acid. Then came a couple of well-known New South Wales cases, both utilising the alternative rat killer thallium, which was marketed using the brand name 'Thall-rat'. In 1952, Yvonne Fletcher was convicted of dispatching two of her husbands. This was followed the next year by the unlikely old wretch Caroline 'Aunt Thally' Grills, who was convicted of attempted murder, even though she looked more like a woman on her way to bingo than a cold-hearted murderer using thallium to rid herself of unwanted relatives.

The Major Players in the Martha Needle Drama

The Junckens:
Otto Juncken

Once out of the clutches of Martha, Otto would go on to forge a long and remarkably successful life, both professionally and personally.

With economic times improving, his employer – Clements Langford – won contracts to build city theatres and office buildings and also constructed eminent Richmond factories for notable companies such as Rosella as well as Bryant and May. And the firm's star employee, Otto, would prosper throughout this time. During World War I, he unofficially changed the spelling of his surname to 'Yuncken'. Then in 1918, he left his employer to form a partnership with fellow tradesman Lauritz Hansen.

This partnership was the beginning of the firm called Hansen Yuncken, which has constructed some of Australia's most iconic buildings. As a tribute to its founding fathers, the national company Hansen Yuncken is still going strong today, with over 650 staff spread across five Australian States.

And although he was once the great love of Martha's life, Otto ultimately found another woman to marry. In July 1901, Otto married 21-year-old Bertha Arbrecht from nearby Abbotsford, with Herman performing the honours as best man. Otto and Bertha were to have six children and the family contributed readily to community life. Undoubtedly lucky to have survived the carnage in his younger years, Otto passed away peacefully in November 1945 at 80 years of age.

Herman Juncken

The man who had so narrowly avoided a fatal dose of rat poison in 1894 settled in the town of Nuriootpa in South Australia's Barossa Valley the following year and started the Juncken Builders and Joinery business. He married Clara Krieg in 1902 and the couple had two children. Herman took an active interest in the sporting and social life of Nuriootpa right up to his death in 1930, at 68 years of age. His son, named Carl Otto after two of Herman's brothers, was also a carpenter and he took over the family business until his death in 1951. The Juncken Builders and Joinery firm is still thriving today.

Margaret Juncken

The matriarch of the Juncken family was not only Martha's most despised nemesis but she also outlived Martha by a long way. Mrs Juncken eventually passed away in North Adelaide at the ripe old age of 78 in January 1913.

Martha's Beloved Family:

In stark contrast to the successful Junckens, Martha's family members continued to tread their familiar path ...

Mary Foran

Martha's reprehensible mother did not improve her behaviour with age. She also spent a lot of her time hanging around with Martha's half-brother, Daniel Foran Jnr, who ended up being a chronic alcoholic.

Mary Foran also continued to keep her fluids up. On 22 March 1900, South Australia's *Advertiser* reported: 'Mary Foran, aged 63, who said she was a Highland Lady, was charged by M.C. Wells with being idle and disorderly. The evidence showed she was frequently drunk, and earned a small living by knitting and telling fortunes. She was sent to gaol for two months. Daniel Foran was charged with a similar offence, and was sent to gaol for one month.'

Mary died in 1906 at the age of 69 and was buried in the West Terrace Cemetery in South Australia. At no point in her life did she ever attribute any of her own behaviour as a contributing factor towards Martha's dysfunctionality.

Daniel Foran Jnr

Martha's oldest stepbrother did not live as long as his mother, dying mysteriously in a South Australian prison cell on 29 March 1902.

On the previous morning, he had presented himself in a delirious state to farmers at a property in Tickera and told them he wanted to give himself up to police. The last words he mentioned to them were, 'I did not do it', although it was never exactly clear what 'it' was meant to be.

He was ultimately handed over to the police at nearby Wallaroo, who noted that he was insane, before he died in his cell sometime that night. A hastily conducted post-mortem found that his body was very filthy and emaciated; it concluded that he had died due to heart failure, alcoholism, self-abuse and 'reckless living'. He was only 36 years old when he died.[181]

Martha's Stepfather - Daniel Foran Snr

The abhorrent monster who had been convicted of sexually assaulting his stepdaughter, Martha, would live long enough to grow old disgracefully. The late but not great child molester died on 9 January 1927, boasting repeatedly to all those around him that he was 100 years old.

The Witnesses:
Herbert King

In Martha's era, there must have been considerable money to be made from funerals, because after first coming to Richmond virtually penniless in the early 1880s, the undertaker King became one of the area's most wealthy businessmen. When he died at his residence, 'Kingsley', in Lennox Street in 1913, he was heralded as one of Richmond's 'most famous self-made men'. In his estate, he left a massive £15,659 in real estate and £5,235 in savings.[182] The name 'Herbert King' is still synonymous with funeral homes in Melbourne, although in recent times the company has amalgamated with the equally well-known firm Tobin Brothers.

Cuthbert Blackett

Blackett continued working as the Government Analyst until October 1902, when he finally resigned his position at the age of 71 after he found that the increasing workload was causing too much strain. Only a few weeks later he suffered a massive stroke at his residence, 'Ingleby', in Walsh Street, South Yarra – a street later made infamous because of the cold-blooded murder of two police officers in 1988. Blackett died the next morning without gaining consciousness.[183]

Dr William Boyd

The doctor who had brought Martha undone remained a prominent citizen and highly sought-after practitioner for the rest of his days – all on the back of being the man 'who discovered Martha Needle'. A newspaper article announcing his death at Erin Street, Richmond, in November 1933 described him as 'one of the best known medical men in Melbourne'. Boyd's status also didn't harm his bank balance and showed that money could still be made in private practice, even in lowly Richmond. The estate he left to his wife amounted to a staggering £82,799.[184]

Dr George Hodgson

Even though he didn't appear to be able to distinguish between a pimple on someone's backside and a supra-gluteus-maximal lesion, the ever-hospitable Hodgson continued to operate a busy practice as a general practitioner. He was also an active member of the British Medical Association and took a great interest in the progress of the society in Victoria. Hodgson passed away in 1936 at 81 years of age. He was buried at St Kilda Cemetery, near where he was residing at the time.

Dr Donald McColl

As the man who would be forever haunted by one particular death certificate – the wretched one he supplied for Louis Juncken – McColl would pass away in May 1938 at 76 years of age. In the latter years of his life, he would campaign vigorously against the so-called 'faith healers' who were then trying to ply their trade in local churches.

Dr Frederick Elsner

After unsuccessfully treating three-year-old Mabel Needle, Elsner would continue working in the Richmond area for another four years before moving to St Kilda and then Moree in New South Wales. He would cringe every time his saw his name being associated with the Needle case in the newspapers.

To make matters worse, his name had already been extensively sullied on a national basis in the newspapers through his high-profile divorce proceedings. (These were the days when such proceedings could be gleefully and salaciously reported on the front page.) His wife gave evidence that, while living in Richmond, her husband was violent and knocked her down and kicked her several times.

On one occasion, he told her she looked tired and should go to bed. She did so but then she awoke and went downstairs to find him in a compromising position with a local nurse. For this crime, she threw a vase at her husband and severely cut his head, forcing him to consult another doctor to have the wound stitched.

Just as the story was reaching its well-read crescendo, both parties agreed to the divorce without any further findings or admissions.[185]

Somehow, Elsner survived all his personal dramas to continue his medical career. He later became well known for his studies in the emerging field of dermatology.

Dr James Neild

The overworked coroner continued to lecture in forensic medicine at The University of Melbourne until 1904. In between his prolific literary pursuits, he also played a major role in founding and maintaining the Victorian branch of the St John Ambulance Association.

Neild died at his home at 21 Spring Street, Melbourne, in August 1906 at 82 years of age.[186]

Dr Charles Payne

The young doctor who had made a mess of diagnosing May Needle went on to live a prominent life, although much of this would be on the coat-tails of his young wife. Four years before he ventured to Richmond, Payne had married 22-year-old Ellen ('Nellie') in Hobart. It was while she was living in Richmond and sitting bored at home that Nellie had taken woodcarving lessons, the first step to her becoming one of Australia's most prolific and renowned sculptors of the 20th century. Her emerging talent saw her move to England in 1899, where Payne also continued his medical career, firstly as a personal physician for a local Duke and then as the proprietor of a small psychiatric hospital.

The Paynes moved back permanently to Hobart in 1908, where Dr Payne would eventually pass away in 1925.

The Lawyers:
Charles Finlayson

The methodical lawyer, whose prosecution skills helped send Martha to her early grave, continued working as a Crown Prosecutor and was ultimately appointed King's Counsel. He died on 10 September 1909.[187]

David Gaunson

Martha's spirited lawyer continued in his legal practice for some time, representing a range of motley clients, before he returned to political life. In June 1904, he was successful as a Labor candidate, forming an alliance with Thomas Bent, who by this time was the much-maligned and controversial Victorian Premier. (The latter's definitive biography even carried the subtitle *'Bent by name, Bent by nature'*.)[188] Gaunson would remain a vocal and belligerent critic of the Victorian police force for the rest of his days. He died in 1909 at 63 years of age. Among his pallbearers were Thomas Bent and the illegal bookmaker John Wren.

Marshall Lyle

The crusader Lyle not only continued practising as a successful solicitor but he also relentlessly maintained his firebrand campaign against the death penalty. He did not live long enough to witness its abolition in Australia, passing away at the age of 82 on 17 August 1944.[189]

Justice Henry Hodges

The judge who sentenced Martha to hang continued his glittering legal career and, while he eventually became a senior judge, he also continued to attract controversy for his manner in court. Things became so bad that in 1913 a committee of the Victorian bar formally recorded a stinging rebuke about his extreme discourtesy towards those appearing before him.

Nonetheless, Hodges was knighted in 1918. He also became immensely wealthy. In the latter years of his life, he lived in a substantial mansion in Lansell Road, Toorak, and he also owned a country house, 'Dreamthorpe', in the Macedon district. He died at 'Dreamthorpe' in 1919 after a short illness, at 74 years of age.

Ironically, he was buried at Boroondara General Cemetery.[190]

The Cops:
Alfred Whitney

As the Needle matter came to a conclusion, Whitney was dismayed to learn that, due to the harshness of the economy at the time, neither he nor Detective Fryer would receive any additional financial reward or rise in rank for their acclaimed work on the case. Nonetheless, at the age of 50, Whitney would finally be promoted to the rank of Sub-inspector in 1900 – but his career would be marked by uncomfortable controversy from that point on.

Complaints about the police force reached such a pitch that in 1905, the Thomas Bent government appointed a Royal Commission to inquire extensively into the force's efficiency, organisation and administration. One of the main parliamentary mouthpieces leading the charge was David Gaunson, who used this opportunity to ruthlessly hunt down Whitney and Fryer, among others. Both would be called before the Royal Commission to extensively give evidence and be cross-examined.

Whitney's reputation soured at the Royal Commission when an allegation by Mrs Louisa Hogan was exhaustively investigated. Mrs

Hogan suggested that she had been induced to pay Whitney £27 to have a large sum of stolen money returned rightfully to her.

The Commission eventually concluded that 'In this case there was a great conflict of evidence, and we find that the charge was not proven'. But, as the saying goes, 'mud sticks'.

Robert Fryer

Fryer fared even worse than Whitney at the Royal Commission, after he made allegations about another officer – specifically that the fellow detective had accepted a £50 bribe.

The Commission concluded that 'The evidence shows that the statements of Fryer are unreliable. It has also been shown that he had been in the habit of passing valueless cheques, and we recommend that his conduct be brought under the notice of the Hon. Chief Secretary.'

An internal inquiry was conducted the following year and the allegations against Fryer for passing dud cheques were sustained. As a result, he was demoted back to the rank of constable in uniform and ordered that his service should be restricted to a country district. His career in tatters, Fryer would serve his time at Bendigo, where all the scallywags appearing before the local court would constantly remind him of his past indiscretions.[191]

The Prison Workers:
Robert Burrowes

The Governor of Melbourne Gaol at the time of Martha's execution was appointed the following year as a Police Court Magistrate. He would serve in this position throughout the Stawell and Horsham districts until his death from an asthma attack in 1906, at 52 years of age. Burrowes was also buried at Boroondara General Cemetery.[192]

Reverend Henry Scott

The overbearing Reverend continued working as the prison chaplain and also assisted the poor with his 'slum work' throughout the Depression. He later became the chaplain of the Melbourne and Women's Hospitals. He preached right up until his death in 1912, just before his 72nd birthday.

Thomas Pauling

Martha's ghoulish hangman went on to execute others, including another woman – the impoverished prostitute Emma Williams, who murdered her two-year-old son in 1895. But from such humble beginnings, he then slid further downhill and his chosen career path as a hangman came to an abrupt end. After squandering his earnings on heavy drinking and gambling, he fell into massive debt and fled from Victoria to escape his numerous creditors. He was never heard from again.[193]

Robert Gibbon

Pauling's gruesome hanging assistant did not fare any better. Although he happily took over as Chief Executioner after Pauling vanished, by the end of 1897 he was asking for permission to carry a firearm in the street because he believed that his life was 'continually in danger'. His request was refused.

Although he continued in his grisly hangman role, Gibbon was convicted of committing a sexual assault on a young girl in 1901. He was subsequently flogged three times and sentenced to a four-year prison sentence.

By 1909, Gibbon's mental condition had deteriorated to such a degree that he began to suffer from delusions, believing that naked young girls were running along the street in front of him as they shouted obscenities and taunts at him. He even took the step of writing to the police to warn them that unless they took steps to 'prevent these carryings-on', he would have to take the law into his own hands and hang the girls who were cruelly teasing him. The police informed the prison doctors about Gibbon's claims and they examined him before pronouncing him insane. At the age of 58, Gibbons was incarcerated at Yarra Bend Asylum, where he would die a 'raving lunatic' several years later.[194]

A Real-Life Drama Queen

The melodramatic Martha may have been pleased to know that her life story would ultimately be the subject of a theatrical production – a play conducted at the famous La Mama venue in Carlton during the 1993 Melbourne Fringe Festival. Said to be 'based on a true story', the production entitled *The Eye of the Needle* was acclaimed among critics and went on to win the Best Production Award for that year.

But Martha may have been dismayed in equal measure to know that the play didn't particularly immortalise her reputation for romance. It focused instead upon the tension between the two Juncken brothers vying for her attention and portrayed her abruptly as a flirty 'notorious local poisoner who was hanged'.

All in the Family

The spookiest footnote of all to the Martha Needle story involves her nephew, Alexander Newland Lee, the son of Martha's older sister, Ellen. At the age of 31, he was hanged in Adelaide Gaol on 15 July 1920 for poisoning his wife, Muriel, and three of their children, who were aged six, five and three.

Apparently inspired by his infamous aunt, his crimes were said to be among the most horrendous ever recorded in South Australia. He killed his family with the pesticide strychnine, mainly because they had become a burden to him after he became enamoured of a young nurse. Just as his aunt had done many years before, he brazenly signed the Poison Book to comply with the prevailing regulations.

At his trial, Lee suggested that the strychnine must have been dislodged from an overhead shelf and accidentally fell into some milk that his family members had consumed before going to bed. For some remarkable reason, the jury opted not to accept this version of events and he was found guilty. He remained impenitent to the last, made no confession of any kind and went to his death unflinchingly, the 53rd person executed in South Australia.

Perhaps the art of poisoning and the propensity for murder ran in Martha's family after all.

Sometimes the strangest stories are the ones that are true.

Time Line of Events

- 9 April 1864 - Martha Needle born near Morgan, South Australia (as Martha Charles)
- 4 April 1876 - Stepfather Daniel Foran convicted of sexually assaulting Martha
- 15 May 1882 - Martha marries Henry Needle in North Adelaide, South Australia
- 13 November 1882 - Mabel Needle born in Sydney, New South Wales
- 6 October 1884 - Elsie Needle born in Adelaide, South Australia
- Mid-June 1885 - The Needle family moves to Richmond, Victoria
- 28 December 1885 - Mabel Needle dies
- 28 April 1886 - May Needle born in Richmond, Victoria
- 24 April 1889 - Sophia Gilroy dies
- 22 June 1889 - Henry Needle takes out £200 life insurance policy
- 4 October 1889 - Henry Needle dies
- 5 October 1889 - Martha makes £200 insurance claim
- 9 December 1890 - Elsie Needle dies
- 27 August 1891 - May Needle dies
- 30 September 1891 - Dr John Singleton Snr dies
- Early January 1892 - Martha begins living as housekeeper at 137 Bridge Road
- 16 April 1892 - Martha first becomes 'engaged' to Otto Juncken
- 4 December 1892 - Thomas Gilroy dies
- 18 August 1893 - Louis Juncken falls ill for the first time
- 7 October 1893 - Annie Robinson dies
- 25 April 1894 - Louis Juncken falls ill for the second time
- 30 April 1894 - Emma Jones assists with Louis Juncken's care and he recovers
- 8 May 1894 - Emma Jones departs Bridge Road
- 10 May 1894 - Martha purchases a new box of 'Rough on Rats'
- 11 May 1894 - Louis Juncken falls ill again
- 15 May 1894 - Louis Juncken dies

- 22 May 1894 - Martha threatens the life of Margaret Juncken, via letter
- 2 June 1894 - Pharmacist James Stiles dies
- 6 June 1894 - Herman Juncken falls ill
- 13 June 1894 - Martha arrested
- 23 June 1894 - Body of Louis Juncken exhumed
- 10 July 1894 - Bodies of Henry, Elsie and May Needle exhumed
- 12 July 1894 - Commencement of Martha's Police Court hearing
- 16 July 1894 - Lily Stiles dies
- 24 September 1894 - Commencement of Martha's Supreme Court trial
- 27 September 1894 - Martha convicted of murder and sentenced to death
- 10 October 1894 - Executive Council review of Martha's case
- 22 October 1894 - Martha hanged at Melbourne Gaol
- 15 July 1920 - Martha's nephew, Alexander Newland Lee, hanged at Adelaide Gaol for the poisoning murder of his wife and three of his children

END NOTES

Chapter 1: The Life and Crimes of Martha Needle

1   *Sydney Morning Herald (SMH)*, 25/7/1894, p.7; *Herald* [Melbourne], 24/7/1894, p.1

2   *Herald*, 2/8/1894, p.2

Chapter 2: As the Twig Is Bent - A Miserable Early Existence

3   SA Police Report, 16/9/1894, Public Records Office of Victoria (PROV) VPRS 264, P0001, Unit 2

4   *Advertiser* [SA], 4/4/1876, pp.4 and 6; *South Australian Register* 13/7/1876, 3 April 1875, 15/3/1877, both p.3

5   SA Police Report, 16/9/1894, PROV VPRS 264, P0001, Unit 2

Chapter 3: Early Marriage and Baby Carriage

6   NSW Registry of Births, Deaths and Marriages: Records of Mabel Needle (3651/1882)

7   Births, Deaths and Marriages Victoria: Records of Elsie Needle (17379)

8   Richard Broome (with Richard Barnden, Don Garden, Don Gibb, Elisabeth Jackson and Judith   Smart), *Remembering Melbourne 1850–1960*, 2016, p.339; Janet McCalman, *Struggletown – Public and Private Life in Richmond 1900–1965*, 1998

9   *Argus*, 15/6/1894, p.5

10   The University of Melbourne, 'Diseases and Epidemics', www. emelbourne.net.au. It was the growing death toll from this disease and a final acceptance throughout the 1890s of the role played by germs in spreading it that finally led to the development of a proper sewerage system throughout Melbourne.

Chapter 4: 'Rough on Rats' … and Just as Harsh on Humans

11   The longevity of arsenic was demonstrated in the case involving French 'Emperor' Napoleon Bonaparte, who met his maker way back in 1821 after reportedly succumbing to cancer. Some historians preferred to believe that Bonaparte had been poisoned by someone close to him and, due to their urging, surviving locks of Bonaparte's hair were tested for contaminants in 1962. The detection of trace residues of arsenic was sufficient to launch a new conspiracy theory around the world.

12   Crime Hub, 'Beware the bite of the Black Widow', Criminology in Oz, 10/6/2014, www.criminologyinoz.wordpress.com

13   ibid.

Chapter 5: Mabel Needle - The Loss of a Young Life

14   Geoffrey Blainey, *Odd Fellows: A History of IOOF Australia*, 1991

15   *Evening News* [Sydney], 22/11/1898, p.4; *South Australian Chronicle*, 13/5/1893, p.10; *SMH*, 8/5/1893, p.1; *Express and Telegraph* [SA], 9/5/1893, p.3

16   *Age*, 18/6/1894, p.5

Chapter 6: A Bit of Flightiness

17   *Barrier Miner* [Broken Hill], 9/10/1894, p.3

18   *Herald* 16/7/1894, p.1

19   *Herald* 12/7/1894, p.1; *Advertiser* (SA) 16/6/1894, p.5; *Sun* 29/1/1975, p.14

20   *Advertiser* (SA) 16/6/1894, p5. Whilst the surname was always reported as 'Juncken', some members of the family often spelt it with a 'Y' – as in 'Yuncken'. Nonetheless, most of the family still residing in South Australia always retained the original spelling.

21   ibid. and *Argus*, 14/6/1894, p.5

22   Police Court Transcript (hereafter PC Transcript), p.43, Criminal Trial

Brief, PROV VPRS 30, P0006, Unit 1

Chapter 7: Untimely Demise of a Husband

23   *Argus*, 18/6/1894, p.5

24   ibid.

25   *Argus*, 6/7/1894, p.5

26   *Herald*, 16/7/1894, p.1

Chapter 8: Mummy Dearest - Elsie and May Needle

27   *Advertiser* [SA], 16/6/1894, p.5

28   ibid. and *Herald*, 18/6/1894, p.1

Chapter 9: A Fresh Beginning and a Besotted New Man

29   PC Transcript, pp. 48-9

30   Ibid., p.5

31   *Age*, 14/7/1894, p.7

32   Exhibit A17, Criminal Trial Brief, PROV VPRS 30, P0006, Unit 1

33   *Herald*, 13/7/1894, p.1

34   W. Stanton Lowe, 'The Needle Case – One Murder Too Many', *Townsville Daily Bulletin*, 19/11/1952, p.5

35   PC Transcript, p.11

36   *Argus*, 16/6/1894, p.7

37   *Herald*, 13/7/1894, p.1

38   *Argus*, 19/6/1894, p.5

39   ibid., p.6

40   *Age*, 19/6/1894, p.6; *Argus*, 19/6/1894, p.5

Chapter 10: An Obstacle No More - The Destruction of Louis Juncken

41   *Herald*, 16/7/1894, p.1

42   *Age*, 14/7/1894, p.7

43   PC Transcript, pp.15–17

44   ibid., p.12

45   ibid., pp.20–24

46   *Herald*, 13/7/1894, p.1

47   *Argus*, 14/7/1894, p.1

48   PC Transcript, pp.15–20

49   *Herald*, 16/7/1894, p.1

50   Supreme Court Transcript (hereafter SC Transcript), pp.4 and 26,
      Capital Case File PROV VPRS 264, P0001, Unit 2

51   SC Transcript, p.51; PC Transcript, pp.24–5

52   SC Transcript, p.4

53   *Advertiser* [SA], 16/6/1894, p.5

Chapter 11: More Dreadful Misfortune

54   SC Transcript, pp.5 and 26; *Herald*, 16/7/1894, p.1

55   *Argus*, 16/6/1894, p.7

56   SC Transcript, p.27; *Herald*, 16/7/1894, p.1

57   W.R. Jewell, 'Blackett, Cuthbert Robert (1831–1902)', *Australian
      Dictionary of Biography (ADB)*, Volume 3, 1969

58   SC Transcript, pp.25 and 49–51; *Argus*, 15/6/1894, p.5; *Herald*,
      31/7/1894, p.1

Chapter 12: Setting a Trap for the Black Widow

59   *Advertiser* [SA], 23/6/1894, p.5; *Herald*, 2/8/1894 and 3/8/1894, both p.4

60   *Argus*, 17/7/1894, p.6. The person she had visited was Mr Priestley,
      a local who at that time made a living as a 'Skin Merchant'.

61   SC Transcript, pp.30–1 and 56

62   *Advertiser* [SA], 17/7/1894, p.5

63   *Argus*, 17/7/1894, p.6; *South Australian Register*, 19/6/1894, p.6; *Weekly
      Times*, 16/6/1894, p.23

64   *Herald*, 14/6/1894, p.1; *Argus*, 14/6/1894, p.5

65   SC Transcript, p.56; *South Australian Register*, 19/6/1894, p.6

Chapter 13: A Public Frenzy

66   *Herald*, 18/6/1894, p.1; *Argus*, 20/6/1894, p.5; *Age*, 19/6/1894, p.6

67   *Herald*, 14/6/1894, p.1; *Advertiser* [SA], 15/6/1894, p.5, and 16/6/1894, p.5; *Australasian*, 23/6/1894, p.1089

68   *Argus*, 15/6/1894, p.5

69   ibid.

70   *West Australian*, 5/1/1909, p.2; Geoffrey Serle, 'Gaunson, David (1846–1909)', *ADB*, Volume 4, 1972; James Morton and Susanna Lopez, *Gangland Australia*, 2007, pp.23 and 350–1

71   *Age*, 18/6/1894, p.5; *Argus*, 18/6/1894, p.5; *Barrier Miner* [Broken Hill], 18/6/1894, p.1

Chapter 14: Digging Up the Truth

72   *Argus*, 18/6/1894, p.5

73   *Herald*, 18/6/1894, p.1

74   Bryan Gandevia, 'Neild, James Edward (1824–1906), *ADB*, Volume 5, 1974; Maurice Gurvich and Christopher Way, *The Scarlet Thread – Australia's Jack The Ripper*, 2007, p.161

75   *Advertiser* [SA], 25/6/1894, p.5

76   *Herald*, 19/6/1894, p.1

77   *Herald*, 21/6/1894, p.1; PC Transcript, p.53

78   *Brisbane Courier*, 23/6/1894, p.5; *Advertiser* [SA], 23/6/1894, p.5

79   *Advertiser* [SA], 25/6/1894, p.5

80   PC Transcript, pp.54–55

81   SC Transcript, pp.33–35; *Advertiser* [SA], 23/6/1894 and 25/6/1894, both p.5

82   *Age*, 2/7/1894, p.5

Chapter 15: More Gruesome Business

83   *Herald*, 5/7/1894 and 6/7/1894, both p.1; *Age*, 6/7/1894, p.5

84   *Age*, 5/7/1894, p.5

85   *Age*, 11/7/1894, p.5

86   SC Transcript, p.55

87   *Herald*, 10/7/1894, p.1

88   SC Transcript, p.35

Chapter 16: The Police Court

89   *Australasian*, 21/7/1894, p.120

90   PC Transcript, p.9

91   ibid., pp.9–10; *Herald*, 13/7/1894, p.1

92   PC Transcript, pp.1–12; *Herald*, 13/7/1894 and 14/7/1894, both p.1

93   *Herald*, 14/7/1894, p.1

94   ibid.

Chapter 17: Back by Popular Demand

95   *Advertiser* [SA], 17/7/1894, p.5

96   *Herald*, 16/7/1894, p.1

97   *SMH*, 25/7/1894, p 7; *Herald*, 24/7/1894, p. 1 and 2/8/1894, p.2

98   *Herald* 24/7/1894, p.1

Chapter 18: The Heavily Anticipated Resumption

99   *Herald* 31/7/1894, p. 1

100   PC Transcript, pp.33–34; *Herald*, 31/7/1894, p.1

101   PC Transcript, pp.34–35; *Herald*, 31/7/1894, p.1

102   *Herald*, 1/8/1894, p.4

103   PC Transcript, p.39; *Herald*, 1/8/1894, p.4

Chapter 19: It Pays To Be Insured

104   PC Transcript, p.40; *Herald*, 1/8/1894, p.4

105   PC Transcript, p.42

106   *Herald*, 1/8/1894, p.1

107   PC Transcript, p.42–43; *Herald*, 1/8/1894, p.1

108   PC Transcript, pp.43–44; *Herald*, 1/8/1894, p.4

109   PC Transcript, pp.44–46; *Herald*, 1/8/1894, p.4

110   PC Transcript, pp.46–48; *Herald*, 2/8/1894, p.4

111   PC Transcript, p.49

Chapter 20: The Final Day

112   ibid., pp.50–52

113   PC Transcript, p.54; *Herald*, 2/8/1894, p.4

114   *Herald*, 2/8/1894, p.4

115   *Age*, 3/8/1894, p.6; *Herald*, 3/8/1894, p.4

116   Neither of these men had any way of knowing that this type of conversation was well ahead of its time. Almost 40 years later, Australia's most famous racehorse, Phar Lap, was destined to die suddenly in the United States, sparking a wave of international conspiracy theories. In recent times, a more likely culprit has emerged – namely Fowler's Solution, a commonly used treatment applied to racehorses during that era. Fowler's Solution contained arsenic and it was considered possible that Phar Lap's devoted strapper, Tommy Woodcock, had innocently overdone the doses.

117   *Herald*, 3/8/1894, p.4; *Age*, 3/8/1894, p.6

118   *SMH*, 16/8/1894, p.5; *Advertiser* [SA], 16/8/1894, p.5

119   *Herald*, 8/8/1894, p.1

Chapter 21: The Supreme Court

120   *Herald*, 24/9/1894, p.4

121   *Herald*, 25/9/1894, p.4 and 26/9/1894, p.1

122   *Herald*, 25/9/1894, p.1

123   ibid.

124   SC Transcript, pp.33–41; *Herald*, 25/9/1894, p.1

125   *Herald*, 26/9/1894, p.1

126   *Herald*, 26/9/1894, p.4

Chapter 23: The Final Roll of the Legal Dice

127   *Herald*, 27/9/1894, pp.1 and 4

128   *Herald*, 28/9/1894, p.4; *Argus*, 28/9/1894, p.6

129   *Herald*, 28/9/1894, p.4

130   There were contradictory reports about the amount of time the jury took to reach a decision, with the *SMH* citing '40 minutes' and the *Argus* citing '10 minutes'.

131   *Argus*, 28/9/1894, p.6

132   ibid. and *Herald*, 28/9/1894, p.4

133   *Herald*, 28/9/1894, p.1

134   *SMH*, 28/9/1894, p.5; *Argus*, 28/9/1894, p.4; *West Australian*, 29/9/1894, p.6

135   *Advertiser* [SA], 28/9/1894, p.4

Chapter 24: Pleas To Save Martha

136   Capital Case File PROV VPRS 264, P0001, Unit 2

137   ibid.

138   This document has survived the ravages of time and can still be found stashed away in a dusty government file at PROV: Capital Case File PROV VPRS 264, P0001, Unit 2

139   *Herald*, 10/10/1894, p.1

140   Michael Cannon, *The Woman As Murderer: Five Who Paid With Their Lives*, 1994, pp.118–22

141   *Age*, 22/10/1894, p.5

142   *Barrier Miner* [Broken Hill], 9/10/1894, p.3

143   *Herald*, 10/10/1894, p.1

144   *Fitzroy City Press*, 8/9/1893, p.2

145   *West Australian*, 11/10/1894, p.2

Chapter 25: Preparing to Die

146   State Library of Victoria (SLV) MS 8296. This bible would be retained and still exists in library archives today, as does many of Ada Owen's letters and the replies of Martha and Otto.

147   *Herald*, 22/10/1894, p.1; *Age*, 23/10/1894, p.5 Probate and Administration Files PROV VPRS 28, P0002, Units 394 and 714, item 56/185; Wills

PROV VPRS 7591/P2, Unit 228, item 56/185

148   SLV MS 8296

149   Cannon, pp.70–83; *Smith's Weekly*, 31/5/1919, p.9

150   *Argus*, 21/4/1894, p.9

151   *Herald*, 22/10/1894, p.1

152   Cannon, p.83

153   *Herald*, 22/10/1894, p.1

Chapter 26: Facing the Noose

154   *Argus*, 24/10/1894, p.5

155   ibid.

156   Allan Brennan, 'Poisoned Her Family As A Matter Of Business', *World News Sydney*, 4/9/1935, p.15

157   *Herald*, 22/10/1894, pp.1–2; *Advertiser* [SA], 23/10/1894, p.5

158   *Herald*, 22/10/1894, pp.1–2

159   *Advertiser* [SA], 27/10/1894, p.5

160   SLV MS 8296, letter dated 1/8/1894

161   *Argus*, 23/10/1894, p.5, 24/10/1894, p.5 and 30/10/1894, p.5; *Herald*, 23/10/1894, p.1 and 30/10/1894, p.1; *Advertiser* [SA], 24/10/1894, p.5, 25/10/1894, p.5 and 27/10/1894, p.5

Chapter 27: How Many More?

162   *Herald*, 22/10/1894, p.2

163   *SMH*, 25/7/1894, p.7; *Herald*, 24/7/1894, p.1

164   *Herald*, 16/7/1894, p.1; *Border Watch* [Mount Gambier], 18/7/1894, p.3

165   PC Transcript, p.54; *Argus*, 1/8/1894, p.6

166   *South Australian*, 7/1/1892, p.6

167   SC Transcript, pp.6–7

168   PC Transcript, p.49

169   *Herald*, 16/7/1894, p.1

170   Births, Deaths and Marriages – Victoria: Death records (15229 –1892)

171   SC Transcript, p.7

172 *Morwell Advertiser*, 8/2/1895, p.3. This time the lucky girl was Annie Jones, the daughter of a fellow railwayman, and the local newspaper described Robinson as 'a well-known and esteemed townsman'.

173 *Age*, 8/10/1894, p.1

174   PROV Inquest Files, VPRS 24, Units 627 and 631, 1894, 679, 1019; *Argus*, 17/8/1894, p.7; *Evening Journal* [Adelaide], 5/6/1894, p.611

175   Births, Deaths and Marriages – Victoria: Death records (16396 – 1891); Sylvia Morrisey, 'Singleton, John (1808–1891)', *ADB*, Volume 6, 1976; *Age*, 2/10/1891, p.6; *Mercury and Weekly Courier* [Vic.], 8/10/1891, p.3; *Kilmore Free Press*, 8/10/1891, p.2; *Traralgon Record*, 6/10/1891, p.2

Chapter 28: A Time for Reflection

176 Gurvich and Way, p.239

177 Cannon, p.26

178 *Australasian*, 27/10/1894, p.749

179 Harold Schechter and David Everitt, *The A to Z Encyclopedia of Serial Killers*, 2006, pp.84–5

180 W. Stanton Lowe, p.5

Chapter 29: Life Rolls On

181 *Advertiser* [SA], 31/3/1902 and 1/4/1902, both p.7

182 McCalman, p.14

183 W.R. Jewell, 1969; *Argus*, 20/10/1902, p.6; *Ballarat Star*, 20/10/1902, p.6; *Australasian*, 25/10/1902, p.987

184 *Courier Mail*, 30/11/1933, p.16; McCalman, p.16

185   *Evening News* [Sydney], 22/11/1898, p.4; *South Australian Chronicle*, 13/5/1893, p.10; *SMH*, 8/5/1893, p.1; *Express and Telegraph* [SA], 9/5/1893, p.3

186 Gandevia, 1974

187 Gurvich and Way, p.302

188 Margaret Glass, *Tommy Bent – Bent by name, Bent by nature*, 1993

189 Gurvich and Way, p.302

190 J. Young, 'Hodges, Sir Henry Edward (1844–1919)', *ADB*, Volume 9, 1983; Gurvich and Way, p.302

191 *Bendigo Advertiser*, 1/11/1906 and 17/11/1906, both p.5; *Bendigo Independent*, 21/10/1908, p.3; Royal Commission Report on the Victorian Police Force, 1906, pp.vi, 391

192 *Horsham Times*, 29/6/1906, p.3

193 Cannon, p.144

194 Cannon, pp.144–5; PROV VPRS 515 Volume 55, p.48

SELECTED REFERENCES

ARCHIVAL MATERIAL
Public Records Office of Victoria (PROV)

- Criminal Trial Brief VPRS 30, P0006, Unit 1 – Police Court Hearing, Depositions, Exhibits and Notes
- Capital Case File VPRS 264, P0001, Unit 2 – Supreme Court Trial and associated papers
- Register of Decisions on Capital Sentences VPRS 7583, P0001, Unit 2
- Capital Sentences Files VPRS 1100, P0002, Unit 2
- Central Register of Female Prisoners VPRS 516, Volume 2, p.409
- Central Register of Male Prisoners VPRS 515, Volume 44, p.48
- Women's Suffrage Petition 1891
- Probate and Administration Files VPRS 28, P0002, Units 394 and 714, item 56/185
- Inquest Files VPRS 24, P0000, Units 627, 631, 633, items 1894/679, 1019, 1287
- Wills VPRS 7591/P2 Unit 228, item 56/185

State Library of Victoria

- MS 8296 – Various letters, photographs and papers of Martha Needle and Otto Juncken

Births, Deaths and Marriages - Victoria

- Death records: Elsie Needle (17379), Thomas Gilroy (15229), Sophia Gilroy (9472), Mabel Needle (13690), Annie Robinson (15462), Henry Needle (18486), May Needle (12179), Martha Needle (14018), John Singleton (16396), James Stiles (7401)
- Birth records: James Gilroy (31443)

New South Wales Registry of Births, Deaths and Marriages
- Birth records: Mabel Needle (3651/1882)

Various Records/Correspondence/Photographs from the following:
- Burnley and Richmond Historical Society Archives
- Victoria Police Archives
- National Trust Archives
- Old Melbourne Gaol
- Friends of Boroondara General Cemetery Inc

BOOKS

- Baxter, Carol, *Black Widow – The True Story Of Australia's First Female Serial Killer*, Allen and Unwin, 2015
- Blainey, Geoffrey, *Odd Fellows: A History of IOOF Australia*, Allen and Unwin, 1991
- Broome, Richard, (with Richard Barnden, Don Garden, Don Gibb, Elisabeth Jackson and Judith Smart), *Remembering Melbourne 1850–1960*, Royal Historical Society of Victoria, 2016
- Cannon, Michael, *The Woman As Murderer: Five Who Paid With Their Lives*, Today's Australia Pub. Co., 1994
- Carringbush Regional Library, *Copping it Sweet: Shared Memories of Richmond*, City of Richmond, 1988
- Colquhoun, Kate, *Did She Kill Him? – A Victorian Tale of Deception, Adultery and Arsenic*, Little Brown, 2014
- Cossins, Annie, *The Baby Farmers – A Chilling Tale of Missing Babies, Shameful Secrets and Murder in 19th Century Australia*, Allen and Unwin, 2013
- Dasey, Patricia (ed.), *An Australian Murder Almanac – 150 Years of Chilling Crime*, Griffin Paperbacks, 1993
- Glass, Margaret, *Tommy Bent – Bent by name, Bent by nature,*

Melbourne University Press, 1993

- Gurvich, Maurice and Way, Christopher, *The Scarlet Thread – Australia's Jack The Ripper*, Fairfax Books, 2007
- Haldane, Robert, *The People's Force – A History of Victoria Police*, Melbourne University Press, 1986
- Hempel, Sandra, *The Inheritor's Powder – A Cautionary Tale of Poison, Betrayal and Greed*, Weidenfeld & Nicolson, 2013
- Lawrence, Michael, *They Were Hanged in Melbourne*, Swell Productions, 1970
- Lewis, Wendy, *The Australian Book of Family Murders*, Murdoch Books, 2011
- Mallett, Xanthe, *Mothers Who Murder – And Infamous Miscarriages of Justice*, Ebury Press – Random House, 2014
- McCalman, Janet, *Struggletown – Public and Private Life in Richmond 1900–1965*, Hyland House, 1998
- Morton, James and Lobez, Susanna, *Gangland Australia*, Melbourne University Press, 2007
- Overington, Carole, *Last Woman Hanged – The Terrible True Story of Louisa Collins*, HarperCollins Publishers, 2014
- Saunders, Kay, *Deadly Australian Women*, ABC Books, 2013
- Schechter, Harold and Everitt, David, *The A to Z Encyclopedia of Serial Killers*, Pocket Books, 2006
- Taylor, Bernard, *There Must Be Evil – The Life and Murderous Career of Elizabeth Berry*, Duckworth Overlook UK, 2015
- Tedeschi, Mark (QC), *Eugenia: a true story of adversity, tragedy, crime and courage*, Simon and Schuster Australia, 2012
- Weaver, Rachel, *The Criminal of the Century*, Australian Scholarly Publishing Co., 2008

NEWSPAPERS

- *Advertiser* [SA]
- *Age*

- *Argus*
- *Australasian*
- *Australian Star* [Sydney]
- *Ballarat Star*
- *Barrier Miner* [Broken Hill]
- *Bendigo Advertiser*
- *Bendigo Independent*
- *Border Watch* [Mount Gambier]
- *Brisbane Courier*
- *Bunyip* [SA]
- *Burra Record* [SA]
- *Camperdown Chronicle*
- *Canberra Times*
- *Courier Mail*
- *Evening Journal* [SA]
- *Evening News* [Sydney]
- *Express and Telegraph* [SA]
- *Fitzroy City Press*
- *Herald* [Melbourne]
- *Horsham Times*
- *Inquirer and Commercial News* [WA]
- *Kilmore Free Press*
- *Melbourne Standard*
- *Mercury* [Tas]
- *Mercury and Weekly Courier* [Vic]
- *Morwell Advertiser*
- *New Zealand Herald*
- *Newcastle Morning Herald and Miner's AdvocateOtago Witness*
- *Smith's Weekly*
- *South Australian Chronicle*
- *South Australian Register*
- *Sun*

- *Sydney Morning Herald*
- *Table Talk*
- *Townsville Daily Bulletin*
- *Traralgon Record*
- *Weekly Times*
- *West Australian*
- *Western Mail* [WA]

ARTICLES

- Carland, Rebecca, 'Otto Juncken, Builder 1865–1945', www.collections.museumvictoria.com.au
- Crime Hub, 'Beware the bite of the Black Widow', Criminology in Oz, 10 June 2014, www.criminology.oz.wordpress.com
- Culture Victoria, 'Martha Needle', www.cc.vic.gov.au
- Gado, Mark, 'Rough on Rats', www.crimelibrary.com
- Kenneally, Christine, 'Ned Kelly and the curious case of the missing tooth', August 2011, www.christinekenneally.com
- Kyriacou, Kate, 'Female serial killer Martha Needle killed husband, three daughters and almost future brother-in-law', 3 December 2014, www.couriermail.com
- Levi, Claire and The Richmond Historical Society, 'Bridge Road Richmond Historical Walk', undated.
- Martin, Tammy, 'My Infamous Ancestors', *The Compass*, Volume 1, No.4, 2009, p.14
- Masters, Tony, 'Forensic Science', *Chem News*, University of Sydney Chemistry Alumni, Issue 3, September 2003, pp.6–7
- Robinson, Russell, 'The Black Widow of Richmond Martha Needle Killed Five with Poison', 2 July 2012, www.media.heraldsun.com
- Robinson, Russell, 'The Hangman's Journal', 4 June 2012, www.media/heraldsun.com
- School of Historical and Philosophical Studies, The University of Melbourne, 'Diseases and Epidemics', www.emelbourne.net.au

- Smith, Jeremy, 'Losing the Plot: Archaeological Investigations of Prisoner Burials at the Old Melbourne Gaol and Pentridge Prison', www.prov.vic.gov.au/publications

JOURNALS/PERIODICALS

- *Australian Dictionary of Biography* – entries for: John Singleton, Cuthbert Blackett, Henry Hodges, James Neild, David Gaunson
- *Sands and McDougall's Melbourne and Suburban Directory,* Sands and McDougall
- *South Australian Police Historical Journal,* September 2006

OFFICIAL REPORTS

- Royal Commission Report on the Victorian Police Force, 1906

IMAGE CREDITS

Public Records Office of Victoria: Front and Back Cover, mug shots of Martha Needle and Robert Gibbon

Supreme Court of Victoria: Martha Needle's page – Particulars of Executions Book

State Library of Victoria: Martha Needle's studio portraits, May and Elsie Needle, Melbourne Gaol, David Gaunson, Supreme Court of Victoria

Australasian Newspaper: Martha and Henry Needle's wedding photograph, Mabel Needle, 110 Cubitt Street, Otto Juncken, Robert Fryer, pictorial during trial, Martha Needle's court portraits

Herald Newspaper: Sketch of Henry Needle, exhumation of Needle family, Dr William Boyd

National Trust of Victoria: Martha Needle's death mask

Bayside Library Service: Grave marker stone – Brighton Beach

Elaine Race/ Tony Michael: Needle family gravesite

PRODUCTION ACKNOWLEDGEMENTS

'The key is to keep company only with people who uplift you, whose presence calls forth your best'.

- Epictetus

Whilst writing a book of this nature - and compiling the necessary information - an author can embark on a considerable and unpredictable journey. From humble beginnings, I have been fortunate to have met a lot of good people along the way, many of whom were only too happy to 'go the extra mile' to provide technical and editorial assistance.

In this regard, I would like to especially thank David Langdon, Katie Potter, Kathleen Toohey Chris Hasdo, Elaine Race, Tony Michael, Colin Kemp, Natasha Kamanev, Zander, Amanda and Nathan Clarke, Natasha Kamanev, Julia Deoki, and Joanne Boyd. This is also not to forget all the other staff at organisations such as the National Trust of Victoria, Old Melbourne Gaol, Public Records Office of Victoria, Supreme Court of Victoria, State Library of Victoria, Bayside Library Service and various other libraries, museums and voluntary institutions around the country for their help whenever needed.

The completion of this book has also required a great deal of effort from a talented team operating behind the scenes. I am extremely grateful to the highly capable professionals at New Holland Publishers for their work and support of this project, particularly noting the contributions of Alan Whiticker, Fiona Schultz and Coral Kuhn.

Kaitlyn Smith deserves special mention for her continual encouragement and exceptional capacity to get the job done.

ABOUT THE AUTHOR

Dr Brian 'Joe' Williams is a highly regarded and exceptionally credentialed writer, lawyer, historian and educator, who can count a Ph. D, LLB 1st Class Honours and Master's Degree among his six university qualifications. He was also awarded a Peter Fensham scholarship at Monash University.

Brian has been called a 'walking encyclopaedia' about all matters related to true crime and criminology, and has always been a proud supporter of the underdog.

His previous books and articles – often produced under the name of his alter ego 'Joe St John' - have been highly commended and covered the areas of true crime, popular history, education, sport, biography and humour. He also has numerous radio credits, and in recent years appeared on the high-rating television series 'Crimes That Shook Britain'.

This is the sixth book that Brian has produced for New Holland Publishers. He can be contacted at: bwproductions27@gmail.com

First published in 2018 by New Holland Publishers
London • Sydney • Auckland

131–151 Great Titchfield Street, London WIW 5BB, United Kingdom
1/66 Gibbes Street, Chatswood, NSW 2067, Australia
5/39 Woodside Ave, Northcote, Auckland 0627, New Zealand

newhollandpublishers.com

A record of this book is held at the British Library and the National Library
of Australia.

ISBN 9781921024955

Group Managing Director: Fiona Schultz
Publisher: Alan Whiticker
Project Editor: Danielle Viera
Proofreader: Kaitlyn Smith
Designer: Catherine Meachen
Production Director: James Mills-Hicks
Printer: Hang Tai Printing Limited

10 9 8 7 6 5 4 3 2 1

Keep up with New Holland Publishers on Facebook
facebook.com/NewHollandPublishers

www.ingramcontent.com/pod-product-compliance
Lightning Source LLC
Chambersburg PA
CBHW020451270326
41926CB00008B/565